# THE GOAL MINE

## Nuggets of Learning Goals and Objectives for Exceptional Children

## Donald Cahill and Maureen Cahill

**iep publishing**
Fork Union, Virginia

# The Goal Mine

### Edition 5

© 1989, 1991, 2003 Donald Cahill and Maureen Cahill
Fork Union, Virginia

# iep publishing

2040 Gold Mine Road
Fork Union, Virginia 23055
(434) 842-2000
www.ieps.net
iep@ieps.net


Printed in USA


Library of Congress Control Number:  2003100308


ISBN 0-941457-22-2

*Dedicated to*
*our children*
*Kathleen, Christine, Patrick, Maura, Eileen,*
*Dennis, Elizabeth, Jeanne, Kerry, and Sheila*
*without whom we wouldn't be parents*

*and to their spouses*
*Kazuo, Richard, Julie, Ron, Jim, Ellen, Tim, Joe, Eric, and Frolian*
*without whom we wouldn't be in-laws*

*and to their children*
*Lan, Mie, Kensei, Brian, Liam, Julia, Conor, Jimmy, Sean, Siobhan,*
*Kevin, Kayla, Kelsey, Claire, Olivia, John, Isabel, Leah*
*and the two waiting to be born, "Li'l Dynamo" and "Catherine"*
*without whom we wouldn't be grandparents*

# About the Authors ...

Donald Cahill served in his education career in the public schools as teacher of math, science, and English, department chairman, computer system manager, curriculum director, business administrator, and superintendent of schools. He graduated from St. John's University, earned his master's degree from the City College of New York, and completed his doctoral studies at New York University. A computer buff since the early 1960's with an ongoing interest in effective use of professional resources he has pioneered the development and marketing of IEP software since 1981.

Maureen Cahill came to the special education field from a career in theatre arts and management. Before joining Don in 1987 as full-time director of marketing at IEP Publishing, she served as an administrator at the Performing Arts Center of Brookdale College in New Jersey. She founded and is active in the Fluvanna Arts Council and administers the Carysbrook Performing Arts Center here in the heart of Virginia. She has written and directed plays for students and for adults in schools and community theatres.

The Cahills enjoy working as a team, travelling across the USA and Canada, lecturing, installing their IEP software, and training teachers and administrators.

Donald and Maureen raised their ten children, eight daughters and two sons, on Long Island, in upstate New York, and on the New Jersey coast. Now grown and all married to wonderful spouses, the families live all across the country from New York, New Jersey, Massachusetts, Maryland and Illinois right on to California. As this goes to press, the Cahills are anticipating the births of their 19th and 20th grandchildren.

The "gold" theme in the *Goal Mine* and their IEP software programs, *Goal Rush* and *Goal Digger,* was inspired by their current location in central Virginia, where gold was first mined in the American colonies. An old gold mine lies within a quarter-mile of their office on, where else, Gold Mine Road!

# Goal Mine Contents

The *Goal Mine* is a four-part guide and reference book written to serve all of the people most closely associated with planning and implementing the individual education plans or IEPs for exceptional children: teachers, teacher-parents, parents, surrogate-parents, parent advocates.                    Page

## Part I  A Primer for IEP Goals and Objectives            1

Clarifies what IEP goals and objectives *are and are not!* Understanding these distinctions aids the teacher and parent in developing meaningful learning plans and realistically measuring student progress.

## Part II  Measuring Learning: Tests, Scores, and Scales            23

Types and limitations of tests used in schools. Makes clear some widely mis-understood ideas about IQ tests, test scoring, passing grades, and teaching to the test.

## Part III  The Parent Advocate            43

Ideas for parents and advocates about choice of schools, parents as teachers, using the Goal Mine Library, preparing for IEP meetings, and getting children to read, to do homework, and to study effectively.

## Part IV  The Goal Mine Library of Goals and Objectives            63

Over 6,000 developmental objectives to encourage appropriate choices based on students' needs in: (a) infancy, (b) later development,  (c) transition to independence, (d) exceptionalities, and (e)  typical elementary school course objectives, and (f) high school course objectives.

## Appendix            315

Lists of additional options for inclusion in IEPs:
- Special conditions for learning objectives
- Criteria for achievement of objectives
- Normed (Standardized) tests
- Non-normed evaluation methods
- Teaching methods
- Accommodations
- Special services
- Placements

# A PRIMER ON IEP GOALS AND OBJECTIVES

2

# THE ESSENTIALS OF A LEARNING PLAN

The "individual educational plan" or IEP is a blueprint for education tailored to the needs of a special student. It describes a child's or student's educational needs, identifies learning and developmental deficiencies, and proposes a set of achievements for the student. It is a document which will serve as a guide to the planners and to those members of the professional staff who will use the IEP for the student's instruction.

The value of an IEP depends on the *quality of its communication*. Poorly written objectives pose problems for (a) the teacher who must follow the plan and evaluate the student's progress, (b) the parent, and (c) the administrator who must justify the plan to state IEP auditors. Attempting to evaluate student progress toward nebulous objectives becomes a futile task.

We frequently use the terms "goal" and "objective" loosely and interchangeably to indicate purpose or intent as:

*My goal is to get a good job, save some money and travel.*
*Our objective is to increase customer satisfaction and profits.*
*My primary objective is to finish college.*
*The goal of most people is to achieve happiness.*

In education **goals** and **objectives** define anticipated or hoped-for learning by a student. They spell out what a student is expected to accomplish, to develop, to be able to do, to improve. Educators often use 'objective' instead of the more precise term 'behavioral objective', which means a result with a pre-specified level of performance or 'criterion'. Throughout this book we will use the term **objective** to mean the precise skill or action apart from its **criterion**.

**Goal:** A general statement of the intention to overcome a deficit in a specific area. It is based on a need identified through an evaluation process.
**Objective:** A specific skill, development, ability, or change within the goal area which the student is expected to achieve. It must be *observable* or *measurable*.

An IEP usually covers one school-year. All the goals and objectives a child is expected to achieve in that time should appear in a student's IEP.

# DEFINING GOALS FOR IEPs

A **goal** statement indicates a clearly defined area of learning or development. It does not have to be observable but it should be limited in its scope. For instance, "Improve in spelling" or "Increase fine motor control" certainly designate limited areas of learning.

However, within each goal there are many specific skills which may be broken out. A goal is achieved for the year when the student shows that he or she can perform a set of such skills.

The same goal wording may be used for students of widely differing abilities. A goal such as 'increase vocabulary' covers a large area. For instance, a K-12 curriculum in a school might have 10 or 20 or more vocabulary 'levels'. A first grade student might be expected to achieve level #2 while a high school senior could be expected to master level #18; yet in the IEPs for both of these students the goal to 'increase vocabulary' would be appropriate.

Therefore, when setting a goal for a student we consider:
    (a) the age of the student, and
    (b) the present level of the student's ability in the area of learning, and
    (c) the disability or limitations the student has to cope with.

There is, of course, a limit to how broad a goal should be. It should not be so all-encompassing as to lack any clear intent, or to cover a vast spectrum of knowledge, development, or behavior.

| <u>Acceptable</u>   (Concise) | <u>Unacceptable</u>  (Too broad) |
|---|---|
| Read with comprehension | Improve his schoolwork |
| Develop singing skills | Show progress in school subjects |
| Learn to swim | Increase in development |
| Improve writing skills | Learn more about the world |
| Increase fine motor control | Become a better person |
| Calculate with decimals | Behave himself |
| Acquire basic carpentry skills | Develop normal attitudes |
| Improve public speaking | Study hard |
| Improve research skills | Pay attention in school |
| Reduce aggressive behavior | Show interest in class |
| Improve test-taking skills | Learn her math |

Note:  Avoid wording which describes what will be done *to* or *for* the student. These wordings do not belong in a *goal* wording since they do not describe *student* behavior:
        Johnny will be taught to ...
                Help in reading will be provided ...
                Greta will receive special assistance in math ...
                Andy will be counselled to ...

# DEFINING OBJECTIVES FOR IEPs

An *'objective'* as used in education is a shortened form of the term *'behavioral objective'*, which clearly defines a specific behavior which a student is to learn.

An *objective* can be thought of as a capability, a demonstrated achievement, or a visible action. We conclude that the intended learning has occurred when the student exhibits the defined behavior.

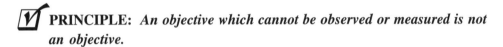 **PRINCIPLE:** *An objective which cannot be observed or measured is not an objective.*

If we set a goal of 'learn to swim' for a student, we might define a final level of performance for the year as any or all of the following:
- *do the 'deadman' float for 3 seconds*
- *dog-paddle for five feet*
- *crawl-stroke for the length of the pool without stopping*
- *float without assistance or flotation gear for 15 minutes*

Without such description of expected performance, you cannot be sure the ***goal*** has been achieved.

In most cases a single IEP goal will have a set of *several* objectives which represent either:
a) a sequential development of skills, or
b) a cluster of closely related but non-sequential skills.

For instance, Larry, a sixth grade student, has an assigned goal of 'improve calculation with whole numbers'. The teacher and his parents need to know his initial level of proficiency in this area. Based on his past performance and his known ability, they can determine which specific skills Larry can be expected to learn within the year.

In Larry's case the objectives within the topic of whole numbers might be the following set:

> *add two 3-digit numbers without any 'carrying'*
> *add two 3-digit numbers with 'carrying'*
> *add three 3-digit numbers with 'carrying'*

An objective describes an *observable* performance. A statement of an objective, at a minimum, must contain:

    **1. a skill**: behavior which can be seen, counted, confirmed, or otherwise observed, and

    **2. a criterion**: the level of skill performance as a quantity: score, measure, count, timing, yes/no, etc.

For example:

| **Skill** | **plus** **Criterion** |
|---|---|
| Speak audibly | every time he responds in class |
| Subtract fractions | with 70% accuracy |
| Broad jump | 4 feet |
| Type | 20 words per minute |
| Clean up his work area | at the end of every class |
| Spell the 3rd grade list | with 90% accuracy |
| Pay attention | as soon as the bell rings for class |

# THE DOMAINS OF LEARNING

Learning is traditionally considered in three *domains:*

**Cognitive Domain:**  The usual academic aspects of  learning
**Affective Domain:**  Attitudes, feelings, socialization, and social behavior
**Psychomotor Domain:**  Control of the body and its parts, including large and small muscle control.

Each domain represents a distinct set of functions:

| <u>Cognitive</u> | <u>Affective</u> | <u>Psychomotor</u> |
|---|---|---|
| Analysis | Acceptance | Balance |
| Calculation | Attraction | Control |
| Comprehension | Enjoyment | Coordination |
| Knowledge | Favoring | Flexibility |
| Memory | Fear | Grace |
| Recognition | Feeling | Lifting |
| Solution | Hatred | Movement |
| Synthesis | Liking | Posture |
| Understanding | Love | Propulsion |
| | Rejection | Strength |
| | Repulsion | Tension |
| | Resentment | Tone |
| | Revulsion | Torsion |

An IEP may contain objectives in any or all of these domains.  It is possible to have objectives under the same goal from more than one domain.  For instance a goal for reading might include an objective related to reading comprehension (cognitive) and another for following the words with a finger (psychomotor) and a third to achieve satisfaction in the reading (affective).

# VERBS FOR OBJECTIVES

The action word in an objective is, of course, a verb. *The verb used in an objective must define an action which can be seen, heard, counted, measured, or otherwise verified. The student must be the subject of the sentence.*

Selecting good action verbs for IEP objectives takes a little practice (even for English teachers). A suitable verb will meet *at least one* of these tests:

Test #1: ***Can I see this action?*** (Did it occur or not?)
Test #2: ***Can I measure it?*** (Test score? Count the number of times? Time its duration?)
Test #3: ***Can I put it on a scale or range?*** (More or less intense? With or without bad language? What degree of provocation? Faster than before?)

☑ **PRINCIPLE:** *If the verb you are considering for an objective fails all of these tests ... throw it out!*

*TEST YOURSELF:* Which of these verbs is <u>not</u> suitable for use in an objective? *(answers are below.)* Try it in the form: "He will ..."

| | | |
|---|---|---|
| 1. recognize | 5. pronounce | 9. smile |
| 2. explain | 6. choose | 10. realize |
| 3. join | 7. understand | 11. learn |
| 4. know | 8. value | 12. appreciate |

ANSWERS: Numbers 4,7,10,11 do not pass the test. Numbers 8 and 12 need very explicit methods of evaluation to make them "visible". See Objectives for Attitudes and Emotions

On the following pages we have listed verbs suitable for IEP objectives in a variety of categories. Look them over to weigh how each one could be used to express a learning achievement which is demonstrable or visible.

# Sample Verbs for Learning

## GENERAL

| | | | | |
|---|---|---|---|---|
| accept | accumulate | acquire | act | adapt |
| adopt | apply | arrive | assemble | associate |
| attend | avoid | balance | bend | calculate |
| clean | climb | communicate | compete | compute |
| compress | cook | correct | count | crawl |
| demonstrate | display | distinguish | divide | elaborate |
| eliminate | employ | endure | enunciate | examine |
| exhibit | explain | express | extend | extract |
| fall | find | fold | follow | furl |
| gesture | grasp | hit | hold | hop |
| hum | identify | indicate | inform | inspect |
| jump | leap | lengthen | lift | list |
| listen | locate | manipulate | make | match |
| multiply | operate | organize | pair (items) | perform |
| pick | play | point | prepare | present |
| pronounce | protect | prove | pull | push |
| put | raise | read | recite | recognize |
| remain | review | revise | roll | rotate |
| run | say | select | serve | shorten |
| show | shop | sign | signal | sing |
| sit | skip | sound (out) | speak | stand |
| state | stay | step | study | subtract |
| suppress | sweep | swing | tell | throw |
| tolerate | translate | tumble | tutor | twist |
| unfold | unfurl | use | utilize | vocalize |
| walk | write | | | |

## MATHEMATICS

| | | | | |
|---|---|---|---|---|
| accumulate | acquire | apply | assemble | associate |
| attend | avoid | balance | calculate | compute |
| correct | count | demonstrate | distinguish | divide |
| eliminate | employ | examine | exhibit | explain |
| extract | find | follow | identify | indicate |
| inspect | lengthen | list | locate | manipulate |
| make | match | multiply | operate | pair (items) |
| perform | pick | point | put | raise |
| recognize | revise | rotate | shorten | show |
| state | study | subtract | use | write |

9

## LIFE SKILLS

| | | | | |
|---|---|---|---|---|
| accept | apply | attend | avoid | clean |
| communicate | compute | cook | count | examine |
| exhibit | find | gesture | grasp | identify |
| indicate | inform | lift | listen | locate |
| make | operate | perform | pick | play |
| point | prepare | pronounce | protect | pull |
| push | put | recite | recognize | remain |
| say | select | serve | show | shop |
| sweep | tell | use | walk | write |

## EXHIBIT

| | | | | |
|---|---|---|---|---|
| demonstrate | display | employ | exhibit | express |
| gesture | indicate | match | operate | pair |
| perform | pick | point | present | prove |
| say | select | show | sign | signal |
| sound | speak | state | tell | write |

## EXPRESSION

| | | | | |
|---|---|---|---|---|
| act | communicate | enunciate | exhibit | explain |
| express | gesture | indicate | list | perform |
| pronounce | recite | say | sign (words) | signal |
| sing | sound (out) | speak | state | tell |
| vocalize | write | | | |

## EMOTIONS

| | | | | |
|---|---|---|---|---|
| accept | acquire | act | adapt | adopt |
| apply | arrive | attend | compete | correct |
| develop | display | eliminate | employ | endure |
| exhibit | express | listen | manipulate | perform |
| play | remain | show | signal | sit |
| speak | stand | stay | suppress | tolerate |

## SYNTHESIS AND ANALYSIS

| | | | | |
|---|---|---|---|---|
| accumulate | adapt | adopt | apply | associate |
| compress | develop | distinguish | elaborate | extend |
| match | organize | pair | revise | translate |

## PHYSICAL ACTION

| | | | | |
|---|---|---|---|---|
| apply | assemble | balance | bend | climb |
| compress | compete | crawl | develop | display |
| employ | exhibit | extend | fall | fold |
| follow | furl | gesture | grasp | hang |
| hit | hold | hop | jump | leap |
| lengthen | lift | manipulate | operate | perform |
| pick | play | point | pull | push |
| put | raise | remain | roll | rotate |
| run | serve | signal | sing | sit |
| skip | stand | stay | step | swing |

## SPEECH

| | | | | |
|---|---|---|---|---|
| acquire | adapt | adopt | apply | attend |
| compress | communicate | correct | develop | display |
| eliminate | employ | enunciate | explain | express |
| hum | lengthen | listen | match | perform |
| pronounce | recite | say | shorten | sing |
| sound | speak | state | suppress | tell |
| translate | tutor | vocalize | use | project |

# CRITERIA FOR ACHIEVEMENT

A **criterion** (the singular of 'criteria') is the measure of performance in an objective. It must be specific enough for other people to verify it. Its wording should clearly indicate *at least one* of the following:

- A count of how many times an action occurs
- A test score: raw, percent, percentile, etc.
- Placement on a scale
- More or less than a known level
- Increase or decrease from an established performance level
- Duration of an action
- An interval between actions
- Consistency
- Physical measurement of distance, volume, weight, time, speed, etc.
- Progressive/regressive change at specified intervals

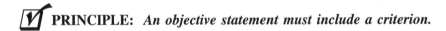 **PRINCIPLE:** *An objective statement must include a criterion.*

### Acceptable Criteria

- *every time*
- *90th percentile*
- *3 times out of 4*
- *at least half the time*
- *50% reduction in absences*
- *60% on a written test*
- *100 yards in 20 seconds*
- *every day*
- *never in class*
- *no more than two times per week*
- *at least five times in 30 seconds*
- *at the rate of ten per day*

## CONDITIONS FOR PERFORMANCE

For the special education student additional factors may have to be considered due to his or her disability. The ability of the student to demonstrate an objective may require additional allowances, assistance, or arrangements. Any such essential **conditions** to performance must be included in the wording of the objective.

**Example:** Consider the differences between the following pairs of objectives:

Swim 10 feet *with assistance*   OR   Swim 10 feet *without assistance*

Speak without stuttering *to another person*   OR   Speak without stuttering *in front of a group*

Essential conditions include any special assistance, physical setting, equipment, or modifications in procedure which are necessary and appropriate to the student's performance. For instance, the student's disability may require:

- prompting
- extended time allowance
- specific stimulus
- Braille copy
- special assistance
- one-on-one setting
- structured or unstructured setting
- adaptive equipment
- large print materials
- visual, auditory, or tactile cues
- model, diagram, or checklist
- small group or large group situation

Of course, the performance of many objectives do not require an explicit condition statement added. For instance, if the objective is to 'recite the alphabet', most of the time there is no need for cues or assistance or special environment.

For many skills, the method of determining whether they have been achieved or not is obvious and implicit. A skill stated as *'count aloud to 10'* implies that the teacher will request it and hear the student perform.

An objective such as *'identify sets of objects having common characteristics with 90% accuracy'* would require a statement of how this measurement will be made.

Certain actions may have a variety of ways in which the achievement can be measured. To measure a student's vocabulary skill level a teacher might use a vocabulary list from a textbook, state syllabus, or a teacher-made list.

If an objective is to be measured using a test it will probably be necessary to specify what kind of test or the name of a particular test as:

> State basic skills test
> Metropolitan Achievement Test
> Criterion-referenced test
> Teacher-made test

It is acceptable practice to indicate a single measuring device or test for all the objectives under a single goal. For example, a set of six objectives under the goal *'improve calculation with decimals'* might have *'textbook test'* indicated at the end of the objectives list.

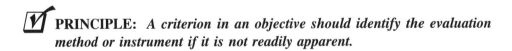 **PRINCIPLE:** *A criterion in an objective should identify the evaluation method or instrument if it is not readily apparent.*

> **HINT:** In determining whether an objective has been achieved, it should never be necessary to resort to ambiguities such as,
> "I think he ..." "She seems to ..." "We believe he can ..."
> Of course, the bottom of the barrel for (non) evaluative statements is,
> > "I / We _feel_ that ..."
> Such expressions indicate  (a) unclear objective statements, or (b) inept evaluations, or (c) fuzzy thinking!

It is far more challenging to verify changes in students' *attitudes* than to measure changes in math, or gym, or reading skills. IEP planners must be more creative and insightful in designing or selecting appropriate observable behaviors which reveal *internal feelings* and *attitudes*.

**Example:** *Does Karen appreciate art?*
We cannot determine Karen's *attitude* toward art merely by asking "Do you like art?" If she wants to please the questioner she may say "Yes, I like art." We will need more substantial evidence that she possesses this quality which we cannot observe directly.

However, people we know who do "appreciate" art show it in observable, concrete ways. If we make up a list of those actions and see if Karen participates in any of them, we can more realistically evaluate her "appreciation" or lack of it.

The more of those activities which we see her perform freely, the more apparent it becomes that she "likes" or "appreciates" or "is interested in" art. Does Karen ...

- Sketch or paint?
- Take lessons in drawing?
- Enroll in art courses?
- Visit art museums?
- Take art books from the library?
- Collect art works for her room?
- Read about arts and artists?
- Discuss art and artists with friends?
- Write class papers on art?
- Belong to an arts association?
- Major in art in school?
- Subscribe to art magazines?

If the answer is "yes" to several of these questions, it indicates some probability that Karen displays a degree of *appreciation* of art. The more "yes" answers, the stronger the likelihood that she truly does "appreciate art".

Goals for improving *emotional* responses must also be defined by observing visible behaviors. Evaluating progress in overcoming an emotional problem means having some before-and-after data on the student's observed behavior.

***Positive observable actions*** include smiling, offers of help, touching, patting, laughing, sharing, spatial proximity, and a variety of 'body language' postures and movements.

*Negative observable actions* which reveal emotions include frowning, striking, shouting, kicking, pushing, avoidance, refusal, hoarding, bad language, and hostile or withdrawal postures. Occasionally, a proposed *objective* within the area of emotional development may be, in fact, a *goal*.

**Example:** *"Exhibit a more positive attitude toward school"* is not an objective because you cannot observe an *attitude* directly. However, used as a *goal* it might be defined by a *set of objectives* dealing with the number of times the student

> ... *was on time/tardy,*
> ... *was present/absent from school,*
> ... *contributed to/disrupted the classroom,*
> ... *attended/cut class,*
> ... *was referred for commendable/disciplinary action,*
> ... *completed/failed to complete assignments.*

A record of such observable behaviors can provide a profile which reveals a student's internalized feeling toward school, or toward a teacher, subject, or situation. Such counts are normally available in school or teacher records.

---

**HINT:** An objective such as '*reduce incidence of outbursts in class*' will probably require the teacher to initiate a system for counting, remembering and recording outbursts for this student. This could become burdensome or even impossible in a classroom setting. Before deciding on this kind of objective, consider the ease or difficulty of evaluating it later on. Avoid selecting an objective whose evaluation will be overly demanding of the teacher's time and attention.

---

# OBJECTIVES FOR GIFTED STUDENTS

In many schools "gifted and talented" students have IEPs or individualized programs of learning prepared for them. For students who have exceptional strengths, the IEPs are not normally designed to remedy disabling deficiencies. Certainly, there is value in helping a student who has an exceptional talent, in music, or mathematics, or art, for instance, to continue to develop in this area. But educators of the gifted must recognize that *more* is not the same as *better*.

Gifted students can profit from *enriched-education* plans attuned to their individual abilities. Planners of such programs recognize that truly gifted students are generally above average in *multiple* areas of study and activity, as opposed to idiot savants.

An IEP for a gifted student can be designed to expand and improve areas in which he or she is below average or less advanced. For instance, students who are computer and math whizzes may be so single-minded in their pursuit of this interest that they ignore music, literature, languages, or physical activity. Providing truly gifted students with opportunities for real improvement in multiple areas will help them to become more well-rounded persons.

Objectives can be chosen for the gifted student which:
    (a) advance within the standard curriculum (acceleration), or
    (b) provide experience outside the common course expectations (enrichment).

 **PRINCIPLE: An IEP for a gifted student should be based on a profile of his or her strengths and (relative) deficiencies, even though any such deficiency may not constitute a disability.**

17

*IEP Objectives For Mainstream Classes*

Most IEP planners attempt to have the IEP include as much participation by the student in regular classes and activities as possible. This is referred to as mainstreaming.

However, if the student is mainstreamed in a course with the same expectations as the rest of the students, that assignment is not *'individualized'* and the *'standard'* course objectives are inappropriate for inclusion in an IEP.

It does make sense for a student's IEP to include the course objectives for a regular class into which he or she is mainstreamed *if they have been modified to reflect his or her limitations.*

### Examples:

... A visually impaired student may be mainstreamed in a math course but may be excused from having to measure lengths with a regular tape measure.

... A student with a speech impediment may be excused from stressful course expectations such as making oral reports to the class.

... A wheelchair-bound student taking a shop course may be excused from such activities prevented by his or her disability such as "pace off the dimensions of a room".

*Replacement* objectives for a course should be included in the IEP where suitable to make use of the student's special abilities to advance within the class.

To facilitate mainstreaming it may also be necessary to identify special study materials or instructional methods to be incorporated for the student enrolled in a course. For instance, an interpreter may be provided for a hearing and visually impaired student, along with Braille or large-print textbooks. A drafting table may be provided to accommodate a student who uses a wheelchair.

 **PRINCIPLE: Because an IEP by definition must be 'individualized', 'personalized', and tailored to the student's identified needs, regular *course objectives* which have been *modified* to adapt to a student's needs or disability are appropriate for an IEP.**

# SUMMARY

- **Goals and objectives are statements of what the _student_ will do.**
  Corollary: A statement of what the _teacher_ will do or what the _school_ will provide is _never_ an objective.

- **A goal addresses a specific _area of learning_ in which the student is deficient.**
  Corollary: A goal must be reasonably _limited_ in its scope.

- **An objective describes _observable_ or _measurable_ learning.**
  Corollary: Any _objective_ which cannot be seen or measured is _not_ an objective.

- **An objective includes a _criterion_ of desired performance.**

- **The statement of any objective has a minimum of two elements, _skill_ + _criterion_.**

- **An objective implicitly or explicitly includes any _special condition_ essential to performance.**
  Corollary: The statement of an objective _may_ include a special condition.

- **An objective implicitly or explicitly includes the _evaluation_ method.**
  Corollary: If the means of _measuring_ the objective is not apparent it must be specified.

- **The statement of an _objective_ may contain _two, or three, or four parts_.**

**Examples:**

| stand on one foot | for 10 seconds | | |
|---|---|---|---|
| **(action)** | **(criterion)** | | |

| clean his work area | every day | with supervision | |
|---|---|---|---|
| **(action)** | **(criterion)** | **(condition)** | |

| identify nouns in sentences | with 90% accuracy | workbook test | |
|---|---|---|---|
| **(action)** | **(criterion)** | **(evaluation)** | |

| multiply fractions | with 80% accuracy | using a model | on quizzes |
|---|---|---|---|
| **(action)** | **(criterion)** | **(condition)** | **(evaluation)** |

## INDIVIDUALS WITH DISABILITIES ACT (IDEA) AND "MEASURABLE GOALS"

As of March 12, 1999 the regulations for the Federal *Individuals with Disabilities Education Act* (IDEA) were finalized. They include the following which directly impacts upon the students' IEPs:

*"<u>Measurable</u> annual goals, including benchmarks or short-term objectives, are critical to the strategic planning process used to develop and implement the IEP for each child with a disability. Once the IEP team has developed measurable annual goals for a child, the team (1) can develop strategies that will be most effective in realizing these goals, and (2) must develop measurable intermediate steps (short-term objectives) or major milestones (benchmarks) that will enable parents, students, and educators to monitor progress during the year, and if appropriate, to revise the IEP consistent with the student's instructional needs.*

*The strong emphasis on linking the educational program of children with disabilities to the general curriculum ... requires that the IEP include a statement of <u>measurable</u> annual goals, including benchmarks or short-term objectives, related to (1) meeting the child's needs that result from the child's disability to enable the child to be involved in and progress in the general curriculum, and (2) meeting each of the child's other educational needs that result from the child's disability.*

*As noted above, each annual goal must include either short-term objectives or benchmarks. The purpose is to enable a child's teacher(s), parents, and others involved in developing and implementing the child's IEP, to gauge, at intermediate times during the year, how well the child is progressing toward achievement of the annual goal. IEP teams may continue to develop short-term instructional objectives that generally break the skills described in the annual goal down into discrete components. The revised statute and regulations also provide that, as an alternative, IEP teams may develop benchmarks, which can be thought of as describing the amount of progress the child is expected to make within specified segments of the year ... An IEP team may use either short-term objectives or benchmarks or a combination of the two depending on the nature of the annual goals and the needs of the child."*

IDEA specifies that a *'measurable'* goal will be measured by its objectives or benchmarks. As you have already read, a goal is defined or becomes operational according to the objectives selected for it. IDEA requires that the goal have relevant or phased objectives or *'benchmarks'* assigned to define that goal. By applying the term *'measurable'* to a goal, IDEA merely emphasizes that *any objectives or benchmarks under that goal are precise and observable*. It may also be done by including a criterion to be applied to all the objectives under that goal, e.g. "Increase reading comprehension *to 80% accuracy*." Each objective for that goal has the same criterion, 80% accuracy.

It seems clear that IDEA intends that evaluation of a child's progress must address each objective or benchmark and must avoid generalized statements that the child has made progress toward a goal.

22

# Measuring Learning: Tests, Scores, and Scales

***HOW DO WE KNOW THEY ARE LEARNING?***

There is a lot of talk today about assessing i.e. measuring what a student has learned. The basic question is "What particular areas of knowledge do you intend to assess?" Up until recently, you could count on most people agreeing that schools exist and are funded to teach children the three C's ... Communication through reading, Communication through writing, and Calculation. (If you are really quite ancient, you'd probably call these the three R's for reading, 'riting, and 'rithmetic.)

## Make Believe Evaluation

Some educator theorists believe that children (and parents) must be shielded from any negatives; to them 'failure' is a bad word; 'honors' belong to everyone. *"What a child knows is not as important as his/her self esteem." "A portfolio of tasks completed has more value than test results."* The attitudes reflected in these statements are based on half-truths, wishful thinking, and a big dose of unreality. Parents owe it to themselves and to their children to take a realistic look at schooling.

## Evaluation Facts

• No one likes to be labelled deficient or a failure but everyone has limitations whether in math, golf, singing, visual acuity, physical strength, reading comprehension, or a million other endeavors. To reduce a standard of performance to the level that everyone is 'superior' is to have no standard at all.

• In any field someone is always the first, the top, the best. In any race everyone is ahead of someone else except for the last one; some have to be in the top half and some in the bottom half. Like it or not, that's the nature of life, of competition, of comparison, of recognition, of business, of sports, of nations.

• No system should injure a child's self esteem. But, neither should it give the child a warped picture of his or her abilities. It cannot shield every child from disappointment, cannot award first place to all, should not pretend that every person is equal in everything, and must not equate participation or mere attendance with excellence.

• The reality of a child's emotional or neurological makeup can limit his/her learning.

• There is more to school performance than test scores and grades. Study habits, cooperation, endurance at a task, competitiveness, truthfulness, creativity, dependability, task completion, are all important in the overall assessment of a person. *But* ... these should not replace the measure of what the child knows and what skills he or she has.

• The mission of the school is to prepare all students to enter the real world where they will be rated, where they may be honored or not, where their self esteem is of little concern to many others, *but* where their ability to read, to communicate, to calculate will be valued as it contributes to their life's work.

## Realistic Evaluation

So then, how to assess learning? Typically, a student is measured (a) against himself, (b) against his peers, and (c) against the population at large.

He can be measured against himself by first establishing a limited and feasible expectation within his ability, e.g. memorizing the spelling of a list of ten words, or the basic addition facts for single digits, to be tested on tomorrow. The test will expose his own personal level of mastery of the facts. It is assumed that the task is not beyond his ability.

In class he can be measured against his peers by test scores and by report card grades. Grades are normally based on multiple tests plus other completed requirements (term papers, projects, experiments, assignments, etc.) Making the honor roll, being chosen student-of-the-week/month/year or class valedictorian are all based on peer comparisons.

The student's achievement is also measured against a large group of other students by using standardized testing which we will discuss later on.

## The "Lake Wobegon" Effect

The town of "Lake Wobegon", creation of author and radio entertainer, Garrison Keillor, is touted as the place "where all the women are strong, all the men are good looking, and the children are all above average." We smile at the switch in phrasing regarding women and men. Most people are probably just a little mystified by the item about the children. All above average in what?

Perhaps people take this humorous claim to mean academic achievement but of course it might also be related to intelligence, physical development, maturity, good looks, or social poise, or all of the above. Whatever the reference is, for an entire group to be above average is statistically impossible unless some deliberate control were being exerted, e.g. only adults who are above average are allowed to move to "Lake Wobegon", or infants who are below average or likely to be below average are deported at birth from the community.

## Averages

Averages are funny things. Whether it is about weights, touchdowns, test scores, or stock values an average will:

    (a) be somewhere between the highest and lowest number, and

    (b) have some items above and some items below the average.

The only exception is when every item in the group being averaged is the same, e.g. the average of *any* number of 5 pound bags of flour is ... *5 pounds!*

As you increase the number of items being averaged the number above and the number below the average *tend* to be about the same. If five six-year-old children weigh 50, 52, 55, 48 and 100 lbs respectively, the average weight is <u>61</u> lbs with only *one child above* the average and *four children below* the average. However, if you weigh 100 six-year-olds you will have *about* half above and *about* half below the average weight.

# STANDARDIZED TESTS

Standardized tests have no passing scores. They are called 'normed' tests because they are *made to fit* within a 'normal' distribution or range of scores. A student's raw score (count of correct answers) is compared to a 'norm' or 'standard' which shows how this score compares to the scores which a large number of students of the same age made on that same test in the past. The questions on the original test are adjusted until, after multiple trials with large numbers of children tested, they produce more 'perfect' distributions of scores, often called a 'bell curve'. The tests most people are familiar with are those where students are given test booklets containing the questions. They then fill in their answers on multiple-choice answer sheets. Commonly administered tests are the California Achievement Test (CAT), Iowa Test of Basic Skills (ITBS), and Metropolitan Achievement Test (MAT). There are many others, too. (See Tests and Measures in the Appendix.)

A standardized test is similar to a foot race in which, let's say 1,000 people run. Everyone is compared to the rest of the group. Fred Smith's performance may be described as '7th place', 'among the first 100 runners', 'better than average time', 'ahead of 993 others'. Even the winner is the 'first of 1,000 runners'. (The times for the first few runners may be recorded but they make no real difference because, no matter how slow everyone is, the first one is still the winner whether he took 5 minutes or 5 hours.) Standardized test scores are usually provided to parents either as *percentiles* (not percents) or as *grade levels*.

## Percentile Scores
A percentile indicates the placement of a raw score (actual count of correct answers) within a total population of student scores. A raw score of 45 out of 90 questions means that 50% of the answers are correct. But, if 45 is the highest score of all who took the test, it would be at the 99th percentile because it would be ahead of 99% of the other raw scores. (It cannot be the 100th percentile because that would mean it was even ahead of itself.) A raw score higher than 60% of the rest of the raw scores would be at the 60th percentile. The *percentage of correct answers* only matters in determining just how much of the tested population had *lower* scores. So, a score at the 24th percentile is in the bottom quarter; the 52nd percentile is in the top half; the 90th percentile is in the top 10% of the tested population.

## Grade Level Scores
The frequently used (and generally misunderstood) term, 'grade level', as applied to achievement of children, is actually based on an average of scores which a large number of children in that grade in many schools achieved.

For example, let's make believe that we give a test with 50 arithmetic questions to 1,000 3rd graders and let's assume that the average number of correct answers turned out to be 29 out of the 50. Then we declare that a score of 29 correct answers on this test is '3rd grade level'. About 500 children will be 'above 3rd grade level' and about 500 will be 'below 3rd grade level' *for this test*.

Now let's give that same test to 1,000 fourth graders and let's say their average score was 42. We then declare that a score of 42 correct answers on the test is '4th grade level'. Again about half of these 4th grade students will be *above* and half *below* that grade level score.

If that *same* test is given next year to a 3rd grade student who scores 28, we say that he is 'below 3rd grade level' *for that test*. A 3rd grade child who scores 42 is 'on 4th grade level'. A score of 36 for a 4th grader is below grade level. A grade level score is *neither passing nor failing*. It simply compares a student's score to the average score and says it is *above* or *below* that average value. A fairly small number of children will ever be exactly *on* grade level.

Statisticians then can wave their magic calculators and divide the initial group results up to create smaller interval grade levels such as grade 3.2 or 3.6 or 4.1 for other scores a child might achieve.

**What does this example tell us?**
* Grade level score refers to the *average score* of a large number of children *at that grade level for that test*.
* A grade level score does not indicate in any way what a *minimum*, or *passing*, or *acceptable*, or *appropriate* score is.
* The fractional grade level scores such as 3.4 or 4.1 are attempts to indicate how much above or below grade level a child's score is on that test. A grade level of 5.7 indicates achievement 7 months above the 5th grade level (based on a 10 month school year).

A common misconception, however, is that grade level represents the standard of *minimal achievement*. How many times have you seen or heard statements by school boards, administrators, or politicians bemoaning the fact that *"Half of our children are below grade level in reading!"* (or math or science or spelling or history or physical ability). Based on these observed *"deficiencies"*, new programs to *"eliminate this problem"* are born and funded.

A radio advertisement for a well-known commercial reading program recently revealed in horrified tones that *"Today almost half the students in the country are below grade level in reading!"* It's kind of fun to surprise people when they make such statements by saying "Gee, that's great!"

For a randomly selected group of students, even less than a hundred, you can assume that the number below (or above) grade level will be about half. It is certainly noteworthy if the average grade level score for an otherwise 'normal' group of students is sharply below or above the appropriate score ... *provided the test represents what the students have been or should have been taught.* For instance, the scores from a *test on dividing fractions* given to children who have only been taught how to *divide whole numbers* are useless. *Throw those scores out!*

## *Intelligence Tests: Real or Bogus?*

A special type of standardized test is designed to measure intellectual *potential*, to predict the ability of students to learn *in the future*. The so-called intelligence test is based on the scores of a large number of children who were given the test and then compared with subsequent learning by that group.

The individual student's score is called an 'intelligence quotient', or IQ. The average or mid-score on such a test is assigned an IQ value of 100.

A group IQ test score produces individual measures with an accuracy (plus or minus) of 10 to 15 points. Thus an IQ score of 115 means the 'true' score is *probably* (though not necessarily) between 100 and 130. Individually administered IQ tests are assumed to be more precise but still have a significant plus or minus factor.

**The Truth About IQ tests**

*Most IQ tests are basically reading tests,* that is the questions must be read from the test booklet. Where it presents multiple choice answers, the choices must be read also. Ask yourself ...
- If this test is given to a child who never went to school will it measure his *intelligence*?
- How dependably will it measure the *intelligence* of a child whose parents speak only a foreign language at home?
- Would you expect the IQ *scores* to be the same for identical twins separated at birth, one raised in a home where everyone reads books and magazines, plays word games, does mathematical puzzles, uses the library, visits museums, and schedules time for computerized learning programs ... the other raised in a home without reading materials, watching TV every afternoon and evening, with no supervision of study and homework?
- How will it measure the ability of a child who has dyslexia?

*An IQ test measures certain already learned concepts related to:* terminology (vocabulary), comparison (greater, less than, or equal), manipulation of numerical symbols (calculation), memorized data (spelling, times tables), logic (relations, cause-effect), analogy (comparable features or attributes), or simple problem solving.

*Most IQ tests do not measure some pretty important abilities:*

| | |
|---|---|
| Creativity | Musical talent |
| Poetic word sense | Foreign language potential |
| Humor | Photographic memory |
| Empathy | Leadership |
| Auditory discrimination | Visual/spatial/color coordination |
| Memorization | Decision-making under pressure |
| Political astuteness | Ethical conceptualizing |
| Learning speed | Adherence to a personal value system |

Surely, a person scoring low on an IQ test but having strength in several of these areas must be *'intelligent'*.

Let's create a parallel to the IQ. Say we wanted to measure a child's 'physical quotient' or 'PQ' and that this PQ would be based solely on an examination restricted to (a) body weight, (b) height, (c) speed in a 100 foot dash, and (d) weight-lifting limit. How much value would the PQ be in deciding a child's potential for swimming, diving, gymnastics, figure skating, ballet, pitching, wrestling, tennis, golf, skiing or white-water rafting. Fitness for these sports would necessitate measurement of many other physical abilities ... eye-hand coordination, balance, fine motor control, gross motor control, reflex speed, muscle tone, recuperative ability, endurance, and flexibility. The PQ would have *limited* value, at best, in identifying likely candidates for school teams or for the Olympics.

So, don't be too impressed with IQ scores. They have real limits in meaning and application to any one individual. They are incomplete guides, at best, to anyone's full potential.

# TEACHER-MADE TESTS

Teacher-made tests are not scientific instruments of high precision. They are most often simple tools which conscientious teachers write and use to assess learning. Typically, such a test is intended to measure a specific scope of material in a subject. The 'quiz' is a brief test which is given at short intervals, every few days or every week, to provide feedback to the teacher on overall achievement in a limited portion of the course. It fulfills several purposes; reinforcement of learning, determination of effectiveness of instruction, identification of any items that require review, or finding those students who may need extra help. Multiple quiz scores plus longer tests provide an ongoing basis for determining marking period grades.

*What does a teacher do when a test's results are disastrous?* ... e.g. 22 students out of 24 fail, or no scores are above 50%, or all the 'A' students got 'D's? The teacher looks for the probable reasons, perhaps ...
- the test wording did not correspond to the terminology used in the textbook, <u>or</u>
- the teacher failed to get the necessary concepts across, <u>or</u>
- the problems were unnecessarily complex, <u>or</u>
- a student rebellion is under way, <u>or</u>
- the students were all at their prom last night, <u>or</u>
- the class is pulling a practical joke on the teacher, <u>or</u>
- the teacher did not spend enough time on the topic, <u>or</u> ...

But, whatever the reason, the test is useless, so it gets thrown out. Few teachers will take the unreasonable stance that the test was perfect and the poor results mean that everyone in the class is too dense to master the work. Instead it's "Oops! Better look into this and possibly to reteach that lesson."

# CRITERION REFERENCED TESTS

Many tests prepared by teachers fall into a category called 'criterion referenced tests'. A criterion referenced test is a test whose content is announced in advance, either in exact detail or at least in the precise skills to be tested. The teacher might describe it as *"a quiz on multiples of all numbers from one to nine"*, or *"the next ten words on the spelling list"*, or *"adding and subtracting fractions"*, or *"listing the freedoms guaranteed by the Bill of Rights"*, or *"reciting the first stanza of the national anthem"*. In other words, everyone knows ahead of time just what they will be tested on.

Some criterion referenced tests are much more extensive, such as a statewide test of basic arithmetic skills required for all third grade students, or a test on the specific skills listed in the school's official curriculum guide for 4th grade language arts. The critical difference in a criterion referenced test is that the required knowledge or set of skills is spelled out in advance. A test which is described just as 'an algebra test', or a general test on American history, or a test which 'covers the basic operations of arithmetic' does not qualify as criterion referenced. The description of the content is too general.

The implication of the criterion referenced test is that the student is expected to prepare by study and practice for each of the stated content criteria. In other words, he or she is expected to score well on the test. A low score usually indicates a failure to do the requisite preparation.

## WHAT'S PASSING...    75%, 70%, OR 65%?

In school subjects and tests there is normally a cut off point designated as a 'passing' grade. This is frequently set at 65%, 70%, or 75%. If a student scores below that point he 'fails' the test or the subject. Are you curious as to how the passing grade is determined? Here's the secret ... *(Sssh!)* ...

**Someone** *(teacher, administrator, committee, publisher, school board, or state education department)* **has decreed** *that (**x%**) shall be the passing score or grade.*

Does a passing grade of 65% indicate lower standards than a passing grade of 75%? Not at all! Test grades and report card grades will be 'tweaked' or adjusted to produce the desired range of outcomes within certain limits. If you find that difficult to accept, consider these common ways that students are given extra help in "measuring up" on tests or report cards:

- "Answer three out of these five questions"
- "Extra credit questions" on a test
- "Extra credit projects" each marking period
- "Partial credit for each of the following
  (a) setting up the problem
  (b) applying the correct formula
  (c) finding the correct answer"
- Option questions: "Describe the character of the hero of *any one* of these three books...."
- Multiple part questions on a single topic
- "Curving" the test results (scaling them upward)
- Essay questions allowing for teacher interpretation
- Dropping (ignoring) the lowest quiz score in calculating the report card grade for this marking period

These are not unethical or even questionable practices since they are fully disclosed, available to all students, evenly applied, and understood by the students, teachers, administrators, and parents. They are merely accommodations to ensure that the failure rate does not exceed an acceptable, though unspoken, value. Few principals would fail to inquire "What's wrong here?" of a teacher of regular classes who has a consistent failure rate of 50% or more.

However, this would not hold true for schools or classes where over half the students are absent on any given day throughout the year. Believe it or not, there are schools where teachers face just this kind of situation and keep on trying. Our hats are off to them for their heroic efforts to help children succeed.

# 'TEACHING TO THE TEST' ... GOOD OR BAD?

Teachers and administrators are sensitive about accusations of 'teaching to the test'. However, this is not the moral equivalent of poisoning your mother-in-law, i.e. an action which is inexcusable under any circumstances. Sometimes such teaching is good and sometimes it's not good. Let's take a look at three situations:

**Example #1:** On Monday, Mr. Wall announces that on Friday on the weekly test students must define and give an example of all the parts of speech. He then proceeds for the rest of the week to teach the parts of speech and he has each student give examples as they proceed. On Friday he gives the test and ... surprise ... the students score very well. They are pleased; he is pleased.

> Q: Did he teach the exact content of the test? *YES*
> Q: Is this dishonest? *NO*

**Example #2:** Mr. Jackson has a copy of the state minimum skills test which his class will be taking next month. The test questions are supposed to be secret. This test will be a sampling of the skills the students should have been taught over the previous several years. Each day Mr. Jackson gives 10 questions taken right out of the test for homework. The following day he reviews the homework questions in class and has the students correct their work. For homework the students must answer 10 more questions from the test plus redo the questions they got wrong the day before. The students score very well on the test. They are pleased; he is pleased.

> Q: Is he teaching the questions from the test? *YES*
> Q: Is this dishonest? *YES*

**Example #3:** Mrs. Grace teaches sixth grade math and her state requires all students in that grade to take a minimum skills math test in April covering basic calculations they should have been taught over the previous several years. The average results of each school will be published in the newspaper. The state has given each school a list of the precise skills which will be tested. Mrs. Grace teaches her classes as usual during the year but for three weeks before the test, she spends 15 minutes a day reviewing each of the types of calculations. Over the period of three weeks she covers all the relevant skills. She gives short quizzes on these skills and assigns extra review work each weekend to those students who need it. The students score very well on the test. They are pleased; she is pleased.

> Q: Is she teaching the skills on the test? *YES*
> Q: Is she teaching the exact content of the test? *NO*
> Q: Is this dishonest? *NO*

What makes the difference among these examples?

1. In Mr. Wall's classroom the test is the motivation and goal of learning for the students. The content is taught as part of the official curriculum. The purpose is to have each student master the *full set* of certain fundamentals. The test is a *mastery* test and is perfectly honest and professional. It is what the students deserve.
*Mr. Wall, you deserve a raise!*

2. Mr. Jackson's intent is to increase the scores of his students without regard for the *full* set of skills he should be teaching and which his students are entitled to. He is teaching the contents of the test rather than teaching all the skills. Using specific test items of this type as a 'teaching' device is plainly dishonest and deserving of professional censure.
*Shame on you, Mr. Jackson!*

3. Neither Mrs. Grace nor her students know the precise questions to be on the test, only the skills or objectives to be tested. She wants her students to have the requisite knowledge to make them and their school look good. Her students are taught the skills, not the test items. She prepared them for a criterion referenced test, a test of previously announced skill objectives.
*An apple for Mrs. Grace, a real professional!*

37

# WHAT DO TEST SCORES REALLY MEAN?

When you are given your child's test scores there are certain basics which you should keep in mind in fairness to the child, the school, and the test itself.

• **The performance of an individual on any one day can vary.** This can occur for a number of reasons, e.g. distractions, personal problems, physical condition, the test setting, hunger, emotional state, etc.

• **Group tests are basically reading tests.** A child with poorly developed reading skills, or who is unfamiliar with the test style or format, or who has a visual or other disability, or some linguistic deprivation may score much below his true knowledge level or ability level.

• **Each standardized test has a content focus.** Most of the common standardized tests compare what these students know as compared to what the norming group knew. This may have no direct relation to what has been *taught* to your child. The curriculum of your child's school may differ from the content of the test. There is no standard curriculum across the nation. The math or science skills required by the test may not have been taught yet because the local curriculum has a different sequence in teaching them. Or the children in your school's 7th grade may have been taught skills in basic algebra which the test may not measure at all.

• **Each test has a middle score.** The mean or average score indicates that about 50% of the group scored above that and 50% scored lower. Critics sometimes expose their ignorance by revealing such 'news' as *"Half our students are below average in reading"* or *"Only 52% of our students pass the reading portion of the Iowa tests"* or *"51% of the students in this school are below grade level in math"*. The term 'grade level' on a test simply means the mathematical average of the scores of the students used to norm the test in that grade. By definition, half of the students in most schools or classes will be *below* that average for the grade level. But on the other hand, half will be *above* grade level. In other words, this is normal.

• **Test results are interpreted.** A wrong answer is *interpreted* to mean that the student does not have the skill or knowledge; a correct answer is *interpreted* to mean he does have the skill.

• **An answer may be both right and wrong**. Do you lack the knowledge if you misread a question but answer correctly what you *thought* you were asked? If you multiplied *12 by 13* instead of *12 by 31* your answer of 156 would be wrong for the test but factually correct *as you understood it.*

• **A correct answer does not necessarily mean you have the requisite knowledge or skill**. On multiple choice tests, which most standardized tests are, some of the correct answers a child chooses may be just guesses. As a matter of fact, on a multiple choice test with four possible answers to each question, you will probably get a score of about 25% correct if you answer every question without even reading it.

• **A test is a sampling.** A test which measures every aspect of a topic would be excessively long. So each student typically knows more than is asked on the test, e.g. Marge might do well in multiplying but frequently gets stuck on 9 x 6 and 7 x 8.

• **No standardized test score is an exact measurement.** Every measurement of any type is 'plus or minus' some amount. Trying to measure something as intangible as *'understanding'* is much less exact than measuring a box with a tape measure. Measuring an esoteric concept like *'intelligence'* to predict future achievement is even more difficult to pinpoint.

39

# Can You Measure Progress Without Tests?

Determining a student's progress is not limited to written and oral questions and answers. There are other, better means available for measuring improvement in certain skill areas or in specific behavior.

For *physical skills* a checklist of attained benchmarks of activity or records of actual measurements of the individual's running speed, distance jumped, accuracy, weight lifted, baskets scored, endurance time and the like are the appropriate measures.

To evaluate a child's *behavioral patterns* it makes sense to use checklists, anecdotal records and counts of relevant events, such as voluntary cooperation, attendance, tardiness, disciplinary infractions, fighting, etc.

Specialized means of judging *improvement* could include pre- and post-therapy records in the form of speech tapes, or photographs, graphs or videotapes of mobility.

A psychologist might use specialized profiles of *attitudes* or *interests* filled out by the student.

IEP objectives will very often require such "non-test" measures. *To paraphrase Gilbert and Sullivan "Let the evaluation fit the task!"*

The reader might find it interesting to consult the list of tests and measures, both standardized and non-standardized, in the appendix.

42

## THE PARENT ADVOCATE

Here are some clarifications and ideas which you may find helpful. They are based on the authors' personal and professional experience. And we sure hope that even long time teachers might profit from some of our observations, too.

## PARENTING BY AMATEURS

All children are raised by amateurs. Parents are often unsure of what's best for their children. Hence, the wide reliance on outside sources of 'expert advice' whether it be Dr. Spock or Dr. John Rosemond or magazine articles or a therapist. A pediatrician is expert in children's medicine, a psychometrician can measure certain narrow aspects of learning, a physical therapist can specify a meaningful program for muscular development.

But, child raising is much more ... it's loving, caring, nursing, guiding, value development, disciplining, supporting, comforting, medicating, soothing, protecting, requiring, restricting, encouraging, educating. In short, it is everything necessary to prepare your child to become an independent adult. In attempting this formidable set of tasks, all parents at times feel overwhelmed, inadequate, uncertain, guilty, and downright depressed. Rest assured that you're in good company; there are few, if any, absolute experts in this field.

The **Goal Mine** is about educating your child and there's no getting away from it ... that work is your responsibility. We hope to provide you with some ideas and procedures to smooth the way to cooperation, to help you in preparing your children, and to give you a bit more confidence in doing that job. Feel free to take it in small bits. Our ideas are not necessarily new and you may not agree with all of them but their concentration in one place will give you a chance to reexamine your role in the thing we call 'education'. These views and conclusions are based on reality, mistakes, successes, discoveries, inventions, and feedback from others, including the authors' own children most of whom are now parents themselves. We hope it will help to remove some of the confusion and uncertainty created by some nonsense movements and current educational fads. Some people (not too many, we hope) may be offended by our views. That's all right. We amateurs are still learning. We invite your thoughts and reactions.

The tools available to you in overseeing the education of your child include schools, public and private, home schooling systems, parent support groups, agencies focused on specific disabilities, libraries, television, computers, books in your home, encyclopedias, periodicals, and study ... your own.

### You Are Your Child's Best Advocate
You have the primary responsibility for your child's well being, education, and development and this gives you the right to choose the secondary agencies to assist you in such care and nurturing. These include your child's school, physician, church, youth group, or sports team.

It is you who must be assured that each agency is doing right by your child.

Some professionals mistakenly think their work serving the child supersedes the right of the parent to see that the job is being done effectively. *You the parent are in control.* This does not mean that you tell the doctor which medication is appropriate, nor that you direct the teacher as to what teaching methods to use, nor that you order the coach about which team position to assign your child. But, it does mean that you have veto power and may not be ignored by any support agency.

There is a vast difference between insisting on being informed of a child's behavior and achievement in school and dictating how the school or classroom must be organized. When legitimate wishes of parents or parent advocates are ignored or rejected in the IEP process, just remember you have an absolute and legal right to
   • Participate actively in the planning process by attending the IEP planning meeting(s),
   • Share in the evaluation of your child's current needs, requirements, abilities and disabilities,
   • Propose specific items for consideration during the planning including goals, objectives, services, and accommodations,
   • Expect clear and unambiguous evaluation of your child's progress, objective by objective,
   • Call attention to any failure to implement the full IEP,
   • Propose revisions in the IEP any time in the year when it seems necessary.

*It's nice to know that you have some control and some options, isn't it?*

 # WHAT SCHOOL IS BEST FOR MY CHILD?

Choosing the school which your child will attend may be a difficult decision for parents due to conditions in your local public school, the availability and cost of alternative private schools, your personal economics, or the necessity for a special program or service due to a learning disability.

## Public School

In most instances, the local public school is the obvious choice, providing it is not under siege from student gangs, nor has the worst academic record imaginable, nor is virtually falling apart from lack of maintenance.

Visit the school and try to get a feeling about:
- its atmosphere: Light and friendly or a prison with books?
- the staff: Do they really like kids?
- the programs: Are they working or are they a lot of glitz?
- achievement: How do the students do on state or standardized tests?

Research over fifty years ago (and since) has revealed that the single most significant factor which determines the quality of a school is its *principal*. A school whose principal is dedicated to student learning and staff development will stand out. Students will learn; teachers will be helped to improve; unsatisfactory teachers will not be recommended for rehiring. This principal will raise some people's hackles but no one will be in doubt about where his or her priorities are. 'Principal', in case you didn't know, is a shortened form of the original title 'principal *teacher*' (not to be confused with 'paper pusher', 'glad-hander', or 'politician'.)

The *advantage* for the child with special needs is that the public schools receive additional funding for special education students and are mandated to provide a "free appropriate public education" under the federal *Individuals with Disabilities Education Act (I.D.E.A.)*. Public school agencies must provide the special programs, services, staffing, accommodations, materials, and busing as needed.

47

But, your local public school *may* have *disadvantages* too.
- Poorly performing principals and teachers, protected by tenure,
- A lack of a cohesive moral value system,
- Administrative reluctance to remove disruptive students from class,
- Toleration of language and behavior repugnant to many parents,
- Inadequate special education programs,
- An over-emphasis on sports and extra curricular activities to the detriment of academics.

However, since the schools are publicly owned, there is always the option of taking individual or group action to pressure or encourage the school board and the administration to improve conditions.

## Private School

If a religious climate is of utmost importance to you then a parochial or church related school is the obvious answer. Private schools, both sectarian and nonsectarian, have some decided attractions.
- A clear-cut value system which can be incorporated in the curriculum,
- Greater control over staff performance,
- Required student manners, dress, socialization, behavior,
- The ability to exclude a student for noncompliance with regulations,
- Greater emphasis on academics,
- Greater demand for quality work from students,
- Significantly higher student achievement,
- Less emphasis on non-curricular activities: sports, cheerleading, pep rallies etc.

But private schools *may* have *drawbacks*, too.
- Professional staff often with less educational and professional preparation,
- Less money available for instructional materials, library, building maintenance, enrichment activities, field trips, music, arts,
- Lack of free school busing,
- High tuition costs, especially difficult if several children from one family are enrolled,
- Need to purchase textbooks and often uniforms,
- Often a lack of programs for children with special needs.

## Home School

Home schooling is a viable option for some families but not all. It is a huge commitment easily equivalent to one parent taking a new full time position. After all, a parent is replacing a full time teacher. Sitting a child in front of a television set with 'educational' videos will not do it. Neither will expecting a computer with a library of programs to take the place of the essential interaction between pupil and teacher.

Teaching is work! A home schooling parent must plan lessons, lead the student through appropriate materials and procedures, evaluate results, and reteach when necessary. If you cannot devote a daily minimum of five hours of active planning, record keeping, testing, personal supervision and instruction, forget it. Remember the old saying about good intentions!

Although home schooled students compete and score well when given standardized tests at public schools, home schooling is perceived as lacking advantages the schools, public or private can offer , e.g. socialization with age peers, on-site library, extracurricular activities, staff trained in many disciplines, exposure to multiple staff personalities and teaching styles, electives such as art, music, shop, foreign languages, and advanced placement courses.

The parent-teacher may need to seek out occasions and opportunities to provide socialization and enrichment opportunities for the student. Education at home may sometimes be the best choice but it is a demanding task for the parent and more difficult as the student moves into higher grade levels. In some instances providing for the specialized educational needs of an exceptional child may be beyond the abilities and resources of the parents.

Whatever your choice of school it is not necessarily a permanent decision. You always have the option of switching if your child's education is not being adequately addressed.

 ## Dick and Jane CAN Learn to Read!

The single most important academic skill for any child is reading. It is the basis for the vast majority of learning for the rest of his or her life whether it be reading for information, entertainment, voluntary self-improvement (newspapers, hobbies, curiosity, computer use, car manuals, assembly instructions, etc.) or just to keep up with the news of the world. It is even the key to taking tests successfully. After all, how can you answer a question you can't read? But you already know how important it is, so let's ask the question ... *why do some young people read so little?*

First ... there's television and films. As entertainment these substitute visual motion and settings for the *imagined* action and situation which the reader enjoys. Pictorial presentations do little to expand vocabulary, allow one to dwell on a thought or problem, as a reader can, to savor an author's imagery, or to go back and reread a telling description.

Next ... there's all those extracurricular activities. But surely, these should not fill *every* night, *every* weekend, *every* vacation.

After that ... the computer. When used for hours of mindless games of action figures and gratuitous violence it is a horrid waste of time. The internet when properly used and parent-directed can be a valuable research tool. It goes without saying that no child should be spending hours on the web and no child should ever be allowed to get into 'chat rooms'. You do have a rule about not talking to strangers, don't you?

But ... the single biggest impediment to young people reading is the example set by the important adults in their lives. That's *you!* Ask yourself if your home is one that encourages reading?
   • Do my children see me read? ... newspapers, magazines, books?
   • Do we ever read aloud to the family from a newspaper, book, or magazine about a particular chuckle, or outrageous political action, or some sad happening?
   • Do we use the public library? ... often? ... with the children?
   • Do (Did) we read books to our young children? ... give them age- appropriate books as gifts? ... buy books ourselves? ... have a family discussion after we all have read a particular book?
   • Do we regularly check the dictionary about the spelling or precise meaning of a word?
   • Do we own a thesaurus? ... know how to use it? ... do we use it?

• Do we solve 'how to do it' problems (learning chess, fixing a hole in the wall, pruning a bush, training a puppy, finding the north star, laying tile) by looking it up in the library or buying a magazine or book on the topic?
• Do we belong to or have we ever joined a book club?
• Do we enjoy reading ourselves?

If the answer to most of these questions is 'no' then don't be surprised if your children do not value reading or want to be more proficient in it.

Read to your children at bedtime when they are little ... *Goodnight Moon, Winnie the Pooh, The Cat in The Hat, Mother Goose, A Child's Garden of Verses,* the *Little Bear* books to name just a few.

Read along with them as they grow up and rediscover the books you enjoyed when you were their age ... *Charlotte's Web, Harriet the Spy, Treasure Island, Tom Sawyer, Little Women, Charlie and the Chocolate Factory, The Chronicles of Narnia.*

Discover new books with them too ... *Harry Potter, The Broadway Ballplayers, The Red Wall* series and many others. Look in your public library for the Caldecott & Newbery Award Winners or browse through a book store as a family group.

Enjoy talking with your children about the books they're reading and let them see *you* reading often and for enjoyment. It's up to *you* to lead the way!

*Readers are winners!*

 *FAMILY LEARNING IS FOREVER!*

It is a terrific boost to your children's development to have them dine with parents and take part in family conversation. Avoid feeding the children first and then dining by yourselves. Once a child can sit up at the table, he or she should share the family dinnertime. This is especially true for the special needs child. They are missing out on a great deal of learning social skills and manners, enjoying humor, participating in conversation... "Please don't interrupt when someone is speaking", "Good dinner, Mom!", "Why do firemen wear red suspenders?", "That's a great idea!", "Did you see that item in the papers today about ...?"

Make it a rule never to eat dinner in front of the television. Your wonderful meal will not be appreciated, conversation dies, and little will be learned. Just about any TV program will be far inferior to what you can give your child or children during a shared family meal.

The secret to real, lifelong learning for all of us is to keep our interests alive; to feel successful in intellectual endeavors; to develop curiosity; to cultivate the challenge of exploring new realms. It does not happen in a vacuum. This is indeed a challenge but who better than you, the parent, can stimulate your children to find joy in mental stretching.

Occasionally, try to get a mind game going at the table. It won't work all the time and you don't have to fill every moment forcing it. There are times to allow for comfortable silence or easy talk.

Here are some of the activities we introduced at our own family dinner table and adapted them to the range of our children's ages. Try one or two and feel free to modify them. Keep it simple enough to get participation and just challenging enough to require thinking, analysis, creativity. If there is a wide spread in ages among the children, you can address specific items tailored to the age of each child. If there is no definitive answer known, have them look it up! ...work it out! ... try it on paper! ... make a model! *Challenge your children to learn.*

**Patterns:** What number comes next ... 1 2 3 4 __ ?    2 4 6 __ ?    1 3 5 __ ?
　　　　1 2 4 7 __ ?    2 4 8 16 __ ?    1 2 4 5 7 8 __ ?    8 4 2 __ ?    5 6 4 7 3 __ ?

**Analogies:** These exercises encourage analysis of the sameness or oppositeness of pairs of ideas. An analogy such as  *dog : paw = boy : ___ ?*
is read as '*dog is to paw as boy is to what*?' The answer, of course, is *hand* or *foot.*
　　　　car : gas = man : ___ ?　　　　　red : cherry = ___ ? : sky
　　　　day : hour = ___ ? : inch?　　　　tall : short = sour : ___ ?

**Story endings:** Let each one create new endings or twists which would have changed a familiar story.
*"How else might the _____ story (book, TV episode, movie, myth, classic, fairy tale) have ended?" "What should the hero or heroine have said/not said (done, wished for, saved, discarded) that would have made it happier/sadder/funnier?"*

**Sequential story building:** *Let's make up a story which is ...* ( funny, scary, adventure, love, kiddie, animal, science fiction, mystery, historical, etc.) One person begins the first few sentences and then each person, in turn, adds on.

**Extremes:** *Who can think of the biggest ___? ... the smallest ____? ... the worst ____? ... the best ____?* (island, state, lake, country, number, fish, animal, tree, insect, sculpture, computer, vehicle, flower, bird, dog, boat, book, story, etc.). This can be the basis for some great research projects.

**Invent a solution:** *How would you ___?* (*weigh* an elephant, a jellyfish, grain of sand, a standing tree; *measure* the length of a whale swimming in the ocean, the height of a tall building, the thickness of a piece of paper; *count* the number of people in a city, flowers in a garden, etc.)

**Inventions:** *How do you think ___ was/were invented?* (shoes, socks, knives, forks, spoons, scissors, hats, wheels, fire, sugar, perfume, roads, haircuts, eyeglasses, salt, fishhooks, string, cloth, boats, sails, oars, rudders, needles, toothbrushes, boomerangs, writing, numbers).

**Measurement:** *If you were marooned on a desert island with no measuring devices, how could you measure things?* (length, weight, temperature, calendar, volume, time, speed).

**Strange foods:** *How do you think people learned to eat ___?* (lobsters, horseradish, hot peppers, seaweed, artichokes, bananas, potatoes, brussels sprouts, peanuts, artichokes, clams, snails) Lot's of good gross fun here!

**Diversity:** *How many different kinds of ___ can you think of?* (bread, wood, nails, wheels, vehicles, windows, shovels, flowers, fish, birds, trees, paper, roads, metals, flying insects, diseases, taxes, money). More curious stuff to research.

**Tom Swiftlies**: Tom Swift, the hero of many children's books was noted for his special style of heroic expressions. The Tom Swiftly uses an adverb, however bizarre, to relate to the subject of its quote. Puns are welcome. If the adults use these occasionally in front of the children they may have to do a little explaining of how it works but the youngsters will catch on after a while. When they do, encourage each to think up new ones.

"Sailing is such fun!", he said breezily.

"I just love sailors", she said fleetly.

"I don't have a thing to wear", she said barely.

"Your checkbook doesn't balance", he said calculatingly.

"Can't we just take a plane?", she asked flightily.

"Put up your sword", he said pointedly.

"I should go on a diet!", she said fatuously.

"You are a snake.", he said venomously.

"Too bad you lost.", she cooed winningly.

"How do you like this, Goliath?", David said stonily.

"Dessert is my favorite.", she murmured sweetly.

**Puns and retorts:** Start a running set of related puns. Here the topic is 'bones'.

| | |
|---|---|
| Mom: | "Breaking an arm is a humerus matter." |
| Dad: | "That cracks me up." |
| Jackie: | "I have a bone to pick with you two." |
| Mary: | "Did you kneed to say that?" |
| Mom: | "I was just ribbing you." |
| Sally: | "That puts you a head of me." |
| Dad: | "That's because you're so hip." |
| Jackie: | "Tibia or not tibia, that is the question." |
| All: | "Ouch" |

**Phrase reversals:** This is another variety of punning. Throw out a phrase and see who can come up with a snappy reversal.

| | |
|---|---|
| "In the nick of time" | Christmas arrives in the "time of Nick". |
| "Wink of an eye" | A flirt has the "eye of a wink". |
| "Up a creek without a paddle" | In a drought you might have a "paddle without a creek" |
| "Punch the clock" | A boxing judge has to "clock the punch". |
| "Justice of the peace" | A cannibal cooking a judge wants a "piece of the justice". |
| "Wring one's hands" | The groom "hands one's ring" to the bride. |

Now try these: make a wish ... stay to the right ... time to go ... right of way
pick a number ... make a face ... ear to the ground ... find a place ... hold on ...

## Pencil and Paper & Family Games

Group games make great gifts for the whole family. Children and adults enjoy games which stimulate thinking, creativity, and healthy competition. Good family games include checkers, chess, backgammon, card games, charades, Scrabble, Monopoly, Pictionary, Trivial Pursuits, Kalah (or Mankalah), Taboo, Masterpiece, Clue, jigsaw puzzles and crossword puzzles ... to name just a few. Crosswords and word games are wonderful for subliminal training in spelling and vocabulary.

**Making up unique license plates:** Adhere to your state maximum number of characters for a license plate, 6, 7, or 8 characters. AVI8R for a pilot ... MOOVER for cow trailer ... 4MULA for a chemist ... SUM GUY for an accountant ... PILLER for a druggist. How about 1DERFUL ... BGD2ME ... 1 4 ALL ... GR8GIRL ... ARTLUVR ... FISH B8 ... I MISS U ... Y NOT ... 1ST R8 ...? Try to figure out the license plates of other cars on the road when the family is out for a drive and even better on a long car trip.

**Letter codes:** Children love secret codes. Move each letter of a word up one letter in the alphabet ('cat' becomes 'dbu') *Who knows what 'eph' is? What will 'boat' become?* Hand out paper and try moving letters up or down two places. Give each child a coded sentence which will decode into something amusing such as 'Walk the dog' or 'Kiss Mom' or rewarding like 'Candy is behind teapot'. The authors used to write clues in code or in rhyme which the children had to decipher first before beginning the search to find where their Easter baskets were hidden. *Cruel parents!*

**Ghost**: Start with one letter. Each person adds a letter at the end of the string until a word is formed. The purpose is *not* to be the one to finish a valid word. The one who adds a letter which completes a word, intentionally or not, *loses*. But, the letter added to the string of letters *must be part of a real word* and may be challenged by anyone else. If the last person to add a letter is challenged and cannot show that the string is part of a real word, he *loses*. If he can give such a word, the challenger *loses*. Keep the dictionary handy. *What a shrewd way to encourage spelling accuracy!*

**Superghost:** Superghost is the same as Ghost except that letters are added to both the front and the back of the string ... a bit more challenging for the older children.

**Scrambled Spellings:** Try to find the word when its letters are mixed up, e.g. what word can be made out of MULP? (answer: PLUM or LUMP). This requires paper and pencil. The number of letters depends on the age of the children, three to five letters are best ... even adults have a difficult time with six letters. Making words out of jumbles is another clever way to teach spelling. Check the puzzle section in your local newspaper for *anagrams* or *jumbles*.

### Quick Arithmetic:
- First one to give me the sum of 23 and 19 gets a peanut.
- If three men are each carrying five jackets and each jacket has four pockets, and each pocket has 2 dollars in it, how many dollars are there altogether?
- 3 boxes contain 13 apples altogether; no two boxes have the same number and one box has three times as many as another box. How many apples in each?   Answers could be [1,3,9] or [2,5,6]
- I have seven coins that add up to 72 cents. What are they? [1,1,5,5,10,25,25] or [1,1,5,5,5,5,50]

These are just some suggestions to get you started. Be on the lookout for puns, diagrams, problems, puzzles, twists, books, etc. which you can bring to the family "think tank" to amaze and amuse. Remember to make games, topics, puzzles appropriate for varying agesand limitations, lots of fun, exciting and challenging.

 *HOMEWORK- TOO MUCH OR TOO LITTLE?*

A child needs to study regularly. How much study time depends on age. It is important that even a Kindergartner begin to develop study habits even if only for five or ten minutes each day. If there is no regularly assigned homework, ask the teacher to help you lay out a sequence of study and/or reading and/or activities which will correlate with and enhance the classwork. Once done, the teacher may wish to provide this guide to all the parents. It is perfectly logical to address the topic of homework in IEP structuring: How much? How often?

**How much study/homework/reading time?** The following are suggested minimal ranges. Actual homework requirements may require more time, especially in upper grades.

| Age | Study time |
| --- | --- |
| 6-7 | 20 - 30 minutes |
| 8-9 | 30 - 45 minutes |
| 9-10 | 45 - 60 minutes |
| 11-13 | 1 - 1.5 hours |
| 14-18 | 1.5 - 2 hours |

People will try to tell you that these expectations are too much; that your children need more 'play time'; that you are laying too much burden on the child. Don't listen to them! If your child is able to complete home work before the time is up he or she can *read a good book*. Establishing a habit of reading is part of his or her education, too, and believe it or not you'll be thanked for it by the adult child!

**When to study?** For the elementary school pupil, probably right after school. A snack and milk or juice on arrival home after school will raise a child's blood sugar level and he or she will be more alert and rested than at any time later in the day or evening. Play time should follow.

**Where to study?** Ideally, upper grade students should have an assigned study time, probably after dinner and chores, and in a quiet place. If possible alone at a desk or table with adequate lighting and without distractions ... *no video, no TV, no earphones, no pop music, no telephone*. If they have no homework, require them to read something of value for that time period. If a child reports 'no homework' too often, a conference with his or her teachers is indicated.

 *You're Scheduled for an **IEP** Planning Meeting*

In many cases, when you go to the IEP meeting you will find that a *draft* version of the IEP has been prepared. This is a reasonable way to start the planning by having something to work from. However, many parents feel inadequate and reluctant to say much, especially in proposing changes in the objectives, accommodations, and services in the draft document. Just remember it is *only a draft* and you have the right to question *everything*, to propose *alternatives,* to suggest *additions*. If the word *'draft'* does not appear on the document presented at the beginning of the meeting, feel free to ask that it be written on each copy. Until you and the other planners have discussed and agreed on the finished form, it is only a *suggested IEP*.

Teachers and other professional staff have a jargon of their own and this can be intimidating to parents. Many fear they will 'look stupid' or say the wrong thing and so they say little or nothing. *This is not the way it is meant to be.* Always bear in mind that the *prime* educator of your child is ... *you!* The person with the *prime responsibility* for your child is ... *you!* So when confronted with unknown terms you must be ready to ask "What does that mean?", "Why do you say that?", "What is the advantage of that?", "What alternatives are there?" You are present at the meeting to share in the planning. The school is legally required to invite you to participate actively in designing the IEP. The real trick is for you to be ready!

Preparation for the meeting will help you to feel more self assured, and stay focused on what you want for your child. Here are some suggestions:

- *Review reports* from the school over the past year. Pay particular attention to any written comments. See if there appears to be a trend up or down in any subject or behavior.
- Acknowledge honestly if behavior problems exist and, if there are, recognize that it is hurting your child's education.
- Make an appointment to talk with the teacher to get a better perspective before the meeting.
- Rough out what you think is needed in the way of feasible learning objectives. Study the objectives under specific deficiency areas which you know apply to your child. Look through the curriculum section in this book for your child's grade level and the objectives for each subject.
- Prepare some sets of goals and objectives on your own. You can go to the meeting with your own suggested IEP. And you can bet your booties *that* will get everyone's attention! But make certain that you keep an open mind to teachers' and others' ideas, observations, and suggestions which they believe will benefit your child. *You are all meeting to cooperate and not to compete.*

There is no set length of time for IEP planning and no requirement that it must be completed in a single sitting. If you are told that the meeting must end by a certain time and you believe that there are more things to be considered for your child's IEP, just ask when the next meeting will be held to complete the task. *You cannot be refused.*

The important thing to remember is that an IEP should be a *substantive* plan for educating your child. It should be *meaningful* to both teacher and parents.

 *How To Use the Goals and Objectives Library*

With the large number of choices in the *Goal Mine Library* which follows, the task of selecting proposed learning objectives may seem overwhelming at first. You will find sets of objectives for specific conditions: vision, hearing, speech, ADD-H, autism, occupational/physical therapy. In addition there are objectives in various growth areas such as infant and child development, vocational/transition, life skills, communication. Finally there are objectives for subjects in Kindergarten through 12th grade. Actually, K-12 course objectives will vary from school to school and even within schools having special programs such as 'gifted and talented', course tracking (slow, regular, fast), etc. Those in this book are a guide to general grade and subject expectations. When appropriate, you are free to incorporate some of them into your IEP draft to bolster your child's academic improvement.

Just approach the task methodically:
- Make a short list of the types of things you want to see addressed in your child's IEP.
- For each item on your list use the table of contents and the index to locate those sections of the library which seem to relate to it.
- Examine the list of possible *objectives* under an applicable *goal* and for each one that seems to fit, ask yourself if it is reasonable to expect your child to attain it to some degree within the year. If yes, write it down. Then ask what *level of improvement* seems possible within the year. Refer to the list of criteria types in the appendix for some ideas. You can always modify the wording of the objective to make it more applicable to your child.
- Make notes of where you believe there is a distinct need for some special consideration or support essential to the child's learning. Consult the lists of special conditions, accommodations, special services, and placements in the appendix.

Searching, weighing and selecting objectives and support considerations in advance will enable you to participate actively and meaningfully in the IEP meeting. Keep an open mind, however, to others at the table who may have a different idea of what is feasible and available for your child. There may be extenuating circumstances which may require other considerations.

Remember, though, that some adjustments may have a price in staffing, effort and dollars and must be justifiable. Mere convenience is not sufficient justification. It is important that everyone's ideas are given consideration and that the team reach consensus on the best educational plan for the child.

62

# THE GOAL: MINE

## A Library of Goals and Objectives

64

# INFANCY-COGNITIVE DEVELOPMENT

**Goal:    Advance 0 to  6 month cognitive development**

1  Calm down when he/she is picked up or held

2  Respond to soothing murmurs

3  Respond to the sound of voices

4  Respond to a loud or sudden sound

5  Respond to the sound of a rattle

6  Focus his/her eyes on his/her caregiver's face

7  Listen to his/her caregiver's voice

8  Look at his/her caregiver's eyes and mouth

9  Look for the source of a nearby sound

10  Turn his/her eyes and head to follow a voice

11  Focus on a slowly moving toy or object

12  Follow movement of a caregiver

13  Hold up his/her own hands and examine them

14  Reach for a toy or object

15  Smile in response to his/her caregiver

16  Respond to being touched and handled

17  Show interest in an object or person for one minute or more

18  Listen to a voice for one minute or more

19  Turn his/her eyes and head to locate a voice or sound

20  Discover and locate a sound source with his/her eyes

21  Show awareness of sounds of objects

22  Respond to caregiver's voice on waking by calming

23  Play with his/her own hands, fingers, feet and toes

24  Use his/her hands and mouth to explore

25  Bring his/her feet to his/her mouth

26  Play with a simple toy or rattle

27  Seek and find a partially hidden toy

28  Reach for a second toy

29  Respond with anticipation to a familiar activity

30  Show enjoyment when repeating a familiar activity

**Goal:  Advance in 6 to 12 month cognitive development**

1  Turn his/her head and shoulders to locate a voice or sound

2  Turn his/her head and shoulders to follow a moving person or object

3  Anticipate and follow a repeated movement

4  Look for his/her caregiver with anticipation

5  Look at other family members or pets when pointed to and named

6  Look at a picture for one minute when shown

7  Respond to facial and vocal expressions

8  Show enjoyment when playing peek-a-boo or blanket-over-the-head games

9  Imitate facial expressions, sounds and body gestures

10  Repeat expressions, sounds or gestures when laughed at

11  Respond with gestures such as "bye-bye" when prompted

12  Listen to familiar words

13  Work to reach a desired toy or object

14  Play two to three minutes with a single toy

15  Reach out for a second toy offered

16  Touch the toy or touch his/her caregiver to start play again

17  Throw toys from his/her crib or playpen

18  Drop objects to the floor one at a time

19  Listen to a caregiver's speech and voice without distraction

20  Respond to "no-no", "da-da", "ma-ma"

21  Respond to simple verbal requests

22  Push or move a toy or object on a surface

23  Play with two toys and reach for a third

24  Stretch out or overcome an obstacle to reach a toy or object

25  Bring a toy within reach by using another object

26  Find a hidden toy or object

27  Push a toy to create action

28  Move his/her own body to regain his/her toy and continue play

29  Take stacking rings or stacking blocks apart

30  Remove a single round piece from a formboard

**Goal:    Advance in 12 to 18 month cognitive development**

1   Respond to sensations such as hot, cold, sweet, tart
2   Look at pictures in books and react with enjoyment
3   Turn pages of a picture book with assistance
4   Hear music and move his/her body in rhythm
5   Learn several new expressions and gestures
6   Know several people other than those in his/her immediate family
7   Hand an object or toy back to a caregiver or other adult when requested
8   Identify primary colors
9   Put two or three rings on a stack
10  Put two or three cylinders in correct holes in a toy
11  Nest two or three blocks together
12  Pull a toy by its string to bring it forward
13  Follow a rolling ball out of sight and retrieve it
14  Retrieve a toy from another room when requested
15  Turn two or three pages of a picture book at a time
16  Identify object pointed to
17  Point to pictures of animals in books and name them
18  Point to pictures of objects in books and name them
19  Use the names of most familiar objects
20  Use the names of family members and friends
21  Look at "him/herself" in mirror and identify "me"

**Goal:   Advance in 18 to 24 month cognitive development**

1  Match like objects
2  Match objects to pictures
3  Match sounds to pictures of animals
4  Point to him/herself when asked, "Where is (name)?"
5  Indicate his/her age by fingers
6  Identify three body parts
7  Identify him/herself in a mirror
8  Recognize him/herself in a photograph

9   Explore drawers and cabinets

10  Point out clothing items, shoe, sock, pajamas, on request

11  Indicate his/her needs with speech and gestures

12  Use two-word sentences

13  Stack four blocks on request

14  Put a triangular piece into a form board

15  Point to parts of a doll on request

16  Point and name outdoor objects

17  Play with play dough and finger paints

18  Turn pages of a picture book one at a time

19  Listen to nursery rhymes and songs with enjoyment

**Goal:   Advance in 24 to 30 month cognitive development**

1   Match textures

2   Match three colors

3   Sort black and white

4   Match shapes, circle, triangle, square

5   Paste cutout shapes onto paper

6   Play in a sandbox

7   Play with water

8   Play with a mechanical toy, starting and stopping it

9   Match identical simple pictures of objects

10  Point to five pictures of familiar objects

11  Point to where those objects belong

12  Pick out pictures of action figures

13  Express action in simple words, run, jump

14  Listen to and enjoy simple stories

15  Use three word sentences

16  Enjoy looking at favorite picture books alone

17  Touch and enjoy tactile books

18  Know his/her own house and his/her room

19  Use "I" meaningfully

20  Identify his/her own gender

21  Know more body parts and how they are used

22  Place objects in, on, and under on request

23  Point to "big" and "little" on request

24  Know his/her routines, mealtime, bathtime, bedtime

25  Pick out and show clothing worn indoors, outdoors

**Goal:    Advance in 30 to 36 month cognitive development**

1  Name objects that make sounds

2  Imitate sounds made by objects

3  Identify six to eight pictures of familiar objects

4  Know what familiar objects are used for

5  Demonstrate the concept of "two" with fingers or hands

6  Point to larger and smaller of two objects on request

7  Put together four nesting blocks

8  Put together a three or four piece puzzle

9  Put rings on a stack in larger to smaller order

10  Match primary colors, red, yellow, and blue

11  Point to several colors when named

12  Sort shapes, circle, triangle, square and put them in toy correctly

13  Enjoy being read and sung to

14  Participate in rhymes and stories

15  Enjoy looking at picture books by (him/herself)

16  Pick out action pictures and say the verb for the action

17  Point to his/her body parts on verbal command, eyes, nose, mouth, chin, ears, legs, feet, arms, hands

18  Use common verbs correctly

19  Use adjectives to describe objects

20  Recite his/her own full name on request

21  Use vocabulary to indicate his/her needs

22  Begin to use short sentences to relate his/her experiences

23  Begin to ask "why", "when", "where" questions

## Goal:  Advance in 36 to 48 month cognitive development

1  Count numbers in imitation

2  Tell if an object is heavy or light

3  Join two parts of a shape together to make a whole

4  Point to longer or shorter of two objects on request

5  Tell his/her name and names of family members and pets

6  Describe two events or characters from a familiar story

7  Describe two events or characters from a film or TV program

8  Repeat finger plays such as "itsy bitsy spider" with words and action

9  Match objects one to one

10  Tell which objects go together

11  Arrange objects into sets or categories

12  Count objects to ten in imitation

13  Name objects as same or different

14  Name three colors on request

15  Name three shapes on request

16  Pick out the longer of two lines drawn on a paper

17  Pick out a specified number from one to five objects on request

18  Describe five textures, smooth, rough, soft, hard, furry, etc.

19  Recall and describe four objects seen in a picture book

20  Name the time of day associated with an activity, morning, afternoon, nighttime

21  Tell what is missing when one object is removed from a group of three

22  Repeat familiar rhymes and songs

## Goal:  Advance in 48 to 66 month cognitive development

1  Name eight colors

2  Match symbols, letters and numbers

3  Retell five main facts from a story heard three times

4  Draw a figure of a person with head, trunk, 4 limbs

5  Sing five lines of a song

6  Build a pyramid of ten blocks in imitation

7  Name objects as "long" and "short"

8  Place objects behind, beside, next to

9  Match equal sets to a sample of up to 10 objects in each set

10  Name ten numerals

11  Count by rote from 1 to 20

12  Name first, middle, last position of a set of 3 objects

13  Count up to 20 items and tell how many

14  Name five letters of the alphabet

15  Say some of the letters of the alphabet in order

16  Print his/her own first name

17  Draw figures of his/her family and pets

18  Draw a picture of his/her house

19  Recite all letters of the alphabet A to Z in order

20  Point to the letters of the alphabet on a chart

21  Name the lower case letters

22  Name the capital letters

23  Match the capital letters to the lower case letters

24  Arrange numerals in sequence visually from 1 to 10

25  Name the position of objects, first, second, third

26  Complete a simple maze

27  Name the days of the week in order

28  Tell the month and day of his/her birthday

29  Use basic grammatical structures

30  Use expressive vocabulary

# *GROSS MOTOR DEVELOPMENT*

**Goal:  Advance  in 0 to 6 month gross motor development**

1  Lift his/her head when held on his/her caregiver's shoulder

2  Turn his/her head side to side when placed on his/her back

3  Lift his/her head up when placed on tummy

4  Hold his/her head to one side when on tummy

5  Hold his/her head up 45 degrees when on tummy

6  Thrust out his/her arms and legs and kick

7  Hold his/her chest up when lying on tummy

8  Hold his/her head in line with his/her body when held upright

9  Hold his/her head in line with his/her body when sitting supported

10  Hold his/her head steady when sitting with support

11  Roll over from back to side

12  Roll from tummy to side

13  Move his/her head actively while held upright

14  Hold his/her head up while leaning forward

15  Bear weight on his/her hands while positioned on tummy

16  Bear some weight on his/her legs with support

**Goal:  Advance  in 6 to 12 month gross motor development**

1  Hold his/her head in line with his/her body in sitting position

2  Hold a sitting position for a few seconds leaning forward on his/her hands

3  Roll over from his/her tummy to his/her back

4  Push up on one hand while on his/her tummy

5  Lift head and assist when pulled to sitting position by his/her caregiver

6  Bear his/her weight on his/her legs and bounce with support

7  Sit up without help

8  Show balance in sitting

9  Sit without support from his/her caregiver for several minutes

10  Put his/her arms behind to support him/herself

11  Go from sitting to lying down

12  Roll over and push up on hands and knees

13  Stay in position balanced on hands and knees

14  Move his/her hands and knees forward in crawl

15  Creep on hands and knees

16  Stand with support from his/her caregiver

17  Stand holding on to playpen side or crib bars

18  Pull (him/herself) up to standing holding on to a chair or other support

19  Lower (him/herself) to sitting using support

20  Take steps holding on to a sofa or other furniture

21  Stand without support for several seconds

22  Lose his/her balance and recover

23  Walk with both hands held by his/her caregiver

24  Walk with one hand held by his/her caregiver

25  Take two to three steps alone

## Goal:  Advance in 12 to 18 month gross motor development

1  Stand alone well

2  Show balance in standing

3  Fall down by sitting

4  Move from sitting to standing position

5  Seat (him/herself) in a small chair

6  Stand up from lying by turning on hands and knees

7  Balance (him/herself) in kneeling position

8  Walk independently without support

9  Take 2 to 3 steps backwards

10  Drop to a creeping position to climb stairs

11  Walk upstairs with aid from his/her caregiver

12  Roll or throw a ball in imitation

13  Roll or throw a ball from sitting position

14  Throw a ball underhand

15  Take steps sidewards

16  Stoop over and regain balance

17  Bend at the waist to pick up a toy

18  Walk faster into a run without falling

19  Stand on one foot with help

20  Pull a toy on a string while walking

21  Throw a ball forward

## Goal:  Advance in 18 to 24 month gross motor development

1  Walk upstairs with one hand held

2  Walk downstairs with one hand held

3  Back downstairs without help on his/her knees using right then left knee on steps

4  Hitch downstairs on his/her backside without help holding on to stair balusters

5  Carry a large toy while walking

6  Push and pull large toys around the floor

7  Kick a ball without losing his/her balance

8  Throw a ball overhand

9  Throw a ball into a box

10  Bend to pick up toys from floor without falling

11  Assume squatting position while playing

12  Maintain balance while running

13  Ride on push-pull toys using his/her legs to move forward

14  Climb forward onto his/her highchair or an adult chair; turn around and sit

15  Stand up from lying by rolling on side

16  Stand on tiptoes

17  Walk upstairs while holding on, with both feet on step with assistance

## Goal:  Advance in 24 to 36 month gross motor development

1  Turn a door knob or television set knob

2  Jump in place with both feet

3  Roll a ball forward

4  Catch a large ball

5  Catch a rolling ball

6  Throw a ball five feet away without moving his/her feet

7  Kick a large stationary ball

8  Climb up a slide and slide down

9  Ride a pedal car pushing pedals right and left

10  Ride a tricycle pushing pedals right and left

11  Walk upstairs alone with both feet on step

12  Walk downstairs holding on with both feet on step

13  Jump from the bottom step

14  Walk on tiptoes a few feet

15  Walk backwards a few feet

16  Stand on one foot

17  Walk forward on a line

18  Stand on 2 inch balance beam with both feet

19  Jump three times with both feet

20  Jump backwards

21  Jump sidewards

22  Jump a distance of 1 foot

23  Forward somersault with aid

24  Hop on one foot

25  Balance on one foot for 2 seconds

26  Walk upstairs using the same foot to lead

27  Walk downstairs using the same foot to lead

28  Throw a ball overhand

29  Kick a large ball when rolled to him/her

**Goal:   Advance in 36 to 48 month gross motor development**

1  Walk upstairs alternating his/her right and left feet

2  Run 10 steps with coordinating arm movement

3  Hop on one foot for 5 steps

4  Walk forward on an 8 foot line

5  Swing on a swing

6  Climb up and slide down a 4 foot slide

7  Climb jungle gyms and ladders

8  Somersault forward

9  March

10 Gallop

11 Catch a bounced ball with two hands

12 Stand on one foot without assistance for 4 seconds

13 Walk backwards

14 Walk a balance beam forward

15 Walk a line for 10 feet keeping his/her feet on line

16 Catch an 8 inch ball

17 Jump a distance of 2 feet

18 Run on tip toes

19 Move to avoid obstacles in path while running

20 Make sharp turns around corners when running

**Goal:   Advance  in 48 to 66 month gross motor development**

1  Run changing directions

2  Jump forward 10 steps without falling

3  Jump over a string two inches off the floor

4  Jump backwards six steps

5  Bounce and catch a large ball

6  Walk downstairs alternating feet right and left

7  Perform walking, running, hopping, jumping, crawling, rolling, marching

8  Hop on one foot for 10 steps

9  Run smoothly and stop on signal

10  Walk the balance beam backwards

11  Walk balance beam sidewards

12  Skip

13  Swing on a swing pumping with feet to initiate and sustain motion

14  Respond to rhythm with appropriate body movement

15  Dribble a ball with direction

16  Catch a soft ball or beanbag with one hand

17  Jump rope by (him/herself)

# INFANCY-FINE MOTOR DEVELOPMENT

## Goal:   Advance in 0 to 6 month fine motor development

1  Look at a colorful toy or object held near his/her face
2  Follow a moving object with his/her eyes
3  Curl his/her fist around his/her caregiver's finger
4  Wave his/her arms in the same direction
5  Look at a colorful toy or object for a few seconds
6  Wave his/her arms at the sight of a toy
7  Follow a toy or colorful object with his/her eyes
8  Look from one object to another
9  Grasp a toy actively
10  Hold his/her fists uncurled
11  Follow with his/her eyes 180 degrees
12  Clasp his/her hands
13  Keep his/her his hands open most of the time
14  Reach for a toy or object with both hands
15  Grasp an object with his/her palm and fingers
16  Look at a tiny object
17  Look at distant objects
18  Drop a toy
19  Recover a toy

## Goal:   Advance in 6 to 12 month fine motor development

1  Hold a small object in each hand
2  Reach for an object using one hand
3  Move an object to his/her other hand
4  Bang a toy or object on a table or on his/her highchair tray
5  Play with a toy actively with wrist movements
6  Hold a block in either hand and bang both on a surface
7  Take an object out of a container
8  Poke at something with his/her index finger

77

9  Let a toy or object go voluntarily

10  Use both hands freely

11  Hold a large crayon in his/her fist

12  Place one block on top of another

## Goal:  Advance  in 12 to 18 month fine motor development

1  Make marks on a piece of paper with a crayon

2  Put two round pegs in a pegboard

3  Put several objects into a box or container

4  Turn a box or container upside down and retrieve objects

5  Point with his/her index finger

6  Use a crayon to make scribbles on a paper

7  Make a tower using 3 cubes or blocks

## Goal:   Advance in 18 to  24 month fine motor development

1  Fill a container with sand and dump it out

2  Make a tower using 4 cubes or blocks

3  Fold a piece of paper

4  Hold a crayon with his/her thumb and fingers

5  Scribble spontaneously with a crayon

6  Imitate a circular motion with a crayon

7  Put 4 large 1 inch beads on a string

8  Hold a scissors and cut a piece of paper

9  Put 6 round pegs in a pegboard

## Goal:   Advance  in 24 to 36 month fine motor development

1  Put one small object into a small container

2  Turn a container upside down to retrieve a small object

3  Fold a piece of paper in two

4  Copy a circle

5  Imitate an X

6  Attempt to draw designs on paper with crayons

7  Hold a pencil with his/her thumb and fingers

8  Scribble with a pencil

9  Make a tower using 6 blocks

10  Take apart a nesting toy by unscrewing it

11  Snip paper with scissors

12  Play with clay and playdough

13  Roll pound and squeeze clay shapes

14  Play with finger paints

15  Put 10 pegs in a pegboard

16  Turn the pages of a picture book one at a time

**Goal:  Advance  in 36 to 48 month fine motor development**

1  Put together a 5 piece puzzle

2  Hold a regular size crayon with his/her thumb and fingers

3  Trace shapes using templates

4  Copy a square shape

5  Copy a triangle shape

6  Copy a diamond shape

7  Snip paper on an 8 inch straight line

8  Cut curves drawn on paper

9  String 4 1/2 inch beads

10  Make a ball and a snake with clay or playdough

11  Make clay shapes with 2 or 3 parts

12  Use crayons with control

13  Add legs and arms to a picture of an incomplete person

14  Add eyes, nose, and mouth to an incomplete head

15  Imitate building a bridge using three cubes or blocks

**Goal:   Advance in 48 to 66 month fine motor development**

1  Copy horizontal and vertical lines

2  Copy angled and perpendicular lines

3  Copy letters H, N, T, V

4   Copy a series of connected V strokes

5   Put together a 10 piece puzzle

6   Begin to draw human figures

7   Draw a person with 2 body parts

8   Cut a 2 inch circle from paper

9   Cut out and paste simple shapes on paper

10   Draw 3 bubbles

11   Make a tower using 10 cubes or blocks

12   Follow a sequence of unnumbered dots

13   Pull a lace through a card following a sequence of holes

14   Draw simple recognizable pictures, man, woman, house, tree

15   Fold and crease a piece of paper two times

16   Copy his/her first name

17   Print his/her first name

18   Print single, large, capital letters anywhere on a piece of paper

19   Color pictures remaining within the lines most of the time

20   Cut pictures from magazines using scissors

21   Fold a 6 inch square in half to make a tent

22   Draw a simple house with roof, windows, door and chimney

23   Add 7 body parts to a drawing of an incomplete person

24   Draw a person with all major body parts

25   Draw a circle, triangle, square, diamond

26   Print simple words

27   Print numbers 1 to 5

28   Make a tracing around his/her hand and fingers

29   Lace and tie his/her shoes

# INFANCY-INDEPENDENT ACTIVITY

**Goal:    Achieve 0 to 6 month independent activity**

1  Respond to food stimulus by opening and closing his/her mouth
2  Nurse at the breast or bottle coordinating sucking, swallowing, breathing
3  Cry to indicate hunger or discomfort
4  Turn his/her head and search with mouth for mother's breast or feeding bottle
5  Bring hand or fist to his/her mouth
6  Swallow pureed cereal
7  Open his/her mouth for pureed cereal or fruit and swallow
8  Use his/her tongue to move food in his/her mouth
9  Recognize mother and anticipate feeding
10  Recognize bottle and anticipate feeding
11  Pat mother's breast or feeding bottle
12  Bring hand to mouth with toy or rattle
13  Place both hands on bottle
14  Stroke mother's breast while nursing

**Goal:    Achieve 6 to 12 month independent activity**

1  Open his/her mouth for food and take bites
2  Hold and bite on a baby biscuit or cracker
3  Take sips from a cup held by his/her caregiver
4  Bite and chew on toys or objects
5  Chew food with a munching pattern
6  Pick up finger foods and feed (him/herself)
7  Hold a spoon in his/her fist
8  Begin to assist in dressing by extending his/her arms and legs

**Goal:    Achieve 12 to 18 month independent activity**

1  Bring the spoon to his/her mouth
2  Hold a cup and drink with assistance from his/her caregiver
3  Hold his/her cup by its handle

81

4  Begin to show lack of interest in his/her bottle

5  Begin to nurse for shorter periods

6  Begin to show a pattern of bowel and bladder control

7  Become aware of a soiled diaper

8  Show he/she is uncomfortable in a soiled diaper by sound or gesture

## Goal:    Achieve 12 to 24 month independent activity

1  Hold a spoon with fingers and palm of hand upward

2  Use a spoon to scoop food from his/her dish

3  Feed him/herself with a spoon

4  Use his/her fingers to feed him/herself bite size foods

5  Drink milk and juice from a cup with assistance

6  Give up his/her bottle

7  Wean from breast feeding

8  Take off his/her own socks

9  Take off his/her hat

10  Put his/her hat on his head

11  Give his/her empty dish to his/her caregiver

12  Know edible and inedible objects

13  Chew food completely with rotary jaw movement

14  Take off his/her own shoes when laces or straps are undone for him/her

15  Pull a large zipper up and down

16  Sit on his/her potty chair or on a toilet seat with assistance from his/her caregiver

17  Begin to anticipate the need to use the potty and tell his/her caregiver

18  Wash and dry his/her hands with assistance

## Goal:    Achieve 24 to 30 month independent activity

1  Hold a small cup in one hand

2  Hold a spoon in his/her hand and fingers

3  Show definite food preferences

4  Unwrap a sandwich or hamburger

5  Turn the knob to open a door

6  Put his/her shoes on with assistance from his/her caregiver

7  Help with simple tasks

8  Help pick up his toys and put them away

9  Pull his/her own pants down with help from his/her caregiver

10  Unfasten large buttons

## Goal:   Achieve 24 to 36 month independent activity

1  Request his/her favorite foods

2  Eat without spilling his/her food

3  Wash his/her hands by himself

4  Brush his/her teeth with assistance

5  Tell his/her caregiver when he/she has to go potty

6  Perform on the potty

7  Pull his/her pants up with assistance

8  Dress him/herself with assistance

9  Wipe his/her nose with assistance

## Goal:   Achieve 36 to 48 month independent activity

1  Use a fork to pick up food

2  Wipe his/her mouth with a napkin

3  Pour milk or juice from a small container

4  Wash and dry his/her hands by him/herself

5  Help to wash and dry him/herself after a bath

6  Know when he/she has to urinate

7  Know when he/she has to move his/her bowels

8  Verbalize the need to use the toilet

9  Blow his/her nose with assistance

10  Dress him/herself with easy items of clothing

11  Button large buttons

12  Zip up zippers

13  Hang his/her clothing on a hook

14  Put his/her own things in the proper places

## Goal:  Achieve 48 to 66 month independent activity

1 Pick out appropriate clothing for an activity or for the weather

2 Dress him/herself

3 Ask for assistance with fasteners when needed

4 Brush his/her hair with assistance

5 Brush teeth

6 Serve him/herself at table

7 Eat using correct utensils

8 Use a napkin

9 Use proper table manners

10 Request food saying "please" and "thank you"

11 Wash hands after eating

12 Show interest in setting the table

13 Help with simple household tasks

14 Take responsibility for toileting

15 Wash hands after using toilet

16 Pick up and put away his/her toys and games

17 Turn on TV and select a favorite program

18 Turn on a computer and select a favorite game

# DEVELOPMENT- LIVING SKILLS

## Goal:   Expand his/her rudimentary communication skills

1  Attend to, stop, or change his/her activity in response to human voice or sound
2  Maintain his/her interest in visual stimulus
3  Exhibit reciprocal interactive patterns
4  Establish eye contact to initiate or maintain interaction
5  Indicate his/her desire to continue communication
6  Vocalize sounds
7  Produce vowel sounds
8  Produce sounds with his/her lips
9  Produce sounds with his/her tongue tip
10  Produce sounds with back of his/her tongue
11  Attempt to imitate speech sounds of others
12  Imitate sounds or patterns of others
13  Respond to speech-gesture games
14  Initiate speech-gesture games
15  Respond to simple questions with "yes/no" gestures
16  Indicate his/her wants and needs
17  Respond to simple commands
18  Give single-word commands
19  Imitate two-word sentences
20  Answer questions with "yes" or "no"
21  Use two-word patterns
22  Develop a basic vocabulary of his/her needs and wants
23  Ask for assistance
24  Express his/her feelings and concerns
25  Give two-word responses to questions

## Goal:   Expand his/her feeding and table skills

1  Finger feed him/herself
2  Reach for his/her spoon when held by another during feeding

3  Bring spoon to his/her mouth after utensil is loaded

4  Assist in scooping his/her food

5  Scoop with spoon without spilling

6  Use rotary motion of his/her wrist to get spoon to mouth

7  Hold his/her spoon with mature finger grasp

8  Feed him/herself with spoon

9  Maintain his/her head in neutral position to feed him/herself

10  Maintain steady pace when eating with his/her spoon

11  Bring cup to his/her mouth

12  Bring cup to his/her mouth without spilling

13  Take consecutive swallows of liquid without coughing

14  Eat with his/her fork

15  Cut with his/her knife

16  Select and use proper utensils for specific food

17  Manage his/her tray and milk carton in cafeteria

18  Use a napkin to wipe his/her face and hands during meals

19  Chew his/her food with mouth closed

20  Swallow his/her food before speaking

21  Use "please" when requesting that food be passed to him/her

22  Use appropriate table manners

23  Exhibit appropriate eating habits

**Goal:   Expand his/her simple language skills**

1  Use a variety of sounds for self-enjoyment

2  Respond to familiar sounds or objects and start babbling

3  Make a variety of sounds and tonal patterns

4  Vocalize actively and purposefully using a variety of sound combinations to communicate about his/her activities

5  Use gestures to indicate his/her wants

6  Say "more" when  he/she wants something to happen

7  Say "no" to indicate nonexistence

8  Say "no" to indicate rejection

9  Use single words

10  Begin to indicate possession through use of "my" or "owner-object" construct ("daddy car" for daddy's car)

11  Use beginning descriptive words (size, shape, color, texture, etc.)

12  Combine words to talk about actions or objects

13  Combine words to indicate locative action

14  Use "not" to indicate nonexistence

15  Express requests by using such words as "like, want, need"

16  Use words to describe location of objects or people

17  Use "can't" to express something that is not possible

18  Combine words to talk about something he/she notices

19  Use "what," "where" and "why" to get information about something happening

20  Use "now" to indicate he/she wants to do something at this time

21  Use "don't" to limit other people's actions

22  Use "and" to link more than one object or situation

23  Describe the actions of others

24  Use "s" to indicate plurality

25  Use "wh" question to get information

26  Use progressive and past verb endings (-ing and -ed)

27  Use "going to" and "have to" to indicate the future

28  Use "'s" to indicate possession

29  Use adjective and adverbs to give "precise" meaning

30  Describe relationship between objects or events by using words such as "to, for, with"

31  Use "a", "an", "the" as a specifier

32  Use "is", "are" to indicate existence and attribution

33  Use "can" to indicate possibility

34  Demonstrate spatial relationships (front, back, beside, etc.)

35  Indicate absolutes through use of "must" and "should"

36  Use pronouns appropriately

37  Sequence events appropriately

38  Discuss two events to indicate causality

39  Use linking relationships "and"

40  Discuss relationships between objects and people

41  Use "when" to indicate a time relationship

**Goal:   Expand his/her oral communication skills**

1  Answer questions and express his/her needs and thoughts orally

2  Answer questions and express his/her needs and thoughts in an audible volume

3  Use oral communication that can be understood to express his/her needs and thoughts

4  Communicate details appropriate to the situation without constant repetition

5  Communicate information appropriate to the situation

6  Be able to relate events from his/her home to school and vice versa

7  Initiate language

8  Repeat sounds made by others

9  Repeat the same syllable 2-3 times

10  Answer simple questions non-verbally

11  Imitate voice intonation patterns of others

12  Use single word meaningfully to label object or person

13  Carry out a series of two related commands

14  Use regular plural forms

15  Use some irregular past tense forms

16  Control his/her voice volume

17  Answer "who" question with name

18  Use the possessive form of nouns

19  Tell his/her full name on request

20  Answer simple "how" questions

21  Tell his/her address and telephone number

22  Name his/her siblings

23  Answer questions beginning with "where", "why"

24  Answer questions beginning with "who", "what", "when"

25  Maintain eye contact when speaking

26  Speak with appropriate voice projection

27  Speak with appropriate intonation

28  Speak with appropriate phrasing

29  Verbally express his/her complete thoughts in clear speech

30  Indicate refusal by saying "no"

31  Increase his/her speaking vocabulary

32  Orally describe a picture in simple words

**Goal:    Expand his/her cognitive skills**

1  Label and point to common objects and pictures

2  Match like objects

3  Label the attributes and functions of objects

4  Classify objects as belonging to a larger group

5  Identify his/her major body parts by pointing

6  Name his/her major body parts

7  Give his/her name, age and gender upon request

8  Name all his/her body parts pointed to

9  State function of his/her senses and body parts

10  Match objects by color

11  Sort objects by color

12  Identify basic colors

13  Name basic colors

14  Complete form-boards and simple puzzles

15  Complete simple puzzles without using trial and error

16  Match and sort objects by shape

17  Complete a variety of interlocking puzzles

18  Identify basic shapes

19  Name basic shapes

20  Identify and label something as "big" or "little"

21  Arrange objects in order by size

22  Identify and label something as "longer" or "shorter"

23  Position him/herself or an object in relation to another object

24  Distinguish between "fast" and "slow"

25 Distinguish between "night" and "day"

26 Distinguish among "today," "yesterday" and "tomorrow"

27 Distinguish among "morning," "afternoon" and "night"

28 Distinguish between the concept "more" and "less"

29 Discriminate between "one" object and "many" objects

30 Compare two sets by matching them up in 1 to 1 correspondence

31 Count by rote

32 Count objects

33 Answer correctly "How many?" after counting objects

34 Distinguish between hot and cold objects

35 Distinguish between hard and soft objects

36 Identify directionality: up, down, left, right

37 Distinguish between dry and wet

38 Demonstrate the difference between push and pull

39 Name the days of the week

40 Name the months of the year

41 Name and describe the seasons of the year

42 Exhibit proper use of the comparative degree of a descriptor

43 Exhibit proper use of the superlative use of a descriptor

**Goal:    Expand his/her time skills**

1 Read numbers on a clock face

2 Distinguish day and night

3 Identify correct order of daily activities

4 Associate meals with time of day

5 Associate activities with time of day: rise, nap, bed

**Goal:    Expand his/her socialization skills**

1 Work in groups of two or more

2 Develop an awareness of recreational skills

3 Take leadership role

4 Exhibit basic and essential physical skills

5  Take directions

6  Develop recreational skills consistent with physical conditions

7  Follow directions

8  Develop recreational skills which contribute to socialization

9  Exhibit self-control and stability

10  Appropriately play with his/her toys

11  Demonstrate respect for others' property

12  Play with one or more persons

13  Take the initiative

14  Share his/her playthings

15  Exhibit appropriate appearance and attire

16  Play with toys or other objects alone or with others

17  Follow a daily routine

18  Play very simple interaction games with others

19  Play with his/her age mates

20  Play with older or younger children

21  Exhibit give-and-take in games

22  Play with others in an unstructured setting

23  Decide to play in a group or by him/herself

24  Participate in at least one game or activity with others

25  Share with age mates

26  Share his/her toys or possessions with others

27  Keep a simple bargain with his/her teacher

28  Ask permission to play with or use a toy or object being used by another

29  Share his/her toys or possessions without being told to do so

30  Choose to play in all areas of the classroom

31  Show more interaction with his/her classmates

32  Show appropriate interaction with his/her classmates

33  Show more interaction with his/her teachers

34  Interact with all of his/her classmates

35 Attempt participation in all group activities that involve singing, imitation tasks, motor tasks, etc.

36  Join in group activities (i.e. songs, imitation activities, motor tasks, etc.)

37  Follow classroom rules

38  React positively to interaction from staff members other than his/her teachers

39  Demonstrate behavior and language appropriate to the school situation

40  Decrease inappropriate "teasing" behavior with adults

41  React appropriately in situations that he/she perceives as causing "high-pressure"

42  Display behavior suitable for his/her age

43  Recognize adults as authority figures

44  Play appropriately in all areas of the classroom

45  Plan for his/her work time

**Goal:   Advance his/her fine motor control**

1  Point to named objects

2  Distinguish objects by shape

3  Cut with scissors

4  Snip paper with scissors

5  Cut in a line with scissors

6  Cut on a line or circle drawn on paper

7  String beads

8  Shape clay

9  Reproduce shapes in clay

10  Use common fasteners

11  Hold and draw lines with a crayon

12  Draw lines connecting points left-to-right

13  Imitate simple strokes with a crayon

14  Copy simple shapes drawn on paper

15  Color picture in lines

16  Copy letters and numbers

17  Write legibly in lettering

18  Write legibly in cursive script

19  Trace shapes and letters with finger

20  Trace shapes and letters with pencil

21  Complete cut-paste exercises

22  Write his/her first name

23  Write his/her last name

24  Write his/her address

25  Write his/her phone number

26  Copy a daily story from the blackboard

27  Imitate finger exercises

28  Make paint brush strokes

## Goal:    Expand his/her measuring skills

1  Associate common measuring devices with type of measure: ruler, cup, scale, thermometer

2  Weigh self on bathroom scale

3  Measure with a cup

4  Measure with a spoon

5  Measure with a ruler

## Goal:    Expand his/her calendar skills

1  Name days of the week

2  Associate days with routine activities: church, daddy goes to work, shopping

3  Name months of the year

4  Find a given date on a calendar: e.g. birthday, Christmas, July 4th

5  Name seasons of the year in order

6  State own age

7  State date of birth

## Goal:    Expand his/her sexuality skills

1  Identify own gender

2  Identify others as male and female

3  Apply appropriate gender pronouns to known individuals

4  Identify correct restroom by word and symbol

5  Identify appropriate places to undress

6  Use correct terms for own sexual anatomy

## Goal:    Expand his/her telephone skills

1  Hold telephone in correct orientation for ear and mouth
2  Carry on a simple telephone conversation
3  Dial 911
4  State home telephone number
5  Answer telephone correctly
6  Dial a local telephone number of a friend or family member
7  Dial the telephone from a written number
8  Distinguish among dial tone, ringing, and busy signal
9  Terminate a telephone conversation correctly

## Goal:    Expand his/her mail skills

1  Affix stamp to a piece of mail
2  Copy an address onto an envelope
3  Deposit mail in mail box

## Goal:    Develop preschool skills

1  Exhibit pleasure at being with others
2  Hop on one foot
3  Run, walk, and stop on signal
4  Catch a large bounced ball
5  Put on his/her coat without help
6  Eat with a spoon or fork
7  Use the toilet independently
8  Share his/her playthings and take turns
9  Accept limits set by parents
10  Make short visits without parents
11  Care for his/her personal property
12  Put his/her toys away when asked
13  Follow one-step directions
14  Sit still for short periods of time
15  Draw simple figures

16  Identify two or more colors

17  Copy a circle and a square

18  Identify common sounds without visual clues such as car horn or dog bark

19  Enjoy listening to stories

20  Relate his/her experiences

21  Give his/her name when asked

22  Differentiate between one object and two

23  Pair objects or pictures with common features

24  Differentiate between big and little

25  Ask questions to gain information

26  Identify common objects by their use

**Goal:   Expand  his/her attending and persisting skills**

1  Attend to giving eye-contact to persons speaking to him/her and to group activities without becoming distracted

2  Attend to individual and group activities without becoming distracted by outside and internal stimuli

3  Attend to tasks without becoming frustrated

4  Complete tasks or answer questions before seeking help or before saying that he/she doesn't know or that he/she can't

5  Sit still during group activities

6  Attend to individual and group activities

7  Attempt to complete his/her tasks showing only minimal frustration

8  Attend to his/her work-time tasks until they are completed before moving on to another task

9  Wait patiently while his/her teacher is working with another student

**Goal:   Expand  his/her reading readiness**

1  Identify colors

2  Identify common geometric shapes

3  Classify objects by categories

4  Classify pictures by categories

5  Recognize his/her own name in print

6  Identify upper case letters

7  Identify lower case letters

8  Match upper with lower case letters

9  Match upper case letters

10  Point to upper case letters when his/her teacher names them

11  Name upper case letters when his/her teacher points to them

12  Match lower case letters

13  Point to lower case letters when his/her teacher names them

14  Name lower case letters when his/her teacher points to them

15  Recite alphabet

16  Develop an environmental awareness (social, family, work, home, school)

17  Develop an awareness of him/herself

18  Match colors

19  Point to colors

20  Name colors

21  Match geometric shapes

22  Point to geometric shapes

23  Name geometric shapes

24  Discriminate visually by finding similarities in patterns of shapes

25  Discriminate visually by finding similarities in letter forms

26  Sequence pictures to illustrate an event

27  Demonstrate directional/positional concepts

28  Read stories and select correct endings

**Goal:  Expand  his/her following directions skills**

1  Follow simple directions on initial request

2  Carry out daily classroom activities

3  Anticipate and follow daily classroom routine

4  Follow multistep directions in the classroom

5  Carry out multistep directions outside the classroom but within the school building

6  Follow two or more directions sequentially

## Goal:    Expand  his/her essential self-care skills

1  Demonstrate the ability to dress him/herself

2  Demonstrate improved personal care

3  Dress him/herself appropriately for specific occasions

4  Dress him/herself appropriately for weather conditions

5  Identify health situations which require treatment

6  Identify specific sources of health care

7  Unfasten his/her coat independently

8  Remove his/her coat independently

9  Put on his/her coat independently

10  Fasten his/her coat independently

11  Put on and fasten his/her coat

12  Identify inside/outside of his/her clothing and turn right side out

13  Identify parts of his/her clothing

14  Completely undress and dress him/herself

15  Cooperate actively in dressing him/herself

16  Undress and dress him/herself

17  Put on "pull-up" garments with elastic waistbands

18  Put on front-opening coat, sweater, jacket or shirt

19  Put on pullover garments

20  Put on both socks

21  Put on his/her shoes

22  Put his/her shoes on correct feet

23  Pull his/her shoelaces tight

24  Attempt to tie his/her shoelaces

25  Keep his/her nails clean and groomed

26  Lace his/her shoes

27  Tie his/her shoelaces

28  Secure velcro closures on his/her shoes

29  Put on his/her hat

30  Put on his/her mittens

31  Put on his/her gloves

32  Take care of his/her clothing

33  Take off his/her coat, hat and mittens or gloves

34  Undress and put his/her clothes in lockers

35  Remove his/her boots or overshoes

36  Put his/her clothes in locker

37  Use toilet facilities appropriately

38  Practice safety in classroom

39  Practice safety in kitchen

40  Practice safety in shopping areas

41  Show how to report an emergency

42  Describe first aid for minor cuts, bruises, burns, in age-appropriate terms

43  Exhibit basic first aid by notifying his/her teacher

44  Protect him/herself in a fight

45  Explain how to avoid a fight

46  Practice personal hygiene and general grooming

47  Exhibit appropriate oral hygiene

48  Practice safety rules in classroom, kitchen, shopping areas

**Goal:   Expand  his/her skills in personal hygiene**

1  Wash his/her hands and face at appropriate times

2  Wash and dry his/her hands

3  Keep his/her fingernails clean and groomed

4  Exhibit pride in a neat appearance

5  Follow a daily regimen of good personal hygiene habits

6  Practice good grooming and personal hygiene

7  Bathe regularly

8  Wash his/her own hair

9  Practice good complexion care

10  Wash his/her face with a washcloth

11  Hold his/her comb or brush

12  Brush or comb his/her hair

13  Keep his/her hair neat and clean

14  Care for his/her hair

15  Exhibit appropriate oral hygiene

16  Hold and raise toothbrush to his/her mouth

17  Put toothpaste on his/her toothbrush

18  Brush his/her teeth

19  Brush his/her teeth on a regular basis

20  Care for his/her nose

21  Demonstrate a healthful method of blowing his/her nose

22  Blow his/her nose

23  Wipe his/her nose

24  Cover his/her nose and mouth to sneeze

25  Indicate by word or gesture his/her need to use the toilet

26  Indicate his/her wet diapers or pants

27  Keep his/her diaper or pants dry in between sittings on the toilet

28  Produce when he/she is placed on the toilet

29  Pull his/her pants down at bathroom time

30  Pull his/her pants up at bathroom time

31  Attempt to adjust his/her clothing in preparation for toileting

32  Reach for and hold support rails during toileting

33  Wipe him/herself after toileting

34  Flush toilet after each use

35  Turn a faucet on and off

36  Wash his/her hands properly after toileting

37  Adjust his/her clothing properly after toileting

38  Use toilet facilities

39  Care for all his/her toileting needs

40  Use toilet facilities appropriately

41  Practice personal hygiene and general grooming

## Goal:   Expand   his/her auditory perception skills

1  Exhibit functional auditory acuity

2  Exhibit functional auditory memory

3  Exhibit functional auditory decoding skills

4  Recall auditory sequences

5  Identify words as sounding the same or different

6  Match spoken words with the same initial consonant

7  Match spoken words with the same final consonant

8  Repeat simple sentences as pronounced

9  Improve his/her auditory discrimination skills

10  Identify rhyming words

11  Increase his/her auditory attention

12  Structure and organize what he/she hears

13  Remember and repeat oral directions

14  Remember and perform oral directions

15  Increase his/her retention so that he/she can take simple notes

16  Increase his/her retention so that he/she can write a summary

## Goal:   Expand   his/her visual perception skills

1  Exhibit functional visual acuity

2  Increase his/her functional visual memory

3  Recall visual sequences

4  Distinguish among visual forms

5  Exhibit left-right motion

6  Demonstrate directionality: left-right, up-down

7  Match similar shapes

8  Match unlike shapes

9  Follow a line of print visually while it is read

10  Exhibit visual discrimination (shapes, letters, numbers, words)

11  Demonstrate visual figure ground differentiation

12  Demonstrate visual motor integration skills

13  Copy designs and figures

14  Copy numbers and letters

15  Demonstrate improved visual-closure

16  Demonstrate improved fine motor skills

17  Demonstrate improved visual sequential organization

18  Demonstrate improved visual form

19  Demonstrate improved ocular motor control

20  Demonstrate improved visual attention and fixation

21  Recognize form from visual cues

22  Color shapes

23  Follow a graphic path and connect a series of dots

24  Trace and copy a form

25  Reproduce a single form from memory

26  Reproduce a series of familiar forms from memory

27  Reproduce series of unfamiliar forms from memory

## Goal:  Expand  his/her safety skills

1  Light a match correctly

2  Light a mechanical lighter correctly

3  Identify poisonous household substances

4  Locate fire extinguisher in home and school

5  Demonstrate correct stairway travel

6  State correct procedure in event of fire

7  Explain need for seat belt in a car

8  State how to report fire or other danger

9  Demonstrate correct handling of cutting instruments

## Goal:  Expand his/her medical care skills

1  Identify own medication by pointing and by name

2  Swallow given dose of medication

3  State why dosage should not be exceeded

4  Identify correct storage place for medication

5 Specify correct dosage of prescription medication

6 Specify correct dosage for nonprescription medication

7 Take his/her temperature with digital thermometer

8 Describe self-treatment for simple cuts

9 Describe self-treatment for nose bleeds

10 Describe self-treatment for a cold

11 Describe self-treatment for his/her chronic condition (allergy, asthma, headache, etc.)

12 Describe procedures and schedule for medical treatment of his/her life-threatening condition (diabetes, high blood pressure, hemophilia, etc.)

13 Describe proper procedure when he/she senses the onset of a seizure

14 Keep a medical diary of medical services, medication, illness, and medication allergies

# *DEVELOPMENT-PHYSICAL DEVELOPMENT*

## Goal:  Demonstrate improved  physical fitness

1 Exhibit improved arm/shoulder girdle strength

2 Exhibit improved abdominal strength

3 Exhibit improved explosive leg strength

4 Exhibit improved cardiorespiratory endurance

5 Exhibit improved appropriate attitudes toward fitness

## Goal:  Demonstrate improved  motor proficiency

1 Establish lateral dominance

2 Perform gross body coordination tasks

3 Perform balance-postural coordination tasks

4 Perform eye-hand coordination tasks

5 Perform eye-hand accuracy tasks

6 Perform eye-foot accuracy tasks

## Goal:   Demonstrate improved  daily living, recreational skills

1 Exhibit basic and essential physical skills

2 Develop recreational skills consistent with physical condition

3 Develop recreational skills which contribute to socialization

4 Develop recreational lifetime-leisure skills

5 Move forward, backward, right, left in his/her own space

6 Walk upright and with even strides

7 Change direction, speed and size of steps

8 Jump with his/her feet together

9 Jump with his/her feet apart

10 Jump sideways from left and right

11 Stand on one foot holding his/her arms out for balance

12 Execute jumping jacks

13 Walk, run, skip to regular or erratic beat of music

14 Clap with hands a simple rhythm

15  Bounce and catch a ball

16  Roll a ball in a straight line

17  Kick a ball

18  Run a distance

19  Skip a distance

20  Hop on both the right and the left foot

21  Toss a ball at a low basket

22  March to music without losing rhythm

23  Demonstrate proper motion for a forward roll

24  Demonstrate proper position for a backward roll

25  Position his/her arms and feet for a proper cartwheel

26  Walk forward on the balance beam

27  Walk backward on the balance beam

28  Climb a rope and hold on

29  Jump rope

30  Punch a balloon with both his/her right and left hands

31  Dribble a ball with his/her feet

32  Kick a ball at a target

33  Bounce a ball waist high while moving in a forward motion

34  Catch a ball 3-4 inches in diameter with one hand

35  Throw a ball

36  Throw a ball at a target

37  Swing a bat at a ball resting on a tee

38  Run around the bases touching every base in order

39  Hold an indoor hockey stick with both hands and run in forward direction

40  Hit a whiffle ball into a goal

41  Execute a proper curl up

42  Move from the sitting cross-legged position to standing without using his/her arms

43  Execute a forward roll

44  Execute a backward roll

45  Walk the length of the balance beam forward and backward

46  Pull him/herself across the overhead ladder

47  Climb the upright ladder and slide down the slide without assistance

48  Pump his/her legs and propel the swings

49  Throw a regulation frisbee

50  Throw a regulation frisbee through a hoop target

51  Dribble a soccer ball with his/her feet

52  Kick a soccer ball into a goal

53  Execute a proper foul shot

54  Execute a lay-up shot

55  Swing a bat in the correct manner making contact with the ball

56  Throw a softball

57  Catch a softball

58  Play a one-on-one hockey game

59  Put a shot

60  Become familiar with water

61  Place his/her face in water and demonstrate appropriate breathing techniques

62  Submerge his/her head in water

63  Flutter kick while holding side of pool

64  Demonstrate appropriate swimming stroke in the standing position

65  Float on stomach without assistance

66  Do the crawl stroke without assistance

67  Swim underwater for a distance

# EMOTIONAL DEVELOPMENT

## Goal: Demonstrate effective functioning as an individual and with others

1 Accept authority

2 Follow directions

3 Accept constructive criticism

4 Respond orally in an appropriate manner

5 Accept the consequences of inappropriate behavior

6 Behave courteously to adults and peers

7 Exhibit respect for the rights of others

8 Participate in class discussion

9 Use acceptable means to gain attention

10 Manage his/her time more effectively

11 Complete his/her assignments within acceptable time limits

12 Complete his/her assigned tasks

13 Control his/her impulsive behavior

14 Decrease his/her hyperactivity

15 Work at a task for a reasonable length of time

16 Cooperate in group activities

17 Exhibit increased sense of security

18 Exhibit increased self-confidence

19 Exhibit increased independence

20 Exhibit self-sufficiency

21 Develop his/her personal independence and social awareness

22 Develop basic survival skills

23 Increase his/her attention span

24 Improve his/her task behavior to the extent that his/her work completion is possible

## Goal: Demonstrate positive attitudes toward him/herself and family

1 Decrease the number of his/her inappropriate emotional outbursts

2 Reduce incidents of his/her willful and oppositional behavior

3  Demonstrate realistic and appropriate perceptions and reactions

4  Demonstrate the effect of his/her behavior on him/herself and others

5  Increase his/her repertoire of coping skills in situations of stress and anxiety

6  Exhibit socially appropriate means of emotional expression

7  Reduce his/her inappropriate attention seeking behaviors

8  Increase the number of positive self-references

9  Decrease the number of negative self-references

10  Develop means of correcting tasks in which he/she has failed

11  Respond to his/her name when called

12  Identify him/herself in terms of name, age, sex, birth-date and address

13  Introduce him/herself appropriately in a given situation

14  Describe physical characteristics he/she associates with him/herself

15  Describe picture of him/herself in terms of appearance, attire and activity

16  Identify four basic feelings

17  Describe a picture of him/herself in terms of feelings

18  Describe things he/she feels he/she is good at and things that are hard for him/her

19  Identify several emotions as illustrated in pictures

20  Select from several emotions the ones he/she might feel in response to specific events or situations

21  Verbally identify objects and events that have a special meaning to him/her

22  Discuss character traits that he/she values

23  Identify his/her feelings and reactions to an experience

2  List character traits that he/she associates with him/herself

25  Distinguish between personal space of him/herself and others

26  Determine why personal space is important to him/herself and others

27  Describe consequences when personal space is respected and violated

28  Identify and describe various approach gestures

29  Distinguish between appropriate and inappropriate approach gestures

30  Describe the consequences of utilizing appropriate and inappropriate approach gestures

31  Identify the emotional and social consequences of substance abuse

32  Identify the emotional consequences of sexually exploitative behavior

33  Distinguish between socially acceptable and unacceptable behavioral response to various situations and environments

## Goal:  Demonstrate effective behavior for assimilation into society

1  Participate in group activities

2  Communicate his/her personal feelings and perceptions

3  Demonstrate continuing growth in his/her social interaction

4  Accept the give and take of interactions with peers and adults

5  Take leadership role

6  Take the initiative

## Goal:  Demonstrate effective reactions

1  Exhibit more mature emotional responses to stress

2  Exhibit appropriate reactions to his/her environment

3  Exhibit his/her coping skills in situations of stress and anxiety

4  Interact appropriately with peers and adults

5  Exhibit mature social skills

6  Use appropriate language when confronted with correction

7  Exhibit reduced tension in a nonthreatening and supportive environment

8  Exhibit improved self-image through success in school

9  Exhibit cooperative and agreeable patterns of behavior

## Goal:  Increase his/her self-confidence, assertiveness, and verbal expression

1  Reduce his/her passive aggressive behavior

2  Increase his/her verbal expression

3  Increase his/her confidence in his/her abilities

## Goal:  Increase his/her self-control

1  Wait his/her turn in games

2  Wait his/her turn in the performance of daily routines

3  Wait his/her turn before speaking

4  Recognize situations in which his/her self-control is lacking

5  Recognize provoking situations in which his/her self-control is needed

6  List ways for him/her to avoid being persuaded by others to misbehave

7  Distinguish between acceptable and unacceptable expressions of his/her feelings

8  Identify the consequences of appropriate and inappropriate expressions of his/her feelings

9  Verbalize his/her feelings in an acceptable manner

10  Recognize cues from an adult to change his/her behavior

11  Identify and demonstrate techniques to control his/her own behavior

## Goal:  Increase his/her verbal communication skills

1  Respond appropriately when called

2  Identify questions

3  Identify commands/requests

4  Identify statements

5  Distinguish among questions, commands and statements

6  Listen to a message before responding

7  Provide opportunities for listener to respond

8  Use statements to relay information

9  Use commands/requests to obtain information

10  Use questions to obtain information

11  Identify "You blaming messages"

12  Identify "I messages"

13  Use "I messages"

14  Describe a recently experienced event

15  Communicate effectively with peers and adults

## Goal:  Increase his/her nonverbal communication skills

1  Establish and maintain eye contact

2  Use appropriate signals to gain the attention of others

3  Identify nonverbal cues that communicate feelings and messages

4  Describe how nonverbal cues can be misinterpreted

5  Use nonverbal cues to convey a simple message

## Goal:   Increase his/her self-disclosure skills

1 Identify when his/her self-disclosure is appropriate or inappropriate

2 Determine when his/her self-disclosure is appropriate or inappropriate

3 Identify feelings which may be experienced when disclosing information about him/herself

4 State possible consequences of self-disclosure

5 State appropriate persons to whom specific information should be disclosed

6 State his/her likes or dislikes about a given person, place or thing

7 Describe his/her personal feelings about a given topic

8 Disclose his/her experiences during a sharing session

9 Disclose information about him/herself to appropriate sources during sharing sessions

## Goal:   Increase his/her interpersonal relationship skills

1  Share his/her objects and toys

2  Ask to be included in an activity

3  Ask permission to use another's property

4  Assist others when needed

5  Accept the denial of a request

6  Deny the request of another politely

7  Respond constructively to name calling or teasing

8  Respond correctly to constructive criticism

9  Ask for an explanation when he/she perceives criticism or punishment is unjust

10  Introduce him/herself to another person

11  Introduce two people

12  Compliment another person

13  Respond appropriately to praise or compliments

14  Respond sympathetically to a peer with problems or difficulties

15  Help defend a peer in trouble

16  Describe methods of accepting others who are different

17  Demonstrate how to initiate interactions with adults

18  Demonstrate how to assist others when needed

19  Explain how to seek assistance when needed

20  Accept the denial of a request appropriately

21  Demonstrate how to deny the request of another

22  Respond appropriately to name calling or teasing

23  Respond appropriately to constructive criticism

24  Demonstrate how to ask for an explanation when he/she perceives criticism or punishment

25  Demonstrate how to compliment another person

26  Demonstrate how to respond appropriately to praise or compliments

27  Demonstrate how to respond sympathetically to peer problems or difficulties

28  Identify when it is appropriate to help/defend a peer in trouble

29  Describe methods of accepting others who are difficult

30  Identify desirable traits in him/herself and others

31  Describe various ways of establishing and maintaining meaningful interpersonal relationships

## Goal:  Increase his/her controlled problem-solving skills

1  Regain/maintain his/her self control

2  Identify a problem situation

3  State his/her feelings about a problem

4  Sequence the events leading to the problem

5  Identify appropriate and inappropriate solutions to the problem

6  Select and implement the best solution to the problem

7  Identify several choices of behavior in his/her response to the situation

8  State possible consequences of different behavioral responses

9  Select his/her best response to the behavior of others

## Goal:  Increase his/her skills in handling critical situations

1  Identify a critical situation

2  State examples of critical situations

3  Describe how he/she feels in a critical situation

4  List physiological changes which may occur while confronted with a critical situation

5 Discuss ways to reduce his/her physiological changes involved in a critical situation

6 Demonstrate effective coping behavior in response to critical situations

## Goal: Increase his/her risk taking skills

1 Identify risk taking situations

2 State importance of his/her appreciation of positive and negative impacts of risk taking

3 Identify situations in which his/her risk taking is appropriate

4 Identify situations in which his/her risk taking is inappropriate

5 Expose him/herself to situations involving risks

## Goal: Demonstrate his/her creative thinking ability

1 Identify real situations

2 Identify fantasy situations

3 Distinguish between fantasy and reality

4 Identify situations where his/her creative thinking is appropriate

5 Demonstrate his/her creative thinking in specific situations

## Goal: Increase his/her skills for group rules and roles

1 State reasons for group rules

2 Identify some rules he/she follows for his/her personal safety

3 Identify rules he/she follows which are necessary for the safety of others

4 Identify group to which he/she belongs (family, class, school, neighborhood or city)

5 Identify rules for each group

6 Participate in the development of group rules with his/her peers

7 Follow group rules in a variety of situations

8 State the function of each group member

9 Identify specific roles in a given group

10 Identify the positive and negative behavior attributed to a particular role

11 Verbalize feelings regarding roles

12 Assume a role as a productive and positive group member

## Goal: Increase his/her skills in cooperating in groups

1  Follow directions during play activities
2  Manipulate his/her toys appropriately
3  Share his/her objects/toys
4  Put his/her toys in a specified area
5  Wait his/her turn
6  Engage in cooperative play for at least five minutes
7  Accept winning or losing without loss of his/her self-control
8  Play cooperatively as a member of a team
9  Ask to be included in an activity
10  Express his/her feelings of group rejection
11  Express his/her feelings of group acceptance
12  Describe his/her feelings when group decisions conflict with individual desires
13  Identify characteristics of a good leader
14  Follow directions given by a group leader
15  Lead small group activity
16  Ask his/her teacher or group to change activity in an appropriate manner
17  Complete his/her part of a group project
18  Demonstrate the techniques of compromise by accepting group decisions
19  Express his/her opinion appropriately when  he/she disagrees with a group decision
20  Cooperate with group to attain common goal

## Goal: Increase his/her negotiation skills

1  State his/her position and reasons for his/her position
2  Restate an opposing view on a given issue
3  Discuss an issue with a person taking a different position
4  Use persuasive skills to convince a group to share his/her position
5  Identify and implement a mutually agreeable solution

## Goal: Increase his/her persuasion skills

1 Identify three types of persuasion skills
2 Describe appropriate persuasion skills to be used in specific situations
3 Identify persuasion skills used in specific relationships
4 Identify persuasion skills used negatively or positively
5 Describe objective persuasion skills to persuade others to adopt a position
6 State his/her position and reasons for his/her position
7 Determine the position of the group
8 Identify the reasons for the group's disagreement with his/her position
9 Restate his/her position and reasons for his/her position in another way
10 Use his/her persuasive skills to convince a group to share his/her position

## Goal: Increase his/her planned ignoring skills

1 Identify those situations which are stress-provoking for him/her
2 Discuss ways to avoid stress-provoking situations
3 List ways to cope with stress-provoking situations he/she cannot avoid
4 Identify "setup"
5 Identify situations in which one person is "setup" by another
6 Demonstrate appropriate and inappropriate response to being "setup"
7 Define planned ignoring
8 Identify situations in which planned ignoring is appropriate and inappropriate
9 Ignore a behavior in a "setup" situation

## Goal: Increase his/her group problem-solving skills

1 Identify and define specific types of group problems
2 Identify and discuss the elements of a group problem
3 State his/her feelings about a group problem with other group members
4 Sequence the events leading to a group problem
5 Identify appropriate and inappropriate strategies to solve a group problem
6 Identify when there is a need to go beyond the group for assistance
7 State outcomes to specific solutions
8 Express his/her feelings and opinions on alternative problem solutions
9 Identify a mutually agreeable solution to a group problem
10 Cooperate with a group in the implementation of an agreed-upon solution in a contrived or natural setting

# CHILDHOOD-ORAL COMMUNICATION

## Goal: Demonstrate pre-language skills

1 Make gurgling sounds

2 Coo and chuckle

3 Make growling sounds

4 Become quiet at the sound of noise

5 Become quiet at the sound of someone humming, singing, chanting or talking

6 Turn his/her eyes and head in the direction of noise

7 Turn his/her eyes and head in the direction of someone vocalizing or speaking

8 Turn his/her head and shoulders in the direction of noise

9 Turn his/her head and shoulders in the direction of someone vocalizing or speaking

10 Vocalize in response to the vocalization of others

11 Vocalize "m" and other single consonants

12 Initiate vocal play with toys

13 Initiate vocal play with people

14 Vocalize consonant-vowel combinations during play

15 Imitate the consonant-vowel combinations vocalized by others

16 Articulate consonant-vowel combinations during play

17 Imitate the duplicated consonant-vowel combinations vocalized by others

18 Articulate duplicated consonant-vowel combinations without imitation

19 Echo words and phrases in songs and rhymes

20 Echo individual words and phrases spoken by others

## Goal: Respond to and use facial expressions

1 Respond to a smile by smiling in turn

2 Respond to a smile by continuing his/her activity

3 Smile when receiving a favored object or upon seeing a favorite person

4 Smile when told good news

5 Respond to the facial expression of sadness by comforting the individual expressing it

115

6  Make a sad face when told sad news

7  Cease an activity when presented with an angry face

8  Respond to the facial expression of fear by comforting that person

9  Respond to a peer's facial expression of fear by removing the frightening stimulus

## Goal:  Respond to and use gestures appropriately

1  Respond by looking at an individual who is waving a hand or arm for attention

2  Gain a person's attention by waving his/her hand or arm

3  Respond to the warning signal of a shaking finger by stopping an activity

4  Respond to the "no" head shake by stopping an activity

5  Point to desired objects or favorite people

6  Look at the object or person pointed to

7  Point to a desired location

8  Indicate that he/she has to go to the bathroom by gesturing toward the area of his/her lower abdomen

9  Indicate that he/she is hungry by directing a flexed finger or fingers in and out of his/her slightly opened mouth

10  Indicate that he/she is thirsty by gesturing with the hand, imitating drinking out of a glass or cup

11  Indicate that he/she is tired or sleepy by rubbing his/her eyes

12  Wave good-bye when he/she is leaving someone

13  Indicate "give me" by extending his/her arm and hand toward the desired object

14  Shake his/her head when he/she does not want an object or does not wish something to happen

15  Indicate that he/she is not feeling well by rubbing the part of his/her body that hurts

16  Encourage people to approach him/her by gesturing "come here" (bending of the index finger)

17  Respond to the "ssh" gesture by becoming quiet

18  Indicate "be quiet" by using the "ssh" gesture

19  Indicate  to the "shooing" gesture by moving out of the way of the person who is making the gesture

20  Indicate "get away from me!" by using the "shooing" gesture

21  Stop an activity when gestured to stop (hand raised with palm facing the person to be stopped)

22  Resume the activity when given the "go ahead" gesture (sweeping motion of the hand)

23  Direct someone first to stop an activity and then to resume it by making the appropriate gestures

24  Respond to the "leave" or "get away" gesture by moving away

25  Respond to someone nodding his/her head by continuing an approved activity

26  Respond to the "hi" or "hello" gesture by gesturing "hi" in return

27  Shake hands when a person extends his/her hand when greeting him/her or when saying "good-bye"

28  Shake to indicate that he/she is cold by using the "I am cold" gesture

29  Respond by standing up when signaled to do so

30  Respond by sitting down when signaled to do so

31  Select an object by size when gestures are used which indicate that an object is "big" or "little" (hands or fingers are held parallel to each other at different distances i.e. close = little and far apart = big)

32  Indicate the size of a desired object by using the size gesture that indicates "big" or "little"

33  Respond to the finger gesture that indicates the number of objects desired (one through five) and select the correct number of objects

34  Indicate the number of objects desired by holding up the appropriate number of fingers (one through five)

## Goal:  Respond to and use vocal tone patterns

1  Respond (with or without words) to the vocal utterance of happiness or pleasure by continuing the activity in which he/she is engaged

2  Respond to the vocal utterance, with or without words, by imitating the happy vocalizations of others

3  Express happiness or pleasure vocally, with or without words, upon receiving a favorite object or seeing a favorite person

4 Express happiness or pleasure vocally, with or without words, upon hearing that he/she is going to participate in a favorite activity

5 Respond to the vocal expression of sadness, with or without words, by comforting the individual expressing sorrow

6 Express sadness vocally, with or without words, by imitating the sad vocalizations of others

7 Vocalize sadness, with or without words, when denied participation in a favorite activity

8 Cease an activity when presented with a vocal pattern, with or without words, that indicates anger

9 Back away from the angry individual while signaling for intervention from a significant person when he/she hears an angry utterance

10 Express anger vocally, with or without words, by imitating the angry vocalizations of others

11 Express anger vocally, with or without words, when aggressively interfered with by others

12 Express fear vocally, with or without words, by imitating the fearful vocalizations of others

13 Express fear vocally (with or without words) when confronted with a fear-evoking situation

## Goal:  Respond appropriately to spoken language

1 Look at the object named

2 Look at the person named

3 Carry out the simple command "show me the _____" by pointing to the object named

4 Carry out the command "give me the _____" by giving the object named

5 Terminate a behavior when told "no!"

6 Turn and look at the person calling his/her name

7 Point in response to the simple question "where is the _____?" when objects are named

8 Point in response to the simple question "where is the _____?" when

pictures of objects are named

9  Carry out simple one-part commands containing verbs

10  Carry out simple one-part commands containing adjectives

11  Carry out simple one-part commands containing prepositions

12  Carry out simple one-part commands containing pronouns

13  Carry out simple one-part commands containing adverbs

14  Carry out simple one-part commands containing the numbers one through five

15  Carry out simple one-part commands containing color words

16  Carry out a sequence of two or more commands

17 Carry out commands containing idiomatic, colloquial, and figurative speech

18  Say a first word with meaning

19  Say the names of several common objects

20  Answer in response to the question "What is this?" by naming the object

21  Indicate his/her wants and thoughts by using nouns

22  Identify and name the parts of his/her face and the primary parts of his/her body

23  Identify and name objects when shown pictures of them

24  Refer to him/herself by his/her first name

25  Refer to others by their first name

26  Use plural nouns in his/her speech

27  Identify and name sounds that are made by persons or objects that are out of his/her sight

28  Identify and name the actions of people around him/her by using a verb form

29  Identify and name the actions taking place in pictures by using a verb form

30  Indicate his/her wants by saying noun/verb combinations

31  Refer to him/herself by saying the pronouns "me" and "my"

32  Indicate his/her wants by saying adjective/noun combinations

33  Say, sing or chant short rhymes and songs from memory

34  Indicate amounts by saying the numbers one through five

35  Use prepositions to describe the position of people and things

36  Indicate his/her wants and thoughts by saying simple declarative sentences

37  Indicate his/her wants and thoughts by asking simple questions

38  Use pronouns to refer to other people

39  Refer to him/herself by using the pronouns "mine" and "I"

40  Identify and name the primary colors and identify objects that are these colors

41  Identify and name objects that are colors other than the primary ones

42  Identify and name colors in pictures

43  Identify and name objects in terms of their use

44  Say his/her age and the month and date of his/her birthday

45  State his/her address and telephone number

46  Say the days of the week

47  Say the date by giving the month and the days

48  Classify objects into categories and use categorical nouns in his/her speech

49  Respond appropriately to questions beginning with the question markers:  when, who, what, whose, how, where, and how many

50  Relate the details of stories told to him/her

51  Carry out simple conversations, including telephone conversations, on a one-to-one basis

52  Use language courtesies

53  Describe experiences in sequential order

54  Describe pictures, using a variety of sentences in sequential order

55  Participate in group conversations

56  Speak in the patterns of acceptable adult speech

**Goal:  Demonstrate his/her speech/language skills at the pre-verbal level**

1  Attend to, stop, or change his/her activity in response to human voice or sound

2  Maintain his/her interest in visual stimuli

3  Demonstrate reciprocal interaction patterns

4  Establish appropriate eye gaze to initiate or maintain a conversation

5  Indicate his/her desire for further communication

6  Vocalize sounds

7  Produce vowel sounds

8  Produce speech sounds with his/her lips

9  Produce speech sounds with his/her tongue tip

10  Produce speech sounds with back of his/her tongue

11  Attempt to imitate speech sounds made by others

12  Imitate sounds or patterns made by others

13  Respond to speech/gesture games

14  Initiate speech/gesture games

## Goal:  Demonstrate  his/her speech language skills at the one-word level

1  Produce first word

2  Use three or more words with meaning

3  Develop a listening vocabulary of 10-25 words

4  Use vocabulary of 10-25 words

5  Demonstrate action words

6  Respond to simple questions

7  Indicate wants and needs

8  Respond to simple commands

9  Give simple commands

10  Respond appropriately to "no" and "yes"

## Goal:  Demonstrate speech/language skills characteristic of the two-word stage

1  Imitate two-word sentences

2  Answer questions "yes" or "no"

3  Use two-word patterns

4  Use basic concept words

5  Demonstrate basic concept words

6  Ask for help and assistance

7  Express his/her own feelings and concerns

8  Give two-word responses to questions

9 Use two-word combinations including noun-noun, noun-verb, adjective-noun, and verb-noun

10  Combine any two words with a rising inflection as question

11  Answer basic questions

## Goal: Demonstrate appropriate pragmatic language involving interactional/conversational skills

1 Open conversation appropriately
2 Engage in conversation for interaction purposes
3 Reduce his/her echoic behavior
4 Establish a topic
5 Maintain a conversational topic for two or more interchanges
6 Provide information that is relevant to the conversation
7 Observe rules of conversational turn-taking
8 Demonstrate appropriate interrupting skills
9 Respond to requests to clarify
10 Ask others for clarification when necessary
11 Close conversations appropriately

12 Maintain appropriate social distance when speaking with another
13 Answer telephone with appropriate greetings and introductions
14 Initiate telephone calls with appropriate greetings and introductions
15 Make telephone calls asking appropriate questions
16 Use tact and politeness markers in conversation
17 Code-shift as appropriate
18 Use situationally appropriate rules for conversation
19 Attend to speaker
20 Relate stories, personal experiences, or activities
21 Explain reasons/excuses
22 Signal topic shifts
23 Use logical sequencing
24 Role-play

## Goal: Demonstrate appropriate pragmatic intents

1 Respond to directions
2 Give directions
3 Answer a variety of questions
4 Give expanded answers to questions

5  Ask a variety of questions

6  Use appropriate social statements/politeness markers

7  Request objects

8  Respond correctly to indirect requests

9  Participate in storytelling

10  Relate a story

11  Participate in informal group dramatizations

12  Initiate/maintain/end a group game or activity

13  Request permission

14  Use language as an effective means of regulating the environment

15  Reject inaccurate information

16  Express hypothetical statements

17  Make experimental statements

18  Use humor

19  Use language to effectively communicate own thoughts and feelings

## Goal:  Demonstrate appropriate semantic skills: associations/categorizations

1  Associate similar objects varying in one or more attributes

2  Categorize pictures according to functions

3  Match items commonly used together

4  Complete open-ended sentence with word based on common association

5  Answer questions related to functions

6  Describe similarities and differences of given objects/pictures

7  Complete analogies

8  Use language to demonstrate the interrelationship of words and concepts

## Goal:  Demonstrate appropriate semantic skills: cause and effect sequencing

1  Explain basic cause and effect relationships

2  Sequence series of related pictures/events

3  Describe his/her personal events, experiences, stories with appropriate sequence

4  Give main idea of story

5  Identify feasible cause and effects of events

123

6  Summarize stories giving important details and correct sequence of events

7  Complete stories with appropriate and probable endings

8  Create his/her own story using logical sequence and plausible cause and effect

## Goal:  Demonstrate his/her appropriate verbal reasoning skills

1  Identify absurdities

2  Describe differences and similarities

3  Complete sentences from verbal analogies expressing varied relationships

4  Complete sentences with comparisons

5  Complete sentences expressing spatial, temporal, familial relationships

6  Answer conditional statements

7  Identify problems and determine solutions

8  Identify the cause of problematic situations

9  Predict outcomes

## Goal:  Increase his/her auditory processing skills

1  Increase  his/her auditory discrimination

2  Increase  his/her synthesis of sequencing/patterning sounds

3  Increase his/her figure-ground discrimination

4  Increase  his/her auditory sequential memory

5  Draw logical conclusions and inferences from orally presented materials

6  Summarize material orally presented

7  Determine cause and effect in material orally presented

8  Follow directions orally presented

9  Use compensatory skills in processing information

## Goal:  Demonstrate appropriate semantic skills: word relationships

1  Use word relationships

2  Make associations

3  Categorize items

4  Describe similarities/differences

5  Complete analogies

6  Sequence a series of events

7  Express cause-effect relationships

8  Give the main idea in a story or conversation

9  Relate experiences

10  Make comparisons

11  Give examples of antonyms/synonyms/multiple meanings

## Goal:  Demonstrate appropriate semantic skills: vocabulary

1  Use basic concepts

2  Label objects, people, events, things, actions, pictures

3  Use descriptive words

4  Use attributes of feeling

5  Use vocabulary for daily living skills

6  Use vocabulary for vocational skills

7  Define objects, events, etc.

8  Use common figurative speech

9  Use figurative language

## Goal:  Demonstrate appropriate rules of morphology

1  Use plurals

2  Use possessives

3  Use suffixes

4  Use prefixes

5  Use negation

6  Use contractions

7  Use noun-verb agreement

8  Use noun-verb agreement

## Goal:  Increase his/her receptive/expressive vocabulary and language relationships

1  Use categories, classifications, associations, opposites

2  Use similarities and differences

3  Use analogies

4  Exhibit functional vocabulary

5  Use story sequencing skills

6  Use part-whole relationships

7  Use comparative relationships

8  Use temporal and spatial relationships

9  Classify objects by categories

10  Classify pictures by categories

11  Use synonyms for common words

12  Orally define words

13  Use new words in sentences and discussions

14  Identify and use homonyms

15  Identify analogies

16  Orally identify parts of compound words

17  Orally identify root words

18  State meanings of common prefixes

19  State meanings of common suffixes

20  Identify and use antonyms

21  Combine simple sentences into complex sentence structures

22  Arrange a set of words in a meaningful sentence structure

**Goal:  Increase communication skills necessary to interact appropriately**

1  Develop a community resource vocabulary (i.e. grocery store, bank, doctor, etc.)

2  Develop communication skills necessary to acquire community services

3  Interact appropriately with community workers in order to obtain services

4  Use appropriate social greetings

5  Respond to social greetings appropriately

6  Use circumlocution technique to make his/her needs and wants understood

7  Provide the information needed to obtain a specific service

8  Discuss a specific topic without making tangential comments

9  Engage in conversation for interactional purposes

10  Observe rules of conversational turn-taking

11  Demonstrate appropriate interrupting skills

12  Respond to requests to clarify

13  Ask others for clarification when necessary

14  Close conversations appropriately

15  Maintain appropriate social distance when speaking with another

16  Attend to speaker

17  Respond to directions

18  Give directions

19  Answer a variety of questions

20  Give expanded answers to questions

21  Ask a variety of questions

22  Use appropriate social statements/politeness markers

23  Request objects

24  Respond correctly to indirect requests

25  Participate in storytelling

26  Relate a story

27  Participate in informal group dramatizations

28  Initiate/maintain/end a group game or activity

29  Request permission

30  Use language as an effective means of regulating his/her environment

31  Use humor

## DEVELOPMENT-WRITTEN COMMUNICATION

### Goal:  Demonstrate improved study skills

1  Alphabetize by the first letter of a word

2  Alphabetize by the first two letters of a word

3  Locate words in the dictionary using guide words

4  Use a dictionary to identify an appropriate meaning for a word

5  Use the table of contents of a book

6  Use the index of a book

7  Use the glossary of a book

8  Use the alphabetical guides on the spine of an encyclopedia

9  Interpret a line graph

10  Interpret a circle graph

11  Interpret a pictograph

12  Interpret symbols on a map

13  Use directions on a map

14  Use a scale of distance on a map

15  Use a dictionary to determine part of speech

16  Use a dictionary to identify accented syllable

17  Use a dictionary to pronounce words

18  Use a dictionary to divide words into syllables

19  Use a card catalog to locate books by author's name, title, subject

20  Interpret a paragraph

21  Develop outlines

22  Develop note-taking

23  Develop better study habits

24  Complete his/her homework assignments when given

25  Develop outlining skills

26  Develop note-taking skills

27  Bring appropriate materials to school

28  Prepare material for class

29  Share material

30  Work cooperatively in a group

31  Complete his/her assigned work

32  Work without interrupting his/her teacher

33  Change his/her activities without incident

34  Undertake a new task without incident

35  Use his/her time productively

## Goal: Demonstrate improved writing skills

1  Write his/her own name

2  Write the alphabet

3  Write in cursive letters

4  Use capital letters appropriately to begin sentences

5  Capitalize proper nouns

6  Use the period in abbreviations

7  Use apostrophes in contractions

8  Use apostrophes in possessives

9  Use the appropriate punctuation to end sentences

10  Use quotation marks around direct quotations

11  Use commas correctly

12  Identify complete sentences and sentence fragments

13  Indent the first line of a paragraph

14  Distinguish singular and plural forms of nouns

15  Distinguish singular and plural forms of verbs

16  Write in a friendly letter format

17  Write in a business letter format

18  Write a simple narrative

19  Write a book report

20  Apply common spelling rules

21  Identify the parts of speech of given words

22  Print personal data (age, phone number, address)

23  Print uppercase letters sequentially

24  Print lower case letters sequentially

25  Print upper case letters dictated

26  Print lower case letters dictated

27  Print simple sentences

28  Identify and use abbreviations

29  Use semicolon between main clauses of compound sentences

30  Use a colon to introduce a list

31  Address an envelope with his/her return address

32  Write a letter requesting information, material

33  Express a complete thought using a sentence

34  Develop a basic outline

35  Proofread his/her written work

## Goal:  Demonstrate improved spelling skills

1  Spell words from a basic word list

2  Spell initial consonant sounds

3  Spell initial consonant cluster sounds

4  Spell base word with suffix

5  Spell base word with prefixes

6  Spell number words

7  Spell days of week and abbreviations

8  Spell months of year

9  Spell months of year and abbreviations

## Goal:  Demonstrate improved word-attack skills

1  Associate consonant sounds with appropriate letters

2  Associate a sound with the appropriate beginning consonant

3  Associate a sound with the appropriate medial consonant

4  Identify vowels in the medial position

5  Identify short vowels in the medial position

6  Identify vowels

7  Identify the use of "y" as a vowel

8  Identify soft and hard "c" sounds

9  Identify soft and hard "g" sounds

10  Apply vowel rules (single syllable, final "e", double vowel)

11  Relate sounds to digraphs

12  Relate sounds to diphthongs

13  Practice the phonetic approach

14  Vocalize letter sounds

15  Produce vowel sounds

## Goal:  Demonstrate improved syllabication skills

1  Explain syllabication concepts

2  Apply rules of syllabication

3  Apply accent rules

4  Associate initial consonants with pictures

5  Identify initial consonants presented visually

6  Identify initial consonants presented audibly

7  Pronounce short vowel sounds

8  Pronounce long vowel sounds

9  Read color words

10  Read number words

11  Pronounce words with consonant, vowel, consonant

12  Pronounce words with consonant, vowel, consonant, vowel

13  Pronounce words with consonant, vowel, vowel

14  Identify the number of syllables in words

## Goal:  Demonstrate improved structural analysis skills

1  Identify parts of compound words

2  Identify the parts of contractions

3  Identify common abbreviations

4  Identify plurals

5  State meanings of common prefixes

6  State meanings of common suffixes

7  Identify possessive forms of words

8  Pronounce common word endings

9  Pronounce prefixes

10  Determine place relationships in stories read

11  Identify root words

12  Read stories and determine time relationships

## Goal:  Demonstrate improved sight-word recognition skills

1  Pronounce the pre-primer Dolch list

2  Pronounce the primer Dolch list

3  Pronounce the first grade Dolch list

4  Pronounce the second grade Dolch list

5  Pronounce the third grade Dolch list

6  Recognize words related to warning, safety, signs

7  Recognize words related to informational signs

8  Recognize words related to direction

9  Recognize words related to food

10  Recognize words related to food preparation

11  Recognize basic recipe directions

12  Recognize medicine labels

13  Recognize warning labels

## Goal:  Demonstrate improved functional word recognition

1  Interpret common warning/safety signs and symbols

2  Interpret common informational signs and symbols

3  Interpret directional signs and symbols

4  Interpret words related to food

5  Interpret words related to food preparation

6  Interpret basic recipe directions

7  Interpret medicine labels

8  Interpret warning labels

9  Interpret clothing labels

10  Interpret traffic signs and symbols

## Goal: Demonstrate improved vocabulary skills

1 Use context clues to define words
2 Use synonyms for common words
3 Identify homonyms
4 Identify analogies
5 Identify synonyms
6 Label objects, people, events, things, actions, pictures
7 Use descriptive words
8 Use attributes of feeling
9 Use vocabulary for daily living skills
10 Use vocabulary for vocational skills
11 Define objects, events, etc.
12 Interpret common figurative speech
13 Use figurative language

## Goal: Demonstrate improved reading comprehension skills

1 Recall the main idea from a reading selection
2 Recall details from a reading selection
3 Sequence events in a reading selection
4 Draw logical conclusions from material read
5 Summarize material read
6 Draw inferences from material read
7 Determine cause and effect relationships in material read
8 Distinguish between fact and opinion
9 Identify a topic sentence in a paragraph
10 Predict outcome of a narrative
11 Identify time span, period
12 Distinguish between reality and fantasy
13 Select correct endings of stories
14 Determine place relationships in stories
15 Determine time relationships in stories
16 Describe setting of a story
17 Describe characters of a story
18 Describe story plot

## *DEVELOPMENT-CALCULATION*

### Goal: Demonstrate improved numeration skills

1   Count by rote to ten

2   Count objects to ten

3   Count by rote to one hundred

4   Match one-to-one

5   Match equivalent sets

6   Use language of sets

7   Write numerals in sequential order

8   Read number words to ten

9   Recite ordinal numbers to "tenth"

10   Read and write numerals to nine

11   Read and write numerals to ninety-nine

12   Read and write numerals to 999

13   Read and write numerals to thousands

14   Read and write numerals to millions

15   Read and write numerals to billions

16   Count by twos to twenty

17   Count by fives to fifty

18   Count by threes to thirty

19   Count by fours to forty

20   Count by sixes to sixty

21   Count by sevens to seventy

22   Count by eights to eighty

23   Count by nines to ninety

24   Read Roman numerals to X

25   Read Roman numerals through M

26   Read fractional numerals

27   Distinguish between numerator and denominator

28   Distinguish place value of decimals to hundredths

29   Round whole numbers

## Goal: Demonstrate improved arithmetic skills

1  Recite addition facts 1-10

2  Add numbers horizontally

3  Add numbers vertically

4  Add two digits without regrouping

5  Add three digits without regrouping

6  Add two or more digits with regrouping

7  Recite subtraction facts 1-10

8  Subtract numbers horizontally

9  Subtract numbers vertically

10  Subtract two digits without regrouping

11  Subtract three digits without regrouping

12  Subtract two or more digits with regrouping

13  Recite multiplication facts to 81

14  Multiply two digits by one digit without regrouping

15  Multiply two digits by one digit with regrouping

16  Multiply two digits by two without regrouping

17  Multiply two digits by two digits with one regrouping

18  Multiply three digits by three digits

19  Recite division facts to 9

20  Divide using multiples of ten

21  Divide by a two-digit divisor with a remainder

22  Divide three digits by two digits with a zero in the divisor

23  Divide four digits by three digits

24  Solve word problems involving addition, subtraction

25  Recite multiplication facts

26  Solve simple word problems

27  Add without the use of fingers or chart

28  Solve word problems involving multiplication and division

29  Add three digits with a carry

30  Add four digits with a carry

31  Subtract three digits with a remainder

32 Subtract four digits with a remainder

33 Multiply three digits by two digits with carrying and no zero in multiplier

34 Multiply three digits by two digits with carrying and zero in multiplier

35 Multiply three digits by three digits with carrying and no zero in multiplier

36 Multiply three digits by three digits with carrying and zero in multiplier

37 Divide two digits by one with a remainder

38 Divide two digits by two without a remainder

**Goal: Demonstrate improved computational skills with fractions**

1 Add like fractions

2 Add unlike fractions

3 Add mixed numbers without regrouping

4 Add mixed numbers with regrouping

5 Subtract like fractions

6 Subtract unlike fractions

7 Subtract mixed numbers without regrouping

8 Subtract mixed numbers with regrouping

9 Multiply fractions by a whole number

10 Multiply fractions by a mixed number

11 Multiply fractions by fractions

12 Multiply whole numbers by a fraction

13 Divide whole numbers by mixed numbers

14 Divide mixed numbers by mixed numbers

15 Convert a whole number to a fraction

16 Convert fractions to mixed numbers

17 Convert mixed numbers to improper fractions

18 Reduce a fraction to lowest terms

19 Convert a fraction to higher terms

20 Convert fractions and decimals

21 Multiply mixed numbers by mixed numbers

22 Divide whole numbers by proper fraction

23 Identify fractional part of a shape

24 Solve word problems with fractions

25 Review computational skills with fractions

## Goal: Demonstrate improved computational skills with decimals and percents

1 Identify the place value of a digit
2 Write decimals
3 Change decimals to fractions
4 Change fractions to decimals
5 Add one-place decimal fractions
6 Add two-place decimal fractions
7 Add one and two-place decimal fractions
8 Add two and three-place decimal fractions
9 Add three-place decimal fractions
10 Multiply whole numbers by decimals
11 Multiply decimals by decimals
12 Divide whole numbers by decimals
13 Divide decimals by decimals
14 Convert fractions to decimals
15 Convert percents to decimals
16 Compute a percentage of a whole number
17 Subtract decimals with tenths
18 Subtract decimals with hundredths
19 Subtract decimals with tenths and hundredths
20 Subtract decimals with thousandths
21 Subtract decimals with hundredths and thousandths
22 Sequence decimals in order of value
23 Complete word problems that require computation of %
24 Convert fractions to percent
25 Round decimal numerals through the thousandths
26 Subtract three-place decimal fractions
27 Solve word problems with decimals and percents

## Goal: Demonstrate improved understanding of money as units of value

1 Recognize monetary units by name
2 Identify and count pennies up to 10
3 Identify and count nickels up to 40

4   Count nickel and penny combinations up to 30

5   Identify and count dimes up to $1.00

6   Count dime, nickel, penny combinations up to $1.00

7   Identify and count quarters up to $1.00

8   Count quarters, dimes, nickels, penny combinations

9   Identify and count half dollars up to $1.00

10  Count half dollar, quarter, dime, nickel, penny combinations up to $2.00

11  Identify and count one dollar bills up to $5.00

12  Count one dollar, half dollar, quarter, dime, nickel, penny combinations up to $5.00

13  Count by tens to one hundred

14  Associate written monetary symbols with value

15  Compare the relationship among coins

16  Make change

17  Explain the use of checks

18  Explain the uses of credit cards

19  Explain the uses of certified checks

20  Describe information on a pay stub

21  Demonstrate the proper completion of a check

22  Demonstrate the maintenance of a checkbook register

23  Interpret a simple checking account statement

24  Compute the cost of a loan at interest

25  Recognize money by name

26  Recognize money by value

27  Complete equation on equivalent values of coins and bills

28  Compare similar items for the better buy

29  Add two items with total less than $1.00

30  Add two items with total less than $10.00

31  Add two items with total less than $100.00

32  Add three items with total less than $1.00

33  Add three items with total less than $10.00

34  Add three items with total less than $100.00

## Goal: Demonstrate improved use of time concepts

1  Tell time to the nearest  hour
2  Tell time to the nearest half hour
3  Tell time to the nearest quarter hour
4  Tell time to the nearest minute
5  Convert hours, minutes
6  Convert days, weeks
7  Convert days, year
8  Convert months, year
9  Recite the names of the weekdays in sequence
10  Recite the names of the months in sequence
11  Recite the seasons in sequence
12  Show the direction in which the clock hands turn
13  Identify numerals on the clock face
14  Identify time on a digital as well as a conventional clock
15  Tell hour hand from minute hand
16  Convert days and hours
17  Convert minutes and seconds
18  Use calendar to find days in month
19  Write dates numerically and nominally

## Goal: Demonstrate improved  skills in measurement

1  Measure to the nearest unit
2  Measure to the nearest half-unit
3  Measure to the nearest quarter-unit
4  Measure to the nearest tenth-unit
5  Convert linear units
6  Distinguish among various units of measurement
7  Estimate the height of objects
8  Estimate the length of objects
9  Convert weight units
10  Convert volume units

139

11  State appropriate metric, English conversions

12  Read a thermometer

13  Explain the relation of temperature to freezing and boiling

14  Measure to nearest 1/8 unit

15  Convert feet, inches

16  Convert yards, feet

17  Convert yards, inches

**Goal:  Demonstrate improved  ability to apply geometric concepts**

1  Distinguish among geometric shapes

2  Define perimeter

3  Define area

4  Define volume

5  Compute the perimeter of a square

6  Compute the perimeter of a rectangle

7  Compute the perimeter of a triangle

8  Match geometric shapes and names

# EARNING A LIVING-PREVOCATIONAL

## Goal:  Increase his/her rudimentary pre-vocational skills

1 Initiate and receive telephone calls in a businesslike manner

2 Demonstrate his/her mastery of one means of public transportation

3 Sit at his/her desk/work area

4 Keep his/her desk/work area neat

5 Use the word "not" to indicate nonexistence

6 Bring appropriate materials to school/work

7 Leave inappropriate materials at home

8 Listen to directions

9 Follow simple oral directions

10 Follow simple written directions

11 Improve his/her work using teacher's corrections

12 Change his/her activities without incident

13 Refrain from disrupting others' activities

14 Answer or attempt to answer a question

15 Accept authority

16 Enter a room without incident

17 Walk in line

18 Walk properly through hall

19 Avoid excessive physical contact

20 Initiate informal interaction

21 Participate in informal interaction

22 Respond to and make greetings and farewells

23 Use correct titles when addressing people

24 Make and respond to introductions

25 Demonstrate manner appropriate to dining situations

26 Clean table before and after eating

27 Clean spills on floor after eating or whenever appropriate

28 Wash dishes thoroughly

29  Dry dishes

30  Make his/her own bed

31  Dust without breaking things

32  Wipe up spills on counters at appropriate times

33  Put away his/her clothes, shoes, toys and games

34  Keep his/her personal areas neat and clean

35  Hang up his/her clothes

36  Use a water fountain properly

37  Open and enter doorway

38  Close door

39  Use simple office materials

40  Place cards and papers neatly in a pile

41  Transport materials through a building

**Goal:   Increase his/her essential pre-vocational personal qualities**

1  Attend to and follow directions from authority figures

2  Increase his/her on-task time to an acceptable duration

3  Follow his/her daily routine

4  Respect others' possessions

5  Participate willingly in a two-person or three-person joint task

6  Use adjective and adverbs to give more precise information

7  Appear for his/her scheduled appointments on time

8  Use acceptable vocabulary in speaking with others

9  Maintain his/her personal hygiene

10  Dress neatly and appropriately for a variety of situations

11  Speak respectfully to all people

12  Show consideration of work mates' space, tools and possessions

13  Use appropriate behavior when eating in public

14  Use appropriate vocal volume in speaking

15  Maintain appropriate space/distance from others

16  Express his/her emotions in an appropriate manner

17  Write/print/state his/her name clearly

18  Write/print/state his/her address

19  Write/print/state his/her telephone number

20  Verify receipt of correct change

21  Make change

22  Identify at least one means of transportation suitable to get to work

23  Memorize essential addresses and phone numbers

24  Demonstrate the recognition and reporting of emergencies:  accident, injury, fire, catastrophe

25  Read a calendar

26  Tell time

## Goal:    Increase his/her effective employee qualities

1  Exhibit punctuality in his/her scheduled appointments

2  Exercise proper care of his/her own tools

3  Increase and maintain his/her auditory discrimination skills

4  Exercise proper care of others' tools

5  Accept constructive criticism

6  Take turns with peers at pleasant activities

7  Take turns with peers at unpleasant necessary activities

8  Complete his/her tasks

9  Respect the property of others

10  Report dangerous or criminal situations

11  Cooperate with peers in joint efforts

12  Expend reasonable effort in working at a task

# EARNING A LIVING-VOCATIONAL PREPARATION

**Goal:** **Increase his/her vocational safety skills**

1 Recognize signs of danger from other people
2 Recognize signs of danger from fumes, smoke, fire
3 Recognize physical/sexual aggression or threat
4 Indicate how to report danger, crime or threat to the appropriate authorities
5 Recognize and avoid life-threatening situations
6 Observe safety rules in using tools and equipment
7 Observe safety rules in using transportation
8 Comply with safety signals

**Goal:** **Increase his/her computer skills**

1 Demonstrate proper start-up procedure for a computer
2 Use keyboarding with touch-type method
3 Use keyboarding with hunt-and-peck method
4 Perform simple data entry
5 Operate a word processing program
6 Load paper into printer
7 Handle and store disks properly
8 Copy disks for backup

**Goal:** **Increase his/her qualifications for self-employment**

1 Select a field of self-employment in which he/she can expect to be successful
2 Identify training requirements for his/her field of self-employment
3 Identify financial requirements for his/her field of self-employment
4 Acquire skills essential to his/her field of self-employment
5 Identify sources for financial backing
6 Identify essential services and tools which he/she must have in order to be self-employed in this field
7 Identify legal and insurance requirements applicable to his/her field of self-employment

# EARNING A LIVING-ON THE JOB

**Goal:** **Demonstrate his/her compliance with authorities at work**

1 Comply with his/her supervisor's directions
2 Respond correctly when criticized
3 Obey rules and regulations when the supervisor is not present

**Goal:** **Demonstrate good communication with his/her supervisors at work**

1 Make his/her basic needs known to his/her supervisor (hunger, thirst, pain, sickness, toileting needs)
2 Seek help from his/her supervisor when needed
3 Let his/her supervisor know when a mistake has been made
4 Let his/her supervisor know when more materials are needed
5 Let his/her supervisor know when a job is finished
6 Communicate his/her needs and progress to his/her supervisor in a manner that is understood

**Goal:** **Demonstrate acceptable demeanor at work**

1 Do what is asked without protest
2 Establish eye-contact or smile when spoken to
3 Refrain from saying "I can't" when presented with a task
4 Accept mistakes or disappointments
5 Show enthusiasm for his/her work

**Goal:** **Demonstrate cooperation at work**

1 Share his/her work materials
2 Work as a part of an assembly line
3 Help others when needed
4 Exhibit control when provoked by others
5 Demonstrate cooperation by participating in tasks requiring shared responsibility without creating conflict

### Goal: Demonstrate respect for others at work

1 Refrain from disturbing or distracting others
2 Refrain from antagonizing others
3 Demonstrate honesty and truthfulness in the work situation
4 Demonstrate respect in his/her interactions with coworkers

### Goal: Demonstrate the ability to deal with sexuality at work

1 Express his/her affections appropriately
2 Refrain from engaging in flirtations, provocative behavior
3 Refrain from engaging in sexual practices in public
4 Avoid sexual exploitation of others
5 Identify the legal and social consequences of sexually aggressive or exploitative behavior
6 Practice socially and sexually acceptable behavior with others

### Goal: Increase his/her production level

1 Work for increasingly longer periods of time
2 Complete more work within a specified time
3 Reduce the incidence of rejected tasks

### Goal: Increase the quality of his/her work

1 Differentiate between high quality and low quality work
2 Complete his/her jobs with attention to neatness
3 Complete his/her jobs with attention to thoroughness
4 Correct his/her mistakes when noticed
5 Complete a specified amount of work with a decreasing number of mistakes

### Goal: Demonstrate punctuality at work

1 Begin his/her work without hesitation
2 Return from his/her breaks or disruptions promptly
3 Refrain from absence without good cause
4 Report to his/her work station on time
5 Demonstrate punctual behavior during the working day

**Goal:   Demonstrate his/her adaptability at work**

1  Accept changes in his/her routine without undue protest
2  Respond appropriately to a new supervisor
3  Adjust to new environments or routines without decreasing production rates

**Goal:   Demonstrate concentration at his/her work**

1  Demonstrate attention to his/her task
2  Complete a task without stopping
3  Complete his/her jobs with decreasing amount of idle time between task related movements
4  Interact with others without letting his/her work suffer
5  Refrain from overreacting when others display inappropriate behavior
6  Work without emotional or behavioral interference
7  Refrain from demonstrating undue frustration
8  Concentrate to complete difficult tasks within a predetermined time frame

**Goal:   Demonstrate safety practices at work**

1  Identify dangerous items/places in the work environment
2  Wear safe clothing and protective devices
3  Keep his/her work area neat and free from hazards
4  Refrain from creating safety hazards
5  Obey shop safety rules

**Goal:   Demonstrate independence at work**

1  Complete a task with a minimum of prompting
2  Work for increasingly longer periods of time without contact from his/her supervisor
3  Maintain steady rates of production without contact from his/her supervisor
4  Refrain from sitting and waiting for others to direct him/her
5  Complete difficult tasks without supervisor intervention

## Goal: Reduce inappropriate behavior at his/her work

1 Refrain from disruptive behavior during work time

2 Refrain from bizarre behavior during work time

3 Decrease the frequency of his/her inappropriate behavior

# BASIC EMPLOYMENT

## Goal: Demonstrate basic skills in tool use

1  Use a hammer effectively
2  Use a screwdriver effectively
3  Use pliers effectively
4  Use a saw effectively
5  Use a broom effectively
6  Use a mop effectively
7  Use a pencil sharpener effectively
8  Use a paint brush effectively
9  Use sandpaper effectively
10  Use a shovel effectively
11  Use a rake effectively
12  Use a power mower effectively
13  Use an electric drill effectively
14  Use a wrench effectively
15  Use an adjustable wrench effectively
16  Use a paint scraper effectively
17  Use a toilet brush effectively
18  Use tools effectively

## Goal: Demonstrate basic skills in light housework

1  Dust furniture and woodwork
2  Strip a bed
3  Dispose of litter properly
4  Wash windows and mirrors
5  Make a bed
6  Straighten the dining room
7  Straighten the living room
8  Straighten the kitchen
9  Straighten the bathroom

149

10 Straighten the bedroom

11 Straighten the house within a predetermined time period

**Goal:   Demonstrate  basic skills in heavy cleaning**

1 Empty waste basket and garbage can

2 Wash waste basket and garbage can

3 Line trash cans and garbage cans with plastic liner

4 Clean walls by wiping

5 Clean glossy surfaces

6 Wash windows

7 Demonstrate heavy cleaning of a specified area within a predetermined period of time

**Goal:   Demonstrate basic skills in floor care**

1 Sweep a floor

2 Use a dust pan

3 Use a dust mop

4 Use a vacuum

5 Mop a floor

6 Wax a floor

7 Buff a floor

8 Clean a floor within a predetermined time period

**Goal:   Demonstrate basic skills in bathroom care**

1 Clean a toilet

2 Clean a bathtub and shower

3 Clean a sink

4 Wash the floor

5 Clean the mirrors

6 Straighten the towels and washcloths

7 Clean walls

8 Clean a bathroom within a predetermined time period

## Goal: Demonstrate basic skills in kitchen care

1 Clear the table

2 Wash dishes by hand

3 Dry dishes

4 Put dishes away

5 Load and unload an automatic dish washer

6 Clean small appliances

7 Clean an oven

8 Clean the stove top

9 Clean the refrigerator

10 Order cupboards and drawers

11 Store foods in the proper place

12 Clean kitchen garbage can

13 Clean and straighten the kitchen within a predetermined time period

## Goal: Demonstrate basic skills in laundry services

1 Sort clothes

2 Hand wash clothes

3 Use an automatic washing machine

4 Use an automatic dryer

5 Fold clothes

6 Launder a family-sized load of clothes within a predetermined time period

## Goal: Demonstrate basic conceptual skills

1 Distinguish dirty and clean

2 Distinguish wet and dry

3 Distinguish hot and cold

4 Distinguish up and down

5 Distinguish on and in

6 Distinguish alike and different

7 Distinguish over and under

8 Distinguish through and around

151

9  Distinguish behind, in front of, and beside

10  Complete tasks that entail these concepts

## Goal:  Demonstrate basic skills in sorting

1  Distinguish between alike and different objects

2  Sort a group of two very dissimilar objects into two piles or containers

3  Sort a group of three or more dissimilar objects into corresponding containers

4  Sort several different kinds of slightly dissimilar objects into corresponding containers

5  Sort a large collection of dissimilar objects into corresponding containers within a predetermined time period

## Goal:  Demonstrate basic skills in moving objects

1  Lift objects so as not to injure him/herself

2  Move heavy furniture

3  Move objects with a dolly

4  Move different sized objects in a safe and efficient manner

# SHELTERED EMPLOYMENT

## Goal: Demonstrate skills for sheltered employment in mailing services

1 Demonstrate one-to-one correspondence

2 Prepare stacks

3 Crisscross stacks

4 Collate on an assembly line

5 Independently collate various stacks of paper

6 Prepare material for stapling or paper-clipping

7 Identify areas for staple or paper clip placement

8 Load stapler

9 Apply necessary pressure to stapler for closure

10 Use electric stapler

11 Attach paper clip

12 Place stapler or paper clip in specified area

13 Open envelope

14 Fold and crease using specific folds

15 Align and insert object or item

16 Insert items in envelope for mailing or transferring

17 Identify object or item to be labeled

18 Detach label from sheet

19 Attach label to item

20 Cut with scissors on a designated line

21 Use a mat knife to cut on a designated line

22 Use the paper cutter to cut paper

23 Select the proper tool and cut the material

24 Tie item

25 Tape item

26 Glue item

27 Operate sealing machines

28 Secure items by sealing

29 Package on an assembly line

30  Package paper goods

31  Package various containers

32  Align corners in stacking

33  Stack objects of different weights and sizes

34  Stack various items

35  Group same or different items

36  Sort slightly dissimilar objects

37  Sort various items

**Goal:   Demonstrate skills for sheltered employment in assembly**

1  Select items for assembly

2  Arrange parts in specified sequence

3  Assemble an item

**Goal:   Demonstrate skills for sheltered employment in bagging**

1  Bag one or more items

2  Close the bag

3  Bag a specified number of items

4  Bag a specified number of a variety of items

**Goal:   Demonstrate skills for sheltered employment in greenhouse horticulture**

1  Prepare a container for planting

2  Make and prepare plant cuttings

3  Plant cuttings in a pot

4  Care for house plants

5  Transplant house plants

6  Transplant bushes

7  Perform greenhouse and horticulture tasks

**Goal:   Demonstrate skills for sheltered employment in building maintenance**

1  Sweep floor areas

2  Clean stair wells

3 Mop floors

4 Wash surfaces

5 Wash walls by hand

6 Wash and clean venetian blinds

7 Clean toilets

8 Clean sinks

9 Clean tubs and showers

10 Police floors

11 Empty waste baskets and garbage cans

12 Line waste baskets and garbage cans

13 Disinfect floors

14 Clean windows

15 Vacuum rugs

16 Dust

17 Scrub floors with a floor care machine

18 Wax floors with a floor care machine

19 Buff floors with a floor care machine

20 Strip floors with a stripping machine

21 Perform building maintenance custodial duties

**Goal:  Demonstrate skills for sheltered employment in grounds maintenance**

1 Water lawns and shrubs

2 Rake grass, leaves and debris

3 Use a shovel to do necessary digging around shrubs and plants

4 Dig out weeds

5 Sweep appropriate debris

6 Paint small exterior objects

7 Trim hedges and bushes

8 Mow a lawn

9 Perform grounds maintenance duties

# REGULAR EMPLOYMENT

## Goal: Demonstrate skills for office employment

1 Sort mail

2 Collate

3 Fold in thirds (business letters)

4 Stuff envelopes

5 Deliver oral/written messages

6 Handle incoming calls

7 Operate copier machine

8 Operate ten-key adding machine

9 Independently perform basic office skills

## Goal: Demonstrate skills for employment in building maintenance

1 Police floors

2 Collect and dispose of litter

3 Vacuum a carpeted floor

4 Dust furniture and woodwork

5 Mop a floor

6 Sweep a floor using a broom

7 Straighten a given area

8 Empty a trash can

9 Empty a garbage can

10 Paint small areas

11 Clean mirrors and windows

12 Safely use a stepladder

13 Clean bathroom fixtures

14 Wash wallpaper and painted walls

15 Use a hand truck

16 Operate an automatic floor cleaning/buffing machine

17 Use floor cleaning machine to strip a floor

18 Use floor cleaning machine to buff and wax floors

19  Wash venetian blinds

20  Properly store equipment

21  Perform building maintenance tasks

## Goal:   Demonstrate skills for employment in outdoor maintenance

1  Collect and remove litter and trash

2  Rake leaves and grass

3  Care for walkways and driveways

4  Remove snow and ice

5  Paint small outdoor objects

6  Edge flower beds and lawns

7  Water flower beds and lawns

8  Fertilize and seed lawns

9  Mow lawns

10  Weed lawns

11  Perform outdoor maintenance tasks

## Goal:   Demonstrate skills for employment in horticulture

1  Prepare soil mixtures

2  Identify common house plants

3  Describe individual plant needs

4  Maintain house plants

5  Maintain lawns

6  Employ pest control measures

7  Identify common cut flowers, flowering plants and florist greens

8  Assist and prepare pre-patterned floral arrangements

9  Perform horticultural tasks

## Goal:   Demonstrate skills for employment in food services

1  Maintain a safe working environment

2  Clean garbage cans

3  Maintain a clean working environment

4  Separate, scrape, stack and remove dishes from table

5  Transport dishes, trays and pans safely

6  Wash pots, pans and utensils

7  Load, operate and unload dishwasher

8  Stack dishes, pots, pans and utensils

9  Operate a garbage disposal

10  Clean and sanitize kitchen equipment

11  Clean and sanitize dining area

12  Clean and stack food trays

13  Care for serving carts and kitchen furniture

14  Set up tables and chairs for serving meals

15  Store food correctly in proper storage areas

16  Refill counter and table dispensers

17  Grease and prepare pans for cooking

18  Fill beverage dispensers

19  Dispense and serve beverages

20  Wash fruits and vegetables

21  Core, peel, slice and dice fruits and vegetables

22  Make toast

23  Make sandwiches

24  Wrap sandwiches

25  Assist in serving in a cafeteria line

26  Clear tables of used plates and utensils

27  Fill table condiment holders

28  Pour water, coffee, juice

29  Use appropriate social courtesies with customers

## Goal:   Demonstrate skills for employment in retail sales

1  Use proper courtesies with customers

2  Record sales on a register

3  Count and make change

4  Locate items requested by customer

5  Wrap or bag customer's purchase properly

6  Make refunds and exchanges

7  Replace merchandise from storeroom

8  Stock shelves

9  Tag and price stock

10  Weigh item to find price

11  Conduct inventory

## Goal:  Demonstrate skills for employment in laundry services

1  Load and unload laundry carts

2  Move heavily loaded hand trucks and carts

3  Sort soiled linen

4  Load and unload commercial washing machines

5  Load and unload commercial dryers

6  Fold and stack flat-work by hand

7  Operate a laundry folding machine

8  Stack laundry folded by a machine

9  Operate a pressing machine

10  Press garments with a pressing machine

11  Fold, bag and box pressed garments

12  Perform basic laundry skills

## Goal:  Demonstrate skills for employment in homemaker services

1  Straighten bedrooms

2  Straighten living and dining room

3  Clean bathroom

4  Clean kitchen

5  Make an occupied bed

6  Prepare simple foods

7  Serve simple meals

8  Answer the telephone

9  Make telephone call with assistance

10  Assist responsible person with child care

11  Perform homemaking services

**Goal:  Demonstrate skills for employment in hotel housekeeping**

1  Dust furniture and woodwork

2  Sweep floors and hallways

3  Mop floors

4  Vacuum rugs and carpets

5  Dispose of trash

6  Make beds

7  Load a hand truck

8  Unload a hand truck

9  Clean sink, bathtub/shower, and mirrors

10  Clean toilet bowls and urinals

11  Clean and fill washroom dispenser

12  Straighten a bathroom

13  Demonstrate honesty in the work setting

14  Load and unload a hand-operated dolly

15  Clean a hotel room

16  Replace lights when burned out

17  Replace complimentary items

**Goal:  Demonstrate skills for employment in automotive services**

1  Wash and dry a car

2  Wax and polish a car

3  Clean the interior of a car

4  Check and replenish fluids

5  Flush and refill radiators

6  Prepare surfaces for painting

7  Apply masking tape and paper

8  Assist in preparing a vehicle for delivery

9  Maintain the service station exterior

10  Maintain the service station interior

11  Perform basic automotive services

## Goal:  Demonstrate skills for employment in warehousing

1  Stack boxes

2  Load and unload truck

3  Load and operate hand truck

4  Handle and store warehouse contents

## Goal:  Demonstrate skills for employment in furniture refinishing

1  Remove paint and finishes from furniture

2  Sand wooden surfaces

3  Apply paint, stains and finishes

4  Refinish furniture

## Goal:  Demonstrate skills for employment in building trades

1  Recognize common building materials

2  Move materials

3  Perform general labor tasks

4  Assist in insulation work

5  Perform building trades tasks

## Goal:  Demonstrate skills for employment in painting

1  Prepare work area with necessary protective materials

2  Prepare interior and exterior surface by scraping, sanding, patching

3  Apply prime and finish coats using a brush

4  Apply prime and finish coats using a roller

5  Apply prime and finish coats using a sprayer

6  Clean painting equipment

7  Clean up spills, drips, overspray

## Goal: Demonstrate skills for employment in a service station

1 Identify safety requirements for employees

2 Pump gas

3 Check and fill tires

4 Check and fill oil

5 Check and fill coolant

6 Check and fill transmission fluid

7 Clean windshield

8 Register payment and make change

9 Use appropriate courtesies with customers

# *INDEPENDENCE*

**Goal:   Demonstrate personal care skills for independence**

1  Take a bath or a shower
2  Shave when necessary
3  Use deodorant
4  Care for menstrual needs
5  Use public rest rooms
6  Demonstrate appropriate personal care practices
7  Keep his/her body clean
8  Keep his/her clothing clean
9  Keep his/her clothing neat
10  Select appropriate and matched clothes
11  Care for his/her hair
12  Maintain a suitable appearance as part of daily routine

**Goal:   Demonstrate clothing skills for independence**

1  Sort dirty clothes
2  Use a washing machine
3  Use a dryer
4  Fold clothes
5  Iron simple garments
6  Put away clothes
7  Identify clothing in need of mending
8  Mend clothes
9  Care for shoes
10  Shop for clothes with assistance
11  Demonstrate proper care of clothing

**Goal:   Demonstrate shopping skills for independence**

1  Identify local stores in which to purchase food, clothing, household goods
2  Count change after paying for a purchase

3  Seek assistance from a salesperson

4  Select appropriate amounts or sizes of food

5  Specify own sizes for clothing items

6  Identify and use "sell by" or expiration dates

**Goal:   Demonstrate  food preparation skills for independence**

1  Plan simple menus

2  Shop for food with assistance

3  Store food in proper places

4  Identify kitchen utensils by name and function

5  Prepare simple snacks and meals

6  Operate a stove

7  Operate simple appliances

8  Wash hands before handling food

9  Scoop food out of containers

10  Open and close food containers properly

11  Mix ingredients with a spoon

12  Operate an oven

13  Operate a broiler

14  Operate an outside grill

15  Operate a microwave oven

16  Toast bread

17  Make coffee and tea

18  Use a mixer and a blender

19  Use a can opener

20  Use a strainer or colander for food

21  Make a sandwich

22  Set a timer for cooking

23  Prepare a meal from a recipe

24  Plan and prepare a simple meal

25  Serve a meal to others

26  Clean up the kitchen

27  Demonstrate basic food preparation skills

**Goal:** **Demonstrate home sanitation skills for independence**

1  Deposit trash in appropriate receptacles
2  Remove garbage to outside location for pickup
3  Sort and store recyclable materials appropriately
4  Clean eating and cooking surfaces
5  Flush the toilet after use
6  Wash hands after using toilet
7  Clean with broom and vacuum
8  Clean windows and mirrors
9  Wash eating and cooking items after use

**Goal:** **Demonstrate functional reading skills for independence**

1  Track visually from left to right
2  Identify his/her own name in printed form
3  Identify his/her address in printed form
4  Identify his/her telephone number in printed form
5  Identify functional signs and words in printed form
6  Read and derive certain information from schedules, menus and directories

**Goal:** **Demonstrate  money skills for independence**

1  Count twenty-five objects
2  Count by 5's and 10's to 100
3  Identify, read and write numbers to 100
4  Use various quantities to show "more than", "less than" and "equal to"
5  Identify U.S. coins: penny, nickel, dime and quarter
6  Find equivalent set of coins for pennies, nickels and dimes
7  Identify specific paper currency values
8  Select appropriate set of coins to match  price of an object

**Goal:** **Demonstrate paycheck skills for independence**

1  Refrain from giving his/her paycheck to others
2  Endorse paycheck

3  Deposit paycheck with assistance

4  Demonstrate proper care and handling of the paycheck

## Goal:  Demonstrate household repair skills for independence

1  Replace common light bulbs

2  Reset circuit breaker

3  Use a plunger to clear a toilet or sink

4  Turn off water supply at a leak site

5  Reglue small broken object

6  Nail an item to a wall

7  Screw an item to a larger object

8  Paint a vertical surface and a horizontal surface with a roller

9  Paint an object with a brush

10 Clean the tools used to paint

## Goal:  Demonstrate home safety skills for independence

1  Use electricity safely

2  Handle and care for sharp and pointed objects

3  Demonstrate safe care/use of poisons, flammables, etc.

4  Avoid falls and unsafe practices that cause falls

5  Demonstrate safe kitchen practices

6  Demonstrate safe bathroom practices

7  Identify safe home practices

8  Carry fragile items properly

9  Hold handrail on stairs

10 Notify someone when leaving the house

11  Demonstrate use of 911 to call for help

12  Carry a house key

13  Use a step ladder properly

14  Use an extension ladder properly

15  Check and replace battery in a smoke alarm

16  Extinguish a minor fire

17  Describe exit procedure in event of fire

## Goal:  Demonstrate school safety skills for independence

1 Travel safely in halls and stairs

2 Demonstrate safe classroom practices

3 Ride safely on the school bus

4 Play safely on the playground

5 Demonstrate safe behavior during a fire drill

6 Identify safe practices at school

## Goal:  Demonstrate community safety skills for independence

1 Walk on sidewalks without bumping into people

2 Cross streets at corners

3 Look both ways before crossing a street

4 Avoid dangerous places and objects

5 Demonstrate safety skills in snow, rain, lightning and ice

6 Carry personal identification

7 Specify sources of help or information when lost or in danger

8 Find safe shelter during bad weather

9 Locate a rest room

10 Locate a telephone

11 Demonstrate proper entry into a revolving door

12 Demonstrate entry into an automatic door

13 Demonstrate boarding an escalator

14 Demonstrate use of an automatic elevator

15 Demonstrate entry into a turnstile

16 Identify left-right directions

17 Follow multistep directions to go to another room in a building

18 Follow multistep directions to go to another place in a neighborhood

19 Find own way home from anywhere in the neighborhood

20 Identify the meaning of traffic signals

21 Identify specific points in the community

22 State home and street addresses

## Goal: Demonstrate emergency skills for independence

1 Identify situations when police, fire, medical help needed

2 Describe methods of obtaining police, fire or medical assistance

3 Role play appropriate response in emergency situations

## Goal: Demonstrate health skills for independence

1 Describe basic first aid procedures for burns and scalds

2 Describe basic first aid procedures for injuries involving bleeding

3 Participate in a program of daily exercise

4 Identify proper amounts and kinds of foods

5 Seek medical help for persistent health problems

6 Demonstrate through role playing good health practices

7 Identify own medication by pointing and by name

8 Swallow given dose of medication

9 State why dosage should not be exceeded

10 Identify correct storage place for medication

11 Specify correct dosage of prescription medication

12 Specify correct dosage for nonprescription medication

13 Take his/her temperature with digital thermometer

14 Describe self-treatment for simple cuts

15 Describe self-treatment for nose bleeds

16 Describe self-treatment for a cold

17 Describe self-treatment for his/her chronic condition (allergy, asthma, headache, etc.)

18 Describe procedures and schedule for medical treatment of his/her life-threatening condition (diabetes, high blood pressure, hemophilia, etc.)

19 Describe proper procedure when he/she senses the onset of a seizure

20 Keep a medical diary of medical services, medication, illness, and medication allergies

## Goal:  Demonstrate travel prerequisite skills for independence

1  Present an identification card when asked by a stranger

2  Seek an adult during an emergency situation

3  Use a telephone to call the operator or an emergency number

4  Refrain from associating with strangers

5  Refrain from exhibiting bizarre behavior

## Goal:  Demonstrate bicycle skills for independence

1  Ride a bicycle with stable control

2  Walk a bicycle across a street corner

3  Demonstrate riding a bicycle on the right shoulder of a road

## Goal:  Demonstrate school travel skills for independence

1  Locate his/her classroom from the school entrance

2  Locate his/her classroom from various points in the school building

3  Locate the rest room from his/her classroom

4  Locate different points in the school building from his/her classroom

## Goal:  Demonstrate private vehicle travel skills for independence

1  Enter and exit from a vehicle

2  Operate doors, locks, windows and seat belts properly

3  Ride in a safe manner

4  Demonstrate appropriate vehicle behavior

## Goal:  Demonstrate bus travel skills for independence

1  Locate the correct bus stop and bus number

2  Board the bus and pay the fare

3  Observe correct bus behavior

4  Leave the bus at the proper location

5  Follow correct transfer procedures

6  Signal driver to stop at a specified location

7  Dismount from a bus properly

## Goal: Demonstrate Metro travel skills for independence

1  Locate the correct Metro station

2  Enter the station and go to the correct track

3  Observe correct behavior

4  Leave the train at the proper stop and exit the station

5  Follow correct transferring procedures

6  Use Metro services to arrive at a specified location

## Goal: Demonstrate community resource skills for independence

1  Use public eating facilities

2  Use public transportation

3  Respond to various emergency situations

4  Obtain a social security card, public assistance, and supplemental security income with assistance

5  Identify specific community resources

## Goal: Demonstrate interviewing skills for independence

1  Identify appropriate documents and data to bring to an interview

2  Wear appropriate and matched clothes

3  Refrain from bizarre and disruptive _behavior

4  Respond appropriately to questions

5  Submit personal identification card

6  State basic identifying information

7  State vocational preference

8  Complete an interview in a satisfactory manner

## Goal: Demonstrate telephone skills for independence

1  Identify various telephones and their parts

2  Answer the telephone appropriately

3  Dial the telephone

4  Interpret busy signal, wrong number and dial tone

5 Use the telephone to call operator, information or emergency numbers

6 Use the telephone to call a friend or neighbor

7 Use the telephone appropriately in specified situations

## Goal: Describe rights and responsibility skills for independence

1 Identify his/her legal rights

2 Identify his/her legal responsibilities

3 Describe his/her legal rights and responsibilities through role play

171

# SPEECH THERAPY

## Goal: Demonstrate correct production of speech phonemes

1 Improve his/her lingual coordination for articulation purposes

2 Strengthen his/her lingual coordination for articulation purposes

3 Audibly identify the target sound to be worked on

4 Identify the location of a target sound as being in the initial/medial/final position in a word

5 Discriminate the target sound from all other phonemes

6 Discriminate target sound from it's cognate

7 Discriminate target sound from his/her error sound

8 Produce the target sound in isolation

9 Produce the target sound in the initial/final/medial position in syllables

10 Produce the target sound in the initial/final/medial position in nonsense words

11 Produce the target sound in the initial/final/medial position in words

12 Produce the target sound in the initial/final/medial position in phrases

13 Produce the target sound in the initial/final/medial position in sentences

14 Produce the target sound in the initial/final/medial position in conversational speech

15 Produce the target sound in the initial/final/medial position in spontaneous speech

16 Reverse his/her infantile swallowing pattern

## Goal: Increase his/her fluency

1 Demonstrate fluent and non-fluent behaviors

2 Exhibit a normal breathing pattern using diaphragmatic breathing

3 Exhibit pre-voice exhalation

4 Exhibit easy onset of speech

5 Use light contact of articulators

6 Reduce muscular tension

7 Exhibit continuous phonation

8 Exhibit continuous airflow

9 Exhibit reduced rate of speech

10  Reduce the frequency of secondary characteristics

11  Reduce the frequency of interjections

12  Reduce the frequency of part-word repetitions

13  Reduce the frequency of whole-word repetitions

14  Reduce the frequency of prolongation

15  Reduce the frequency of blocks

16  Increase his/her self-confidence in speaking ability

17  Speak with controlled fluency pattern

18  Maintain spontaneous fluency pattern

19  Use appropriate eye contact

## Goal:   Increase his/her articulation skills

1  Use appropriate oral motor movements for articulation

2  Improve his/her ability to identify and discriminate phonemes

3  Produce target phoneme(s) in all positions of words

4  Produce target phoneme(s) in phrases

5  Produce target phoneme(s) in sentences

6  Produce target phoneme(s) in oral reading

7  Produce target phoneme(s) in structured conversation

8  Produce target phoneme(s) in spontaneous conversation

9  Articulate all speech sounds clearly

10  Produce voiceless consonants

11  Produce voiced consonants

12  Produce stop-plosives

13  Produce bilabials

14  Produce lingua-alveolar consonants

15  Produce nasal consonants

16  Produce sibilants

17  Produce correct vowels

18  Produce number of omissions of already mastered phonemes

19  Replace glottal substitutions with appropriate phonemes

20  Produce continuants without the feature of stopping

21  Produce all phonemes within consonant clusters

## Goal:  Increase his/her control of stuttering

1 Identify kinds of stuttering

2 Analyze various stuttering behavior

3 Identify his/her feared speaking situations

4 Reproduce various stuttering behavior

5 Exhibit cancellation and pullout strategies

6 Establish a home management program

7  Reduce rate of his/her speech

8 Exhibit easy onset and inhalation phonation

9 Establish abdominal diaphragmatic breathing patterns

10 Eliminate laryngeal tension

11  Employ rhythmic speech to increase fluency

12 Exhibit continuous phonation

13  Increase his/her self-confidence

14 Employ shadowing/masking techniques

15  Reduce his/her non-fluency

16  Stutter fluently to provide an enhanced communicative atmosphere in the speech setting that allows for maximum verbal output

17  Use a reference for controlling rate of speech

## Goal:  Increase his/her auditory processing skills

1 Expand his/her auditory sequential memory

2  Repeat sentences with an increasing number of word elements

3  Answer questions concerning details, sequences, influences, inferences

4 Improve his/her sound discrimination

5 Improve his/her word discrimination

6 Improve his/her synthesis of sequencing/patterning sounds

7 Improve his/her analysis of sound elements in words

8 Improve his/her figure ground discrimination when following directions

9 Improve his/her figure ground discrimination during sound/word discrimination

10 Improve his/her figure ground discrimination during memory and retention tasks

11 Recall the main idea from an orally presented selection

12  Recall details from an orally presented selection

13  Sequence events in an orally presented selection

14  Draw logical conclusions from orally presented materials

15  Summarize material orally presented

16  Draw inferences from material orally presented

17  Determine cause and effect in material orally presented

18  Recall auditory sequences

19  Identify words as sounding the same or different

20  Match spoken words with the same initial consonant

21  Match spoken words with the same final consonant

22  Increase skills in grammatical and/or auditory closure

23  Follow oral directions

24  Give spontaneous examples of words that begin with a certain consonant/ phoneme

## Goal:   Reduce his/her vocal tension

1  Eliminate vocal abuse/misuse

2  Identify his/her behavior which causes vocal abuse

3  Identify the physical end-product of vocal abuse

4  Demonstrate acceptable vocal behaviors

5  Accept responsibility for changes in vocal behavior

6  Use appropriate loudness levels

7  Exhibit voluntary control of relaxed efficient voice

8  Integrate good voice patterns into personal communication needs

9  Eliminate harsh glottal attacks

10  Encourage appropriate tongue posture

11  Increase his/her oral opening

12  Establish his/her optimal vocal pitch

13  Reduce his/her general body tension and laryngeal tension

14  Establish appropriate breathing patterns

15  Reduce his/her monotonous vocal patterns

**Goal:    Increase his/her vocal tension**

1  Use appropriate voicing elicited non-verbally (coughing, throat clearing, pulling, pushing, lifting)

2  Judge the acoustical characteristics of his/her own voice

3  Expand his/her voiced production into a prolonged vowel

4  Establish consistent voluntary control of his/her voicing

5  Reduce overt tension accompanying his/her vocalization

6  Establish his/her voiced production of words

7  Establish voiced productions of phrases and sentences

8  Establish his/her carry-over of voiced communication in his/her environment

9  Establish adequate breath pressure

10  Exhibit appropriate tongue posture

11  Increase his/her volume

12  Establish optimal pitch

13  Exhibit inhalation phonation

**Goal:    Increase his/her vocal quality for more intelligible speech production**

1  Increase his/her loudness level

2  Decrease his/her loudness level

3  Increase his/her oral opening

4  Increase his/her rate of speech

5  Decrease his/her rate of speech

**Goal:    Demonstrate correct syntactic structures**

1  Combine his/her words meaningfully

2  Use verb tenses correctly

3  Use singular/plural nouns correctly

4  Exhibit correct subject-verb agreement

5  Use present progressive verb tense correctly

6  Use past tense regular verbs correctly

7  Use past tense irregular verbs correctly

8  Use singular and plural correctly

9  Exhibit correct use of modal auxiliaries

10  Use auxiliary and future tense verbs correctly

11  Improve his/her comprehension/usage of adjectives

12  Improve his/her use of articles

13  Improve his/her use of auxiliary verbs

14  Improve his/her use of negatives

15  Improve his/her use of pronouns

16  Improve his/her use of embedded elements

17  Improve his/her use of 'wh' questions

18  Improve his/her use of interrogative reversal forms

19  Improve his/her use of conjunctions

20  Improve his/her use of prepositions and prepositional phrasing

21  Increase his/her use of complex and compound sentence forms

22  Demonstrate his/her use of tag ending in question forms

23  Improve his/her use of comparatives

24  Improve his/her use of "that" and copula

25  Improve his/her usage of possessives

26  Exhibit his/her use of syntactical elements in storytelling

27  Use contractions appropriately

28  Use adverbs correctly

29  Use "er" and "est" suffixes

30  Improve his/her comprehension/usage of active and passive voice

31  Improve his/her usage of "do", "does", "did" in question forms

# OCCUPATIONAL THERAPY-PHYSICAL THERAPY

## Goal: Increase correct oral motor function

1 Accept tactile stimulation around outside of his/her mouth and cheeks

2 Accept tactile stimulation of his/her gums

3 Accept tactile stimulation inside his/her cheeks and lips

4 Assume stable, aligned posture in preparation for his/her oral motor activities

5 Reduce dominance of his/her tonic bite

6 Inhibit his/her tongue thrust

7 Reduce excessive reaction to tactile stimulation of his/her mouth/face

8 Relax his/her oral musculature

9 Allow tooth-brushing

10 Maintain his/her lip closure

11 Maintain his/her lip closure to swallow

12 Decrease his/her drooling

13 Maintain his/her head in neutral to swallow

14 Maintain his/her proper alignment of jaw

15 Maintain his/her position of jaw with manual resistance

16 Move his/her jaw up and down

17 Move his/her jaw laterally

18 Demonstrate rotary movements of his/her jaw

19 Grade movements of his/her jaw

20 Demonstrate voluntary sucking

21 Demonstrate blowing

22 Inhibit protrusion of his/her tongue

23 Inhibit retraction of his/her tongue

24 Elevate his/her tongue

25 Lateralize his/her tongue

26 Suck from a bottle

27 Maintain his/her head in neutral to accept food

28 Remove food from his/her spoon with top lip closure

29  Maintain his/her head in neutral to drink

30  Seal lips on his/her cup to drink

31  Take bites of his/her food

32  Chew his/her food

33  Swallow easy textures of his/her food without choking

34  Eat pureed or soft solid foods

35  Swallow difficult textures of food without choking

36  Swallow liquids without choking

37  Demonstrate a positive attitude toward his/her mealtime

38  Eat a variety of foods

39  Allow several different people to give him/her food

**Goal:    Demonstrate reduction of his/her hypertonicity**

1  Relax when he/she is passively positioned

2  Tolerate patterns of dissociation

3  Inhibit flailing of his/her limbs with voluntary relaxation

4  Maintain a position of reduced hyperextension

5  Maintain patterns of dissociation

6  Maintain relaxation while being positioned

**Goal:    Demonstrate reduction of his/her primitive reflexes**

1  Actively dissociate his/her legs in supported standing

2  Dissociate his/her head from body movements

3  Maintain normal symmetrical muscle tonus while weight bearing

4  Maintain normal muscle tonus regardless of body position in space

5  Integrate his/her primitive reactions

**Goal:    Increase his/her postural tone without overflow**

1  Perform bridging to assist in dressing

2  Maintain his/her head in neutral in supported sitting

3  Maintain his/her head in neutral during active movement transitions

4  Maintain an upright position against gravity with pelvic support

5  Maintain an upright position against gravity with trunk in neutral and arms relaxed with pelvic support

6  Maintain an upright position against gravity with good posture

7  Maintain reduced tone in an upright posture for ADL and fine motor activities

**Goal:   Increase his/her flexion**

1  Perform his/her active flexion without hyperextension of other body parts

2  Decrease his/her head lag in pull to sit

3  Bring his/her hand to his/her mouth

4  Bring his/her hands together

5  Bring his/her head/trunk forward to help in dressing

6  Help in dressing

7  Keep his/her weight forward when tipped back in sitting

8  Assume the supine flexion position

9  Flex while hanging on a flexion bar

**Goal:   Increase his/her head and trunk control in prone and supine**

1  Hold his/her head up in midline momentarily in prone

2  Hold his/her head up in prone, propped on forearms

3  Lift his/her head and chest in prone propped on forearms

4  Maintain his/her head in midline in supine with hands at midline for play

5  Reach out for his/her toys in prone

6  Pivot in prone

7  Push backwards with arms in prone

8  Pull forward with arms in prone

9  Crawl on his/her belly with reciprocal arm-leg movements

**Goal:   Increase his/her righting and equilibrium reactions in a variety of positions and activities**

1  Demonstrate head righting against gravity

2  Roll segmentally

3  Move his/her arm across body to roll

4  Move his/her leg across body to roll

5  Demonstrate body righting against gravity

6  Use an equilibrium reaction to maintain his/her balance in various positions

7  Demonstrate equilibrium reactions in various positions

8  Maintain standing with one foot on a higher surface

9  Stand on one foot

10  Maintain his/her equilibrium on an unstable surface

11  Maintain his/her equilibrium while performing dynamic activities on an unstable surface

12  Shift his/her weight to initiate movement transitions

13  Use his/her equilibrium reactions to prevent falling while ambulating in school environment

**Goal:   Increase his/her skills in sitting and/or  transition to and from sitting**

1  Support him/herself using arms when placed in sitting

2  Sit without arm support, hands free

3  Sit in side sitting with arm support

4  Pivot in sitting

5  Reach to sides in sitting with trunk rotation

6  Sit in side sitting without arm support

7  Go to prone from sitting

8  Come to sitting independently

9  Assume tailor sitting

10  Assume side sitting - both sides

11  Eliminate W sitting

12  Maintain his/her stability in chair or bolster sitting

13  Maintain his/her stability seated on an adaptive toilet

14  Maintain his/her stability in sitting for ADL and fine motor activities

15  Back into small chair to seat him/herself

16  Climb forward into adult chair, then turn around and sit

17  Climb on furniture to look out window, etc. and get down

## Goal: Increase his/her stability with proper alignment in upper extremity weight-bearing

1 Maintain a prone on elbows position

2 Reach with one arm in prone on elbows position

3 Maintain his/her weight on one elbow in side-prop position

4 Maintain his/her upper extremities in proper alignment in weight-bearing

5 Alternate left-right unilateral upper extremity weight-bearing

6 Maintain his/her weight-bearing on one arm while reaching with opposite arm

7 Move his/her body over weight-bearing arm

## Goal: Increase his/her stability with proper alignment in lower extremity weight-bearing

1 Assume a quadruped position from prone

2 Assume quadruped from side sitting

3 Shift his/her weight in quadruped

4 Shift his/her weight to alternate arms in quadruped for fine motor activities

5 Assume an upright kneeling position and maintain

6 Maintain his/her stability in kneeling during dynamic activities

7 Assume a half-kneeling position - both sides

8 Maintain his/her lower extremity dissociation and alignment in half-kneeling during dynamic activities

9 Come to partial standing from bolster sitting

10 Pull or push to stand

11 Rise to standing from chair sitting

12 Assume standing through half-kneeling

13 Maintain his/her stability in standing during dynamic activities

14 Move his/her body over weight-bearing leg

15 Stand with one foot on higher surface

16 Stand on one foot - each side

17 Stand on one foot for dressing activities

**Goal: Demonstrate independent locomotion with normal movement patterns**

1 Roll short distances
2 Scoot his/her body in sitting to move short distances
3 Drag with his/her arms in prone
4 Prone crawl reciprocally
5 Shift his/her weight forward and back on hands and knees
6 Creep on his/her hands and knees
7 Achieve plantigrade position (hands and feet)
8 Creep upstairs
9 Push him/herself downstairs backwards
10 Assume a kneeling position in preparation for locomotion
11 Kneel-walk

**Goal: Increase skill in walking independently with normal gait pattern and graded control**

1 Rise to standing from a seated position
2 Pull or push him/herself up to a standing position
3 Stand at and cruise along a supporting surface
4 Get to the floor from a standing position
5 Walk with a symmetrical gait pattern
6 Demonstrate a heel-toe gait pattern
7 Demonstrate all the components of equilibrium in gait
8 Maintain his/her head, shoulders, trunk, and pelvis in alignment over the base of support in gait
9 Maintain his/her arm(s) in a position of reduced hypertonic posturing in gait
10 Walk sidewards
11 Walk backwards
12 Develop the speed and endurance for functional gait in the school environment
13 Demonstrate sufficient balance and awareness of safety to walk
14 Demonstrate the ability to fall safely
15 Walk on uneven surfaces

16  Walk up and down a ramp

17  Climb stairs using a railing

18  Descend stairs using a railing

19  Climb stairs without a railing

20  Descend stairs without a railing

21  Run

22  Control stopping while running

**Goal:  Increase his/her static and/or dynamic balance**

1  Maintain his/her balance on tiptoes

2  Stand on two inch walking board

3  Stand on one foot, hands out

4  Stand on one foot, eyes closed, hands on hips

5  Balance while walking on a variety of surfaces

6  Maintain his/her balance walking on tiptoes

7  Maintain his/her balance walking between lines

8  Maintain his/her balance walking on a line

9  Maintain his/her balance walking in a circle

10  Maintain his/her balance, hopping on one foot

11  Maintain his/her balance walking on board

**Goal:  Increase his/her advanced body movement**

1  Jump in place

2  Jump forward

3  Jump vertically

4  Broad jump

5  Jump in different directions

6  Jump off box with one foot lead

7  Jump on trampoline

8  Gallop - both leads

9  Skip on two feet alternately

10  Perform forward roll

11 Perform backward roll

12 Stand on his/her head

13 March to beat of music

## Goal: Increase his/her ball skills

1 Roll ball forward from sitting

2 Hurl ball with one hand without falling from standing

3 Throw underhand using two hands

4 Bounce small ball

5 Kick large ball

6 Catch large ball, arms out straight

7 Catch small ball

8 Bounce large ball

9 Throw small ball overhand

10 Toss bean bag at target

11 Bounce ball and catch it

12 Throw small ball up and catch it

13 Hit ball with bat

14 Dodge ball thrown at student

15 Run up and kick ball

16 Kick dropped ball

17 Catch bounced ball

## Goal: Increase exercise, R.O.M., strength, and endurance

1 Tolerate positioning in adaptive equipment

2 Tolerate splinting

3 Tolerate passive range of motion

4 Increase his/her range of motion at specified joint(s)

5 Increase his/her trunk mobility

6 Increase his/her trunk rotation

7 Increase his/her shoulder girdle mobility

8 Increase his/her pelvic mobility

9  Isolate his/her movements at specified joint(s)

10  Increase his/her muscle strength to a specified level (P,F,G,N)

11  Increase his/her strength of the specified muscle(s) to a predetermined level (P,F,G,N)

12  Maintain his/her overall muscle strength and endurance

13  Increase his/her overall muscle strength and endurance

14  Increase his/her strength and endurance of the hemiparetic side

15  Increase his/her strength and endurance of neck musculature for sustained head control

16  Increase his/her trunk symmetry in range and strength to reduce scoliotic curve

17  Increase his/her strength and endurance of trunk musculature

18  Increase his/her abdominal strength

19  Increase upper extremity strength and endurance

20  Increase lower extremity strength and endurance

21  Develop his/her strength and endurance to perform functional activities in the classroom and school environment

**Goal:  Increase his/her skills in the use of advanced equipment**

1  Pull him/herself forward when lying prone on scooter-board

2  Pull him/herself forward reciprocally when lying prone on scooter-board

3  Hold his/her legs off ground while prone on scooter-board

4  Move him/herself on scooter-board maintaining normal muscle tone

5  Move his/her tricycle or pedal car by pushing on floor with his/her feet

6  Maintain his/her feet on pedals of tricycle, holding handles, while being pushed

7  Pedal his/her tricycle forward

8  Steer and pedal his/her tricycle with control

9  Control his/her speed and directions while riding wheeled toys

10  Sit on swing, holding on with his/her hands while being pushed

11  Use his/her trunk and legs in coordination to swing

## Goal: Increase his/her skills in the use of adaptive equipment

1  Move with a scooter board
2  Weight-bear with proper postural alignment in a standing box
3  Walk in a ring walker
4  Walk in parallel bars
5  Walk with a rollator
6  Walk with a geriatric walker
7  Walk with a reciprocal walker
8  Walk with axillary crutch(es)
9  Walk with Lofstrand crutch(es)
10  Walk with quad cane(s)
11  Walk with straight cane(s)
12  Use appropriate gait pattern with assistive devices
13  Stand up and resume sitting with correct placement of assistive devices
14  Walk on uneven terrain with assistive devices
15  Climb and descend a ramp with assistive devices
16  Climb and descend stairs with assistive devices
17  Demonstrate appropriate safety techniques in the use of assistive devices
18  Fall safely while using assistive devices
19  Stand up from the floor with assistive devices
20  Advance from a 4-point to a 2-point gait
21  Advance to ambulating without assistive devices

## Goal: Increase his/her wheelchair skills

1  Sit in his/her wheelchair with proper postural alignment
2  Lock and unlock his/her wheelchair
3  Propel his/her wheelchair forward and backward
4  Propel his/her wheelchair accurately in the desired direction
5  Respond quickly to stop his/her wheelchair
6  Safely ascend and descend a ramp in his/her wheelchair
7  Propel his/her wheelchair on uneven terrain
8  Develop the endurance and control to propel his/her wheelchair in a variety of school activities

9  Demonstrate sufficient control and awareness of safety to use his/her wheelchair

10  Perform transfers between his/her wheelchair and a regular chair or toilet

11  Perform transfers between his/her wheelchair and the floor and return

12  Demonstrate sufficient control and awareness of safety to perform wheelchair transfers

**Goal:   Normalize his/her response to sensory input**

1  Accept his/her body parts being touched or placed in contact with a variety of textures

2  Demonstrate awareness of which body area is being touched

3  Indicate to others his/her desire for tactile stimulation

4  Exhibit his/her enjoyment when he/she is handled, moved around and played with

5  Demonstrate his/her freedom from self-stimulatory behaviors involving touch or movement

6  Demonstrate his/her desire to explore the environment through touch

7  Maintain eye contact appropriately

8  Maintain appropriate attending behavior

9  Recall verbal directions for _____ step task and complete task in correct sequence

10  Cooperate for handling during therapy

11  Increase his/her tolerance to wearing splint

**Goal:   Increase his/her body awareness**

1  Accept his/her body parts being touched or placed in contact with a variety of textures

2  Demonstrate awareness of which body area is being touched

3  Indicate to others his/her desire for tactile stimulation

4  Exhibit his/her enjoyment when he/she is handled, moved around and played with

5  Explore his/her environment through touch

6  Maintain eye contact appropriately

7  Maintain appropriate attending behavior

8  Cooperate for handling during therapy

9  Increase his/her tolerance to wearing splint

10  Move his/her hand to his/her mouth in exploration

11  Show increased awareness of touch

12  Indicate location of body parts

13  Recognize body parts on another person

14  Identify right/left sides of his/her body

15  Follow complex directions

16  Demonstrate his/her internal awareness of laterality

17  Demonstrate his/her knowledge of direction (up/down, over/under, etc.)

18  Recognize spatial relationships of objects

19  Indicate his/her awareness of which body part is being touched

20  Indicate where he/she is touched on his/her arm when his/her vision is occluded

21  Indicate which finger is touched when his/her vision is occluded

22  Identify geometric shape traced on his/her hand when his/her vision is occluded

23  Imitate geometric shape traced on his/her hand when his/her vision is occluded

24  Discriminate a variety of familiar objects

25  Discriminate a variety of geometric shapes when his/her vision is occluded

26  Discriminate a variety of tactile stimuli when his/her vision is occluded

27  Match objects of various sizes, shapes, textures, and weights using tactile cues

## Goal:    Increase his/her motor planning

1  Identify correct motor sequence to accomplish a simple motor task

2  Verbalize motor sequence to accomplish a simple task

3  Perform motor sequence to accomplish a simple task

4  Perform motor sequence to accomplish a complex task

5  Plan and perform multiple complex motor tasks

6  Imitate the actions of another person

7  Imitate the gestures, facial expressions of another person

8  Imitate finger-play

9  Imitate another person's interaction with a toy

10  Demonstrate awareness of body position in space by maneuvering through obstacle course

11  Follow verbal directions regarding assuming body positions

## Goal: Increase his/her postural control, equilibrium, and balance

1 Sustain upright sitting at desk

2 Show improved postural stability in various positions

3 Sustain antigravity extension

4 Sustain antigravity flexion

5 Demonstrate integration of his/her primitive postural reflexes (ATNR, STNR)

6 Demonstrate his/her ability to stand on foot

7 Demonstrate his/her ability to stand on one foot when his/her vision is occluded

## Goal: Increase his/her vestibular-bilateral integration

1 Demonstrate freedom from gravitational insecurity

2 Demonstrate freedom from hypersensitivity to imposed movement/handling by therapist

3 Demonstrate his/her ability to adaptively respond to movement/gravity

4 Demonstrate a normalized response to vestibular stimulation

5 Demonstrate more normal duration of post-rotary hystagmus after spinning

6 Demonstrate visual pursuit past vertical midline

7 Demonstrate rotation in sitting during reach

8 Cross his/her midline during reach with extremities

9 Demonstrate even, two handed activities

10 Demonstrate even jumping on two feet

11 Demonstrate his/her coordination of arms with legs

12 Demonstrate improved bilateral motor integration

## Goal: Increase his/her ocular motor skills

1 Look at objects and persons

2 Look at an object as it is moved in a variety of directions

3 Visually track stimulus in two planes

4 Visually track stimulus in all planes

5 Fixate on visual stimuli

6 Track an irregularly moving object

7 Converge/diverge on a moving object

8  Shift attention between two objects

9  Scan several objects

10  Look at an object to specify choice

## Goal:    Increase his/her visual efficiency skills

1  Locate an object

2  Maintain his/her gaze while moving toward an object

3  Scan area to locate a specific object

4  Count objects without duplication

5  Classify objects by visual attributes

6  Identify objects at a distance

7  Identify action in a picture

8  Describe a picture

9  Match by internal detail

10  Match by external detail

11  Relate single parts to whole

12  Discriminate figure from background

## Goal:    Increase his/her systematic scanning skills

1  Define systematic scanning as "looking carefully"

2  Read across a line from left to right, top to bottom

3  Demonstrate systematic scanning

4  Use systematic scanning to check for completeness

## Goal:    Increase his/her visual perceptual skills

1  Develop his/her functional visual memory

2  Demonstrate figure-ground differences

3  Demonstrate improvement in his/her visual-closure

4  Duplicate peg designs from model

5  Duplicate bead designs from a model

6  Complete shape form-board

7  Build tower of _____ blocks

8  Duplicate _____ block design from model

9  Demonstrate improvement in his/her visual-spatial relationships

**Goal:   Increase his/her play skills**

1  Retain object when placed in his/her hand

2  Group voluntarily

3  Touch one object to another in play

4  Use single movement to cause something to happen

5  Manipulate his/her toys and tools

6  Bring his/her hands to his/her mouth

7  Actively explore by mouthing, shaking, and banging objects

8  Play with his/her hands together

**Goal:   Increase his/her proximal stability as a foundation for his/her arm/hand
use**

1  Demonstrate relaxation of his/her arms

2  Stabilize his/her shoulder girdle to reach

3  Reach across his/her midline

4  Reach with either hand

5  Reach with both hands simultaneously

6  Reach with graded control

7  Stabilize his/her shoulder girdle to grasp

8  Stabilize his/her shoulder girdle to pick up a large object with two hands

9  Maintain his/her shoulder girdle stability for control in fine motor activities

10  Show his/her control in bilateral fine motor activities

11  Show his/her control in fine motor activity

12  Show his/her control in handling a writing utensil with an immature grasp

13  Show his/her control in holding a writing utensil with a digital grasp

14  Show his/her control in holding a writing utensil with a mature grasp

15  Show his/her control in using a writing utensil

16  Show his/her control in cutting with adaptive scissors

17  Show his/her control in cutting with standard scissors

18  Show his/her control in weight bearing and weight shifting on forearms

19  Show his/her control in weight bearing and weight shifting on extended arms

## Goal:   Increase his/her motor skills needed for interaction with his/her environment

1  Use a raking grasp

2  Use a palmar grasp

3  Use a tripod grasp

4  Use a refined pincer grasp

5  Use his/her dominant hand for grasp

6  Grasp with his/her non-dominant hand

7  Use his/her non-dominant hand as an assist

8  Poke or point at an object

9  Transfer an object between his/her hands

10  Hold an object with one hand while manipulating it with the other

11  Demonstrate in-hand manipulation

12  Release an object

13  Release an object with accuracy

14  Place an object

15  Place an object with accuracy

16  Release an object quickly with accuracy

17  Show ability to isolate his/her fingers

18  Exhibit his/her finger dexterity

19  Adjust his/her forearm and wrist to grasp

20  Demonstrate his/her control of supination-pronation of his/her forearm

21  Develop his/her arm/shoulder girdle strength

22  Hold object with both his/her hands

23  Exhibit a visually directed reach

24  Manipulate and explore objects using one or more actions appropriate to the object

25  Demonstrate his/her bilateral hand skills, where his/her hands are used in opposing movements

26  Demonstrate his/her usage of hammer and other tools

27  Place and remove six large pegs in hole with direct placement

28  Place and remove six small pegs in hole with direct placement

29  String beads

**Goal:    Increase his/her visual motor skills**

1  Imitate simple strokes

2  Copy simple strokes

3  Copy geometric designs or figures

4  Snip paper

5  Cut on a wide straight line

6  Cut on a wide curved line

7  Trace a wide line

8  Catch a ball

9  Catch a bounced ball

10  Keep a balloon/ball in the air for a specified number of repetitive hits

11  Perform eye/hand accuracy tasks

12  Perform eye/foot accuracy tasks

13  Demonstrate improved visual motor skills

14  Demonstrate improved ball skills

# VISION

**Goal:** **Demonstrate improved orientation and mobility skills**

1 Locate changes in ground textures
2 Use a sighted guide
3 Follow directions around a familiar location
4 Use protective techniques in moving around environment
5 Demonstrate the trailing technique
6 Move independently around the classroom
7 Move independently around school

**Goal:** **Demonstrate improved ability to gain information using the tactile mode**

1 Demonstrate tactual exploration skills
2 Exhibit Braille readiness skills
3 Exhibit Braille reading skills
4 Exhibit Braille writing skills

**Goal:** **Demonstrate improved skill in using equipment and resources for the visually handicapped**

1 Operate a 4-track cassette recorder
2 Use recorded texts
3 Operate a standard typewriter using the touch system
4 Operate a Braille typewriter
5 Operate a large-type typewriter
6 Operate a computer with voice equipment
7 Use appropriate low-vision aids
8 Identify most useful resources available to low-vision students

**Goal:** **Demonstrate improved ability to maintain personal safety**

1 Demonstrate the operation of a telephone
2 Demonstrate the operation of a cellular telephone
3 Explain the appropriate times to use 911 on the telephone

4  Describe what he/she will do if he/she smells smoke or the smoke sensor beeps

5  Explain the use of a personal safety signal device

6  Describe what to do in the event of a severe injury when alone

7  Describe how to use a variety of safety signal devices

**Goal:  Demonstrate improved understanding of his/her visual impairment**

1  State how his/her own vision is different from peers

2  State adjustments made by teachers due to his/her visual impairment

3  State options available when material presented is not legible

4  State options available when material presented is not available

5  Describe "normal" vision

6  Name major parts of eye anatomy

7  Describe path of light into the eye

8  Describe parts of a routine eye exam

9  Name parts of his/her eye affected by his/her eye condition

10  Name his/her own visual impairment

11  Discuss prognosis for his/her visual impairment

12  Discuss etiology of his/her visual impairment

13  Discuss special needs due to his/her visual impairment with his/her classroom teacher(s)

14  Discuss his/her visual impairment with peers

15  Solicit help when needed

16  Work independently when appropriate

**Goal:  Demonstrate improved understanding of his/her entitlements to assistance in public places**

1  Identify specific rights to assistance in public places under the ADA law

2  Demonstrate how he/she should register a complaint of nonconformity with the ADA law

3  Explain the process for getting assistance in an airport, train station, or bus depot

*HEARING*

**Goal:  Demonstrate improved compensatory skills for aural rehabilitation**

1  Demonstrate hearing-aid use
2  Increase and maintain his/her auditory discrimination skills
3  Increase and maintain his/her speech and reading skills
4  Increase and maintain his/her skills in auditory closure
5  Use situational, contextual and environmental cues

**Goal:  Demonstrate improved understanding of his/her auditory impairment**

1  State  how his/her hearing is different from peers
2  State adjustments made by teachers due to his/her impairment
3  State options available when material presented is not audible
4  State options available when material presented is not available
5  Describe "normal" hearing
6  Name major parts of ear anatomy
7  Describe path of sound into the ear
8  Describe parts of a routine ear exam
9  Name parts of his/her ear affected by his/her hearing impairment
10  Name his/her own impairment
11  Discuss prognosis for his/her auditory impairment
12  Discuss etiology of his/her auditory impairment
13  Discuss special needs due to his/her auditory impairment with his/her classroom teacher(s)
14  Discuss his/her auditory impairment with peers
15  Work independently when appropriate

**Goal:  Demonstrate improved ability to maintain personal safety**

1  Solicit help when needed
2  Demonstrate how he/she can use a telephone to get help
3  Demonstrate the operation of a cellular telephone to get help
4  Explain the appropriate times to use 911 on the telephone

5 Demonstrate the use of the text telephone or TTY (teletype)

6 Demonstrate the use of an installed volume amplification unit on a telephone

7 Demonstrate the use of a portable volume amplification unit on a telephone

8 Explain the use of a personal safety signal device

9 Describe what to do in the event of a severe injury when alone

10 Demonstrate the use of a variety of safety signal devices

**Goal:  Demonstrate improved communication by signing**

1 Sign to indicate his/her toilet needs

2 Sign to indicate his/her food and drink needs

3 Sign to indicate his/her comfort needs

4 Sign to indicate threats to his/her safety

5 Sign words related to a picture

6 Sign an answer to a question

7 Sign words related to reading vocabulary

8 Sign functional sight vocabulary words

9 Finger-spell a given word

10 Sign environmental sounds

11 Sign isolated words

12 Sign vowel sounds

13 Sign consonant sounds

14 Sign the difference among one, two and three syllable words

15 Sign the difference between similar words

16 Sign sentences

# ATTENTION DEFICIT DISORDER-HYPERACTIVITY

(See also Emotional Development, pp. 106-114)

**Goal:  Demonstrate improved duration of his/her attention**

1  Copy assignments given by his/her teacher(s)

2  Underline or highlight key words or phrases in assignments or directions given to him/her

3  Divide his/her assignments into smaller segments

4  Accomplish smaller tasks first

5  Record all assignments given by his/her teacher in one book

6  Keep folders to segment his/her assignments, completed work, drawings, etc.

7  Make up a checklist for a series of things he/she must do

8  Keep a copy of his/her class schedule readily available e.g. pasted or written on his/her assignment pad

9  Make a checklist of what materials/tools he/she will need for a given task

10  Make a checklist of what materials/tools he/she will need to take home

11  Keep a calendar for his/her reference in his/her assignment folder

12  Use a typewriter or word-processor to do his/her assignments

13  Take notes in class when prompted by his/her teacher

14  Repeat his/her teacher's directions when asked

15  Look at his/her teacher's eyes when oral directions are being given to him/her

16  Nod his/her head to indicate that he/she recognizes directions

17  Reduce his/her physical movement while listening

18  Ask questions right away if he/she does not comprehend directions

19  Avoid noisy or distracting environments when he/she is working

20  Complete his/her assigned one-step tasks

21  Complete his/her assigned two-step tasks

22  Complete his/her assigned multiple-step tasks

23  Follow a daily routine

24  Follow a routine for doing his/her written work

25  Follow a routine for storing his/her completed work

26 Follow a routine for storing his/her books

27 Follow a routine for doing homework

28 Refer to prompt cards on books, folders, etc.

29 Keep a chart of his/her accomplishments: tasks, homework, chores,

30 Start working on a task within ___ seconds

31 Start working on a task without disturbing others

32 Ask questions which are on topic

33 Make eye-contact with persons speaking to him/her

34 Complete tasks or answer questions before seeking help or before saying that he/she can't or that he/she doesn't know

35 Sit still during group activities

36 Complete his/her tasks with minimal frustration

37 Sit quietly and look at task materials

38 Listen when other students are speaking

39 Repeat directions when asked

40 Read lists of words or sentences without losing his/her place

41 Perform a relaxation activity before taking a test

**Goal:   Demonstrate improved skills in redirecting his/her hyperactivity**

1 Perform classroom management/housekeeping tasks given to him/her by his/her teacher(s)

2 Perform school bus management/housekeeping tasks given to him/her by his/her bus driver

3 Perform sorting tasks of increasingly large numbers of objects

4 Demonstrate and then lead his/her class in occasional aerobic exercises selected by his/her teacher (jumping jacks, calisthenics, etc.)

5 Stand and stretch during seat-work to relieve tension

6 Cooperate in his/her group activities

**Goal:   Demonstrate improved skills to reduce his/her hyperactivity**

1 Listen to recordings of soothing sounds or stories

2 Practice relaxation of portions of his/her body: hand, arm, shoulders, legs, abdomen, neck

3  Practice relaxation of his/her entire body

4  Daydream about a given non-stimulating topic while in a resting position

5  Accept the give and take of interactions with his/her peers and with adults

6  Exhibit more mature emotional responses to stress

7  Exhibit coping skills in situations of stress and anxiety

8  Exhibit reduced tension in a non-threatening and supportive environment

9  Recognize situations in which his/her self-control is needed

**Goal:  Demonstrate improved  writing legibility**

1  Write his/her letters tall enough to almost fill the space between lines on composition paper

2  Form each letter of his/her written words more slowly and completely

3  Increase the space between each letter of words

4  Reduce the pace of his/her writing

5  Compare his/her writing after his/her writing practice with his/her normal writing

6  Trace letters and numbers from a model

7  Recopy written work after correction

**Goal:  Demonstrate improved planning and sequential organization of thought**

1  Make a list of what he/she needs for a given task or procedure

2  Divide a task into its component parts orally

3  Divide a task into its component parts in writing

4  Write an outline to segment logical parts of a topic

5  Perform sorting tasks of objects

6  Ask teacher to check accuracy or direction of his/her work when partially complete

7  Keep a diary

8  Accept responsibility for taking his/her medication

9  Develop more consistent study habits

10  Complete his/her assigned work

11  Develop his/her outlining skills

12  Develop his/her note-taking skills

13  Bring his/her books and materials to school

14  Complete his/her assignments within acceptable time limits

15  Identify what materials are required for an assignment

16  Repeat information after varying time intervals

17  Memorize sequential data sets: days of the week, months, seasons, alphabet

18 Keep completed work in a specified place: folder, mailbox, etc.

19  Complete a task in sequential order

20 Use complete phrases and sentences in writing

21  Attempt to perform a task before asking for assistance

22  Read instructions, directions, and explanations before asking for assistance

**Goal:    Reduce his/her impulsiveness**

1  Practice daydreaming about a given topic

2  Use selected time-killing activities while waiting for directions: doodling, shaping pipe cleaners, stringing/unstringing paper clips, etc.

3  Make notes or outlines of real or fantasized projects while waiting

4  Start on easier portions of a task or do a substitute task while waiting for help from his/her teacher

5  Practice social routines for greeting, departing, requesting, expressing appreciation

6  Attend to work-time tasks until they are completed before he/she moves on to another task

7  Follow simple directions on request

8  Carry out his/her daily classroom activities

9  Anticipate and follow his/her daily classroom routine

10  Follow multistep directions in the classroom

11  Follow two or more directions sequentially

12  Wait his/her turn

13  Engage in cooperative play for at least five minutes

14  Participate without disruption during lunch

15  Accept responsibility for his/her behavior on the school bus

16  Maintain and use a checklist of safety behavior in class, cafeteria, gym, school bus, crossing streets, biking, swimming, etc.

17  Refrain from making sounds which are inappropriate or disruptive

18  Cease unnecessary body movements when cued by the teacher

19  Stay in line when class moves through the halls

20  Develop a clear routine for normal procedures: arrival at school, going to lunch, attending an assembly, going home, etc.

21  Perform a relaxation activity following a stimulating activity

22  Stop an activity when directed to do so

**Goal:   Reduce his/her dysfunctional behavior**

1  Exhibit give-and-take in games

2  Share his/her playthings

3  Keep a simple bargain with his/her teacher

4  Ask permission to play with or use a toy or object being used by another

5  Join in group activities without disruption

6  React positively to interaction with staff members other than his/her teachers

7  Acknowledge the effect of his/her behavior on him/herself and others

8  Increase his/her repertoire of coping skills in situations of stress and anxiety

9  Develop means of correcting tasks which he/she has failed

10  Describe things he/she is good at and things that are hard for him/her

11  Listen to a message before responding

12  Identify nonverbal cues that communicate feelings and messages

13  Accept winning or losing without loss of his/her self-control

14  Accept the consequences of his/her inappropriate behavior

15  Describe consequences when someone's personal space is respected

16  Describe consequences when someone's personal space is violated

17  Distinguish between appropriate and inappropriate approach gestures

18  Identify the emotional consequences of sexually exploitative behavior

19  Communicate his/her personal feelings and perceptions when asked

20  Use appropriate language when he/she is corrected

21  Respond appropriately to environmental cues: bells, signs, signals, gestures

22  Arrive to class on time

23  Identify school rules for class, attendance, being quiet, and hallway behavior

24  Handle school property correctly

25  Keep food on his/her plate in the lunchroom

26  Settle minor conflicts without yelling, fighting, or crying

26 Await his/her turn in peer activities

**Goal:   Improve personal interaction skills**

1  Allow others take their turns in games and class activities

2  Ask the owner's permission before using materials, equipment, etc.

3  Raise his/her hand to gain teacher's permission to speak

4  Await his/her turn to speak in class or out of class

5  Adapt a tone of voice appropriate to each: class, library, lunchroom, hallway, and school bus

# *AUTISM*

( See also Living Skills pp.85-102, Physical Development pp. 103-105,

Oral Communication pp. 115-127, Written Communication pp.128-133)

## Goal: Develop social skills

1  Make an appropriate response after structured reading of a social story related to waiting

2  Make an appropriate response after structured reading of a social story related to taking turns

3  Make an appropriate response after structured reading of a social story related to transitioning from one activity to another

4  Make an appropriate response after structured reading of a social story related to changing a topic in a conversation

5  Make an appropriate response after structured reading of a social story related to ending an activity with others

6  Make an appropriate response after structured reading of a social story related to initiating social contacts

7  Make an appropriate response after structured reading of a social story related to accepting changes in plans

8  Make an appropriate response after structured reading of a social story related to situations requiring silence

9  Exhibit an appropriate response after structured reading of a social story about being a friend

10  Initiate his/her participation in a group activity

11  Look at the eyes of a person he/she is speaking to

12  Shake hands when introduced

13  Use appropriate forms of apology: "Excuse me", "I'm sorry"

14  Respond correctly to a list of basic social/personal questions, e.g. "What is your (name, ... age, ... family's names, ... pet's name, ...  teacher's name, ...)"

15  Increase time attending to a peer

16  Increase time attending to an adult

## Goal: Develop expressive language skills

1 Suggest words that characters in simple cartoon situations might say

2 Distinguish between funny and sad cartoon situations

3 Distinguish between nice and not-nice behavior in cartoon situations

4 Identify probable responses of characters to other characters' statements in cartoons

5 Repeat standard phrases for social situations: "Thank you", "Excuse me", "I'm sorry", "That's nice", etc.

6 Imitate facial expressions of emotions: liking, disliking, fear, love, humor, etc.

7 Imitate nonverbal sounds for liking, disliking, fear, love, humor, etc.

8 Use one or more words for liking, disliking, fear, love, humor, etc.

9 Respond appropriately to cues and directions in class

10 Respond appropriately to cues and directions at home

11 Reduce inappropriate or irrelevant speech

## Goal: Develop playing skills

1 Complete a simple game with one other child

2 Participate in a simple game with several children

3 Participate in a simple game involving taking turns

4 Participate in a simple game requiring verbal responses

5 Relate a game's activities and outcome to another child

6 Relate a game's activities and outcome to an adult

7 Exhibit enjoyment in game activities

8 Keep a record of games played

9 Exhibit preferences for types of games

10 Mimic animals: cats, dogs, bears, birds

11 Imitate toy and block structures shown by a peer

## Goal: Develop stress management skills to reduce agitated behavior

1 Identify his/her own primary stress situations

2 Use gestures or words to communicate his/her stress

3 Apply stress reduction techniques as directed at times of agitation: deep breathing, humming, successive stretching-relaxing

4 Apply stress reduction techniques independently at times of agitation

5 Demonstrate use of a self-monitoring method when directed to record incidents of applied stress reduction: wrist counter, marks/stars/stickers on a pocket chart

6 Use the self-monitoring method independently

7 Indicate acceptance and rejection by gesture

8 Indicate acceptance and rejection orally

# READING- GRADES 1-8

## 1st grade reading skills

1  Recognize upper and lowercase letters (random order)

2  Identify single consonant sounds

3  Identify short vowel sounds

4  Identify rhyming words

5  Recognize sight words

6  Recognize vocabulary words from basal

7  Explain sentence meaning

8  Recall facts of a story

9  Identify main idea as stated

10  Follow 1 and 2 step oral directions

11  Use table of contents

12  Identify consonant blends

13  Identify consonant digraphs (wh, ch, sh, th)

14  Identify long vowel sounds

15  Select word for given meaning

16  Recognize synonyms

17  Explain the main idea of paragraph or story when inferred

18  Draw conclusions

19  Analyze character's feelings

20  Recall sequence of events

21  Make inferences

22  Identify vowel digraphs (ay, ai, ee, ea, ie, ue)

23  Recognize  compound words

24  Recognize contractions

25  Recognize antonyms

26  Distinguish between real and make-believe

27  Follow district curriculum for all first grade reading skills

**2nd grade reading skills**

1  Identify variant single consonants (c, g, s)

2  Review consonant blends

3  Review short vowel sounds

4  Review long vowel sounds

5  Identify synonyms of given words

6  Identify antonyms of given words

7  Recognize sight words  (1/4 Grade 2 Fry list)

8  Recognize vocabulary words from basal

9  Recognize vocabulary from content areas

10  Recall facts (who, what, where, when, how)

11  Recall order and sequence of events

12  Identify main idea

13  Explain sentence meaning

14  Use context to identify correct word to complete sentence

15  Identify main idea when inferred

16  Analyze character's feelings and motives

17  Follow 1 and 2 step written directions

18  Use table of contents

19  Review consonant digraphs

20  Review vowel digraphs (ai, ay, ee, ea, ie, oe, ue)

21  Identify diphthongs (oi, oy, ou, ow)

22  Recognize rhyming words

23  Blend sounds to form words

24  Recognize inflectional endings (s, es, ed, ing)

25  Recognize compound words

26  Identify base words

27  Identify prefixes (re, un)

28  Identify suffixes (er, y, ful)

29  Recognize synonyms of given words

30  Recognize antonyms of given word

31  Recognize sight words (1/2 Grade 2 Fry list)

32  Recognize vocabulary from basal

33  Recognize vocabulary from content areas

34  Recall facts (who, what, where, when, how)

35  Make inferences

36  Draw conclusions

37  Alphabetize to 1st and 2nd letter

38  Recognize contractions

39  Divide words into syllables

40  Distinguish between fact and fiction

41  Use dictionary to find definition of given word

## 3rd grade reading skills

1 Review initial and final single consonants

2 Review initial and final consonant blends

3 Review short vowel sounds

4 Review long vowel sounds

5 Blend sounds into words - choose correct word for a phonetically spelled word

6 Identify silent letters in words

7 Identify synonyms

8 Identify antonyms

9 Recognize sight words when given an oral clue

10 Recognize vocabulary from basal

11 Recognize vocabulary from content areas

12 Recall of facts (who, what, where, when, how)

13 Identify main idea as stated

14 Recognize order and sequence of events

15 Explain sentence meaning

16 Make inferences about a story or selection

17 Analyze character's feelings and motives

18 Identify main idea when inferred

19 Draw conclusions

20 Recognize figurative language

21 Follow 1 and 2 step written directions

22 Locate and use table of contents

23 Alphabetize to 1st, 2nd, and 3rd letter

24 Locate and use glossary

25 Review initial and final consonant digraphs

26 Review variant single consonants (g, c, s)

27 Review short vowel sounds

28 Identify variant long vowel sounds (ar, er, ir, ur, or)

29  Review vowel digraphs (ai, ay, ee, ea, oa, ie, oe)

30  Review vowel diphthongs (oy, oi, ow, ou)

31  Review rhyming words

32  Review inflectional endings (s, es, ed, ing)

33  Identify base words

34  Identify prefixes (im, in, un, re, non)

35  Identify suffixes (ly, ful, er, est, less, able)

36  Recognize compound words

37  Identify syllables in a word

38  Identify in context correct meaning of multiple meaning word

39  Use context clues to determine meaning of a word

40  Identify topic of a paragraph

41  Recognize contractions

42  Identify, in context, correct meaning of multiple meaning word

43  Use context clues to determine meaning of a word

44  Identify topic of a paragraph

45  Identify sensory images

46  Distinguish between real and unreal elements

47  Distinguish between fact and fiction

48  Use dictionary to find definitions and correct spelling

49  Use the index, maps, tables, graphs, and diagrams

50  Use library catalog cards

**4th grade reading skills**

1 Review all previously taught phonics skills

2 Reinforce all previously taught phonics skills

3 Review blending of sounds to form words

4 Identify base words

5 Identify prefixes

6 Identify suffixes

7 Use syllabication rules

8 Identify and use synonyms

9 Identify and use antonyms

10 Identify and use words with multiple meanings

11 Use context clues to determine meaning of a word

12 Recognize vocabulary words from basal

13 Recognize vocabulary words from content areas

14 Identify and use homonyms

15 Recall facts (who, what, when, where, how)

16 Recognize order and sequence of events or ideas

17 Identify main idea as stated

18 Recognize figurative language

19 Analyze character's feelings and motives

20 Identify and use parts of a dictionary

21 Follow 1, 2, 3 step written directions

22 Use accent

23 Identify and use compound words

24 Identify main idea (inferred)

25 Identify topic of a paragraph

26 Identify and use parts of a book

27 Use maps

28 Use tables

29 Use charts

30 Use diagrams

31  Identify drawing that correctly follows directions

32  Make inferences

33  Identify facts leading to a conclusion

34  Form conclusions

35  Predict outcomes

36  Distinguish real/unreal elements

37  Distinguish fact/opinion

38  Distinguish fiction/nonfiction

39  Distinguish author attitude/position

40  Recognize cause and effect relationships

41  Construct a simple outline

## 5th grade reading skills

1  Review and reinforce previously taught phonics skills

2  Recognize base words

3  Recognize and explain meanings of prefixes

4  Recognize and explain meanings of suffixes

5  Identify syllables in words

6  Use of accent marks

7  Identify and use synonyms

8  Identify and use antonyms

9  Identify correct meaning of a multiple meaning word

10  Use context clues to identify unknown words

11  Recall of facts (who, what, where, when, how)

12  Recognize sequence of events

13  Identify main idea as stated

14  Identify statements supporting main idea

15  Identify main idea

16  Analyze character's motives, feelings, behavior, and traits

17  Identify and use glossary

18  Recognize the title page

19  Use table of contents

20  Identify the copyright page

21  Identify the index

22  Follow 1, 2 and 3 step written directions

23  Recognize compound words

24  Recognize vocabulary from basal

25  Recognize vocabulary from content areas

26  Predict outcomes

27  Identify cause and effect relationship

28  Draw conclusions

29  Recognize figurative language

30  Make inferences

31  Distinguish author attitude/position

32  Distinguish fact from opinion

33  Distinguish fiction from nonfiction

34  Use dictionary to locate definitions

35  Recognize and use library catalog cards

36  Alphabetize to third letter

37  Recognize and use homophones

38  Recognize and use homographs

39  Read and interpret maps

40  Read and interpret tables

41  Read and interpret charts

42  Read and interpret diagrams

43  Review blending sounds to form a word

44  Review use of dictionary (guide words, definitions)

45  Review use of maps, tables, charts, diagrams

## 6th grade reading skills

1  Identify base words

2  Identify prefixes

3  Identify suffixes

4  Identify correct syllabication of words

5  Interpret accent marks

6  Identify synonyms of words in context

7  Identify antonyms of words in context

8  Recognize the correct meaning of a multiple meaning word in context

9  Use context clues to determine meaning of a word

10  Recognize vocabulary words from basal

11  Recognize vocabulary words from content areas

12  Recall facts (who, what, where, when, how)

13  Recognize sequence of events or ideas

14  Identify main idea as stated

15  Identify statements supporting the main idea

16  Identify main idea when inferred

17  Analyze character's feelings, traits and motives

18  Recognize figurative language

19  Draw conclusions

20  Make inferences

21  Identify and use parts of a dictionary

22  Alphabetize to 2nd and 3rd letters

23  Identify and use parts of a book

24  Follow 1, 2, and 3 step written directions

25  Blend sounds (choose correct word for a phonetically spelled word)

26  Recognize compound words

27  Recognize contractions

28  Identify possessives

29  Identify plurals (with changes in roots)

30  Distinguish fact from opinion

31  Distinguish author attitude/position/purpose

32  Distinguish author's technique i.e. persuasion

33  Distinguish fiction/nonfiction

34  Interpret maps (directions, key)

35  Interpret tables

36  Interpret charts

37  Interpret diagrams

38  Identify and use library catalog cards

39  Recognize contractions

40  Review possessives

41  Review plurals (with changes in roots)

42  Summarize a story or selection

43  Identify and use homographs/homophones correctly in context

44  Recognize cause and effect relationships

45  Identify mood of story

46  Identify time span and period

47  Identify Literary forms

## 7th grade reading skills

1 Identify prefixes

2 Identify suffixes

3 Identify base words

4 Demonstrate syllabication

5 Recognize contractions in context

6 Recognize compound words in context

7 Identify synonyms of words in context

8 Identify antonyms of words in context

9 Recognize the correct meaning of a multi-meaning word in context

10 Recognize vocabulary words

11 Recall of facts (who, what, where, when, how)

12 Recognize order and sequence of events or ideas

13 Recognize order and sequence of events or ideas

14 Analyze character's feelings and motives

15 Identify main idea

16 Make inferences

17 Draw conclusions

18 Predict outcomes

19 Identify the appropriate homophone in context

20 Recognize figurative language

21 Identify author/attitude position

22 Identify and use parts of a dictionary

23 Follow directions of three or more steps

24 Recognize transitional words

25 Distinguish fiction/nonfiction

26 Distinguish fact/opinion

27 Interpret maps

28 Interpret graphs

29 Interpret tables

30 Interpret charts

31  Interpret diagrams

32  Identify and use library catalog cards

33  Use a computerized card catalog to locate books

34  Identify and use parts of a book

35  Identify and use appropriate reference sources

## 8th grade reading skills

1  Identify and use prefixes

2  Identify and use suffixes

3  Identify base words and meaning in context

4  Identify correct syllabication of words

5  Identify contractions and meanings in context

6  Identify meaning of compound words

7  Identify synonyms of words in context

8  Recognize correct meaning of a multi-meaning word in context

9  Recognize words from content areas and basal text

10  Identify factual information when stated

11  Identify main idea when stated

12  Analyze characters' feelings, motives, actions

13  Make inferences

14  State main idea in own words

15  Review map skills

16  Identify and use library catalog cards

17  Identify and use parts of a book

18  Identify antonyms of words in context

19  Identify the appropriate homophone in context

20  Identify the appropriate homograph in context

21  Identify the appropriate homonym in context

22  Recognize sequence of events

23  Predict outcomes

24  Draw conclusions

25  Recognize figurative language

26  Summarize narrative and factual selections

27  Identify author's attitude/purpose

28  Identify author's technique of persuasion

29  Compare and contrast narrative selections

30  Distinguish between relevant and irrelevant information

31 Determine validity of author's reasoning

32 Identify and use parts of a dictionary

33 Follow 3 or more step written directions

34 Identify major topic of a reading passage

35 Infer cause and effect relationship

36 Identify and interpret transitional words in context

37 Distinguish fiction from nonfiction

38 Distinguish fact from opinion

39 Relate ideas or information in passage to situation not discussed

40 Interpret graphs

41 Interpret tables

42 Interpret diagrams

43 Identify and use appropriate reference sources

44 Interpret cartoons

45 Recognize the parts of employment and other application forms

46 Distinguish between relevant and irrelevant information

# *MATHEMATICS- PreK To Grade 8*

## Pre-Kindergarten math skills

1  Match objects (shape/color)

2  Rote count 1-5

3  Compare objects "big" and "little"

4  Compare objects "circle" and "square"

5  Count concrete objects 1-5

6  Compare objects "empty" and "full"

7  Identify a triangle

8  Classify objects by size and shape; large/small, circle/square

9  Rote counts 6-10

10  Compare objects same and different

11  Place concrete objects in one to one correspondence (1-5)

12  Identify first and last

13  Identify rectangle

14  Classify by size, shape and color

15  Count concrete objects 6-10

16  Discriminate between circle/square, triangle/rectangle

17  Make comparisons above/below, longer/shorter, bigger/smaller, more/less

18  Identify the seasons and their weather

19  Associate time with events; morning, afternoon, night; in the morning you go to school, at night you go to sleep

## Kindergarten math skills

1  Count to 20 objects and by rote

2  Use vocabulary: in front of/behind, first/last, before/after

3  Use vocabulary: circle, square, triangle, rectangle, oval

4  Use vocabulary: more/less, larger/largest, taller/tallest, longer/longest

5  Place objects in one to one correspondence

6  Identify numbers 0 through 5

7  Trace or print numbers 0 through 5

8  Form sets of 0 through 5 physical objects correctly

9  Uses ordinal numbers to fifth in real life situations

10  Describe time sequence: morning, afternoon, night

11  Recognize the value of penny, nickel, dime and quarter

12  Recognize a dollar bill

13  Identify numbers 6 through 10 (Enrichment 11 -20)

14  Trace or print numbers 6 through 10

15  Form sets of 6 through 10 members concretely

16  Compare and match sets of objects 1 through 10

17  Classify by multiple attributes

18  Recognize the plus (+) sign

19  Join two sets of physical objects with sums up to 9

20  Recognize the equals (=) sign

21  Respond to simple story problems which indicate the joining of two sets or show how many are left

22  Tell time by the hour

23  Recognize 1/2, 1/3 or 1/4 as part of a whole

24  Recognize the minus (-) sign

25  Count sets of 1 through 10 objects

**1st grade math skills**

1 Count to 10; count concrete objects to 10

2 Read and write numerals 0 through 10

3 Read and write word names zero to ten and matches to numerals

4 Locate 0 to 10 on a number line

5 Identify and use ordinal numbers first to tenth

6 Compare sets of 10 or less using equal (=), less than (<) and greater than (>)

7 Name the number before and after a given number 1 to 10

8 Recognize the symbols + and -

9 Add one digit numbers with sums to 10, vertically and horizontally

10 Apply the commutative property of addition

11 Solve simple story problems using addition, sums to 10

12 State the identity property of zero for addition

13 Subtract numbers with sums to 10, horizontally and vertically, including simple story problems

14 State the names of the days of a week and the number of days in a week

15 State the names and number of months in a year

16 Read a calendar

17 Use place value for ones and tens

18 Count, read and write 1 to 100

19 Use place value to 99

20 Skip count by twos, five's and tens.

21 Recognize patterns related to this skip counting

22 Recognize the value of the coins penny, nickel, dime and quarter

23 Identify and use the cent symbol

24 Determine the value of a collection of coins

25 Solve story problems involving money

26 Complete patterns and sequences with geometric figures

27 Add and subtract sums to 18, vertically and horizontally

28 Add three one-digit numbers with sums to 10 and apply the associative property of addition

29  Solve story problems involving three one digit addends

30  Add two-digit numbers with sums to 99 without regrouping

31  Subtract two-digit numbers with sums to 99 without regrouping

32  Solve story problems involving addition or subtraction, sum to 99 without regrouping

33  Add a two-digit number to a one-digit number, vertically and horizontally without regrouping

34  Subtract a one-digit number from a two-digit number, vertically and horizontally without regrouping

35  Read and interpret simple picture graphs

36  Recognize the properties of a straight line, square, rectangle and triangle

37  Measure in centimeters and in inches

38  Define of liter, kilogram and kilometer

39  Find a missing addend or symbol

40  Describe the concepts of 1/2, 1/4, 1/3 as a part of the whole

41  Read, write and recognize word names for fractions 1/2, 1/4 1/3

42  Identify cup, quart, pound and mile

43  Tell time to hour and half hour

44  Differentiate concept of odd and even

45  Demonstrate knowledge of addition and subtraction facts to 18

46  Use ordinal numbers first to twentieth

## 2nd grade math skills

1  Read and write word names zero to ten

2  Recite addition and subtraction facts to 18

3  Solve story problems involving addition and subtraction facts, sums to 18

4  Use greater than (>), less than (<) and equal to (=)

5  Use place value through the hundreds, (0 to 999)

6  Count, read and write numbers to 999 and locate on a number line

7  Add multiples of tens and hundreds with regrouping

8  Add pairs of two or three-digit numbers without regrouping, vertically and horizontally

9  Use ordinal numbers first through twentieth

10  Supply missing addends

11  Add combinations of one, two, or three digit numbers without regrouping and apply the associative property of addition

12  Solve story problems involving the addition of two or three digit numbers without regrouping

13  Count forwards and backwards

14  Skip count by twos, threes, five's and tens

15  Read and interpret simple picture and bar graphs

16  Subtract multiples of tens or hundreds without regrouping, vertically and horizontally

17  Subtract two and three digit numbers without regrouping, vertically and horizontally

18  Subtract mixed one, two or three-digit numbers

19  Solve story problems involving subtraction without regrouping

20  Add a two-digit number to a one-digit with and without regrouping, vertically and horizontally

21  Solve story problems involving addition of one and two-digit numbers, with and without regrouping

22  Identify the number of days in a week and a year and name the days of the week

23  Identify the number of months in a year and name the months

24  Read a calendar to locate day and date

25  Identify the value of all coins

26  Find the value of a collection of coins

27  Make change from a collection of coins

28  Use dollar sign ($), decimal point and cent symbol

29  Solve story problems involving a collection of coins

30  Tell time to the quarter hour and half hour intervals

31  Add combinations of one, two or three-digit numbers with regrouping including more than 2 one-digit numbers

32  Solve story problems involving one, two or three digit numbers with regrouping

33  Subtract a one-digit number from a two digit number with regrouping vertically and horizontally

34  Use related sentences to show the inverse relationship between addition and subtraction

35  Recognize odd and even numbers

36  Measure and draw lengths to the nearest centimeter; measures to the nearest half inch

37  Describe the use of kilometer, liter and gram

38  Describe the use of cup, pint, quart and mile

39  Solves story problems involving measures

40  Identify and compare sizes of 1/2, 1/3, 2/3, 1/4 and 3/4

41  Recognize multiplication symbol (x)

42  Solve multiplication problems, facts to 5, by repeated addition

43  State the commutative law of multiplication

44  Finds a missing factor

45  Divide 2, 4, 6, 8, 10 and 12 in half

46  Recognize and describe points, straight line, triangles, rectangle, square and circle

47  Solve story problems involving multiplication facts to 5

48  Reinforce and/or extend topics of: mastery of addition and subtraction facts to 18, addition and subtraction with regrouping, multiplication, telling time, and working with money

49  Add and subtract using money

## 3rd grade math skills

1 Add and subtract one-digit numbers and use the number line to demonstrate sums and differences

2 Add numbers up to three-digits with and without regrouping

3 Subtract three-digit numbers with regrouping

4 Solve story problems using addition and subtraction of one, two or three-digit numbers

5 Add three or more numbers, with or without regrouping and apply the associative property of addition

6 Subtract one, two or three-digit numbers, with or without regrouping and solve story problems related to subtraction

7 Subtract two or three-digit numbers with zero in the ones and/or tens column, with regrouping

8 Show the inverse relationship of addition and subtraction

9 Demonstrate the commutative law of addition

10 Show the identity property of zero in addition and subtraction

11 Count, read and write numerals to 10,000 and compare their sizes

12 Round numbers 1 to 1,000 to the nearest ten and hundred

13 Identify and apply ordinal numbers first through thirty-first

14 Use place value and expanded notation to 9,999

15 Skip count by twos, threes, fours, five's, tens and hundreds (sequences and patterns)

16 Identify odd and even numbers to 99

17 Find missing addends, boxed or letter format

18 Identify and use symbols greater than (>), less than (<) or equals (=)

19 Match numeral name to word name to 999 (nine hundred ninety nine)

20 Use the calendar to determine dates, day and the passage of time

21 Tells time to five and one minute intervals

22 Recite multiplication facts 0 to 9 and solve story problems using simple multiplication

23 Recite division facts 0 to 9 and solve simple story problems using division

24 Measure in cup, pints, quarts and gallons

25  Measure and convert centiliters and liters

26  Measure in inches, feet and yards

27  Measure and convert centimeters and meters

28  Measure in ounces and pounds

29  Measure and convert milligrams, grams and kilograms

30  Define a dozen

31  Determine value of a collection of coins and paper money and make change

32  Convert money words to numbers

33  Add and subtract money problems, with and without regrouping, vertically and horizontally

34  Solve story problems using money and measurement

35  Read and interpret charts and graphs

36  Multiply a two-digit number by a one-digit number with and without regrouping, including story problems

37  Multiply a three-digit number by a one-digit number with and without regrouping, including story problems

38  Use order of operations

39  Multiply a three-digit number by a one-digit number with zero in the multiplicand, including story problems

40  Apply commutative and associative properties of multiplication

41  Multiply by 0 and 1

42  Find the missing factor in a multiplication sentence

43  Divide a two-digit number by a one-digit number without regrouping or remainders, including story problems

44  Show the inverse operation relationship of multiplication and division

45  Identify 1/4, 1/3, 1/2, 2/3, 3/4 and show them as parts of the whole

46  Identify and write word name for 1/8, 1/6, and 1/5

47  Subtract fractional parts of the whole pictorially

48  Identify and describe straight line, rectangle, square, triangle and circle

49  Recognize angles

50  Compare selected fractions and whole numbers using greater than (>), less than (<) and equal (=)

51  Locate fractions on a number line

52  Read Roman numerals I to XII and apply to clock

## 4th grade math skills

1  Master addition and subtraction facts, sums to 18

2  Use place value and expanded notation to 1,000,000

3  Count, read and write numbers to 1,000,000

4  Add numbers up to five digits with regrouping, given vertically and horizontally

5  Subtract numbers up to five digits with regrouping, given vertically and horizontally

6  Add three or more numbers up to five digits, given vertically and horizontally

7  Apply the commutative and associate properties of addition

8  Find missing addends in addition and subtraction problems

9  Subtract a three-digit number from a four-digit number, with zeros in the minuend and with regrouping

10  Count money and make change

11  Solve story problems involving addition and subtraction, including money

12  Compare numbers using greater than (>), less than (<) or equal (=)

13  Round numbers to the nearest tens or hundreds

14  Estimate sums and differences

15  Skip count by 2, 3, 4, 5, 6, 10 and 100 and determine whether a number is odd or even

16  Read and interpret graphs

17  Recite multiplication and division facts 0 to 10

18  Demonstrate the inverse relationship between multiplication and division

19  State the multiplication property of zero

20  Identify 1 as the identity element for multiplication

21  Multiply a four-digit number by a one-digit number without and with regrouping, given vertically and horizontally

22  Use the commutative and associative properties of multiplication and the distributive property

23  Find the missing factor in a multiplication or division sentence

24  Multiply a three-digit number by multiples of 10 and 100 given vertically and horizontally

25  Multiply a three-digit number by a two-digit number, without and with regrouping

given vertically and horizontally

26  Divide a four-digit number by a one-digit number with and without regrouping given a boxed or symbol format

27  Divide by multiples of 10 with and without remainders

28  Solve story problems using multiplication and division, including money problems

29  Identify and describe: point, line, ray, line segment, parallel and perpendicular lines, angle, triangle, rectangle, square, circle, parallelogram, cube, rectangular prism, pyramid, cone, sphere and cylinder

30  Find perimeter and area of simple geometric figures

31  Show a fractional part of a whole in a diagram

32  Read and write fractions and mixed numbers and represent on a number line

33  Add and subtract fractions and mixed numbers with like denominators given vertically or horizontally

34  Add and subtract decimals, including tenths and hundredths, with or without regrouping given vertically and horizontally

35  Solve story problems involving fractions and decimals

36  Read and interpret calendar

37  Read time to the nearest minute, clock dial and digital

38  Solve story problems involving the passage of time, minute, hours, days, weeks, months and years

39  Describe liter and deciliter; grams and kilograms; centimeter, meter and kilometer and convert in metric system

40  Measure to the nearest centimeters

41  Solve story problems involving measurement

42  Read a Celsius and Fahrenheit thermometer

43  Read and interpret charts

44  Read and write Roman numerals

45  Solve two-step story problems applying all operations

46  Compare fractions using greater than (>), less than (<) and equals (=)

47  Solve story problems involving fractions

48  Define decades and centuries

49  Convert lengths and weights in the standard

50 Relate ounce, pound and ton; cup, pint, quart and gallon

51 Relate inch, foot, yard and mile

52 Measure to the one eighth inch

## 5th grade math skills

1 Count, read, write and identify place value to 1,000,000 including expanded notation and rounding to the nearest tens or hundreds

2 Read and write Roman numerals up to 50

3 Show the inverse relationship between addition and subtraction and express this in related sentences

4 Find the missing factors or addends in a number sentence

5 Use mathematical symbols greater than (>), less than (<), equal to (=) and does not equal

6 Sequence numbers using various patterns including odd and even numbers

7 Describe the commutative and associative properties for addition and that the identity element for addition is zero

8 Add and subtract whole numbers up to five-digits without or with regrouping including money and story problems

9 Exchange one collection of coins and paper money for another and give change

10 Define the commutative and associative properties for multiplication, the multiplication property of zero, and 1 as the identity element for multiplication

11 Multiply up to four-digit numbers without or with zero by a one-digit number

12 Multiply up to four-digit numbers by a two-digit number without or with regrouping, including story problems

13 Describe the inverse relationship between multiplication and division and express this in related sentences

14 Divide numbers up to four-digits by one-digit numbers without or with remainders, including story problems

15 Divide numbers up to four-digits by two-digit numbers without or with remainders, including story problems

16 Identify and give properties of a point, line, line segment, and intersection

17 Distinguish between prime and composite numbers

18 Find common factors for sets of numbers up to 100

19 Describe the concept of a fraction and match points on a number line

20 Identify and work with equivalent fractions

21  Simplify fractions

22  Adds and subtract fractions and mixed numbers with like denominators, vertically and horizontally, and simplify products including word problems

23  Multiply fractions and mixed numbers and simplify products including word problems

24  Divide fractions

25  Add and subtract decimals to tenths and hundredths without and with regrouping

26  Multiply a decimal by a one-digit number or a decimal by a decimal (hundredths x tenths)

27  Identify solid shapes: cube, rectangular prism, cone, sphere, pyramid and cylinder

28  Measure and compute perimeters of polygons, including word problems

29  Compute areas of rectangular regions

30  Describe and convert grams and kilograms; centimeters, meters and kilometers; deciliters and kiloliters

31  Read time to the nearest minute (dial and digital clock)

32  Solve word problems involving the passage of time; minutes, hours, days, weeks, months and years

33  Read a thermometer (Celsius or Fahrenheit)

34  Read and interpret maps and map scales

35  Read and interpret charts and graphs

36  Convert number of items to dozens and vice versa

37  Multiply two 3-digit numbers

38  Add and subtract fractions with unlike denominators

### 6th grade math skills

1  Identify place value to 1,000,000 including expanded notation

2  Round to the nearest 10,100 or 1000

3  Recognize patterns and sequences

4  Recognize symbols for basic operations and symbols for inequality

5  Add whole numbers up to 5 digits, 2 or more numbers, vertically, horizontally, with and without regrouping, including word problems

6  Estimate sums

7  Apply the commutative and associative properties of addition

8  Recognize zero as the identity element for addition

9  Subtract whole numbers up to 5 digits, vertically and horizontally with or without regrouping, including word problems

10  Estimate differences and recognize subtraction as the inverse operation of addition

11  Multiply whole numbers (up to 4 digits by 3 digits) with or without regrouping, including word problems

12  Estimate products

13  Apply the commutative and associative properties of multiplication and the distributive property

14  Recognize 1 as the identity element for multiplication

15  State the multiplication property of 0

16  Divide up to 4 digit whole numbers by 1, 2 or 3 digit divisors with or without remainders, including word problems

17  Estimate quotients and recognizes division as the inverse operation of multiplication

18  Average sets of numbers (one and 2 digit)

19  Identify and apply order of operations

20  Solve simple equations with missing addends or factors

21  Identify point, line, line segment, ray and intersection

22  Recognize geometric figures (circle, triangle, square, rectangle and hexagon)

23  Recognize congruent triangles

24  Measure angles with the use of a protractor and classifies angles according to their size

25  Recognize parallel lines

26  Find prime and composite numbers up to 100

27  Identify multiples of a given number

28  Find area of square, triangle/rectangle

29  Change fraction form to division form

30  Recognize a fraction as a ratio and two equivalent fractions as a proportion

31  Find the sums and differences of fractions and mixed numbers with like and unlike denominators, horizontally and vertically, simplifying answers, including word problems

32  Find products and quotients of fractions and mixed numbers with like and unlike denominators, simplifying answers, including word problems

33  Identify decimal place value to the ten thousandths

34  Locate points on a number line including whole numbers, decimals and fractions

35  Find the sums and differences of decimals with equal or unequal numbers of digits, with or without regrouping, vertically and horizontally including word problems

36  Find the products of decimals and whole numbers (including zero) with or without regrouping, vertically and horizontally, including word problems

37  Find the quotients of a decimal of more than one digit when divided by a whole number, with and without regrouping and remainders, including word problems

38  Convert fractions, decimals and percents one to the other

39  Convert from one metric unit of measure to another in length, weight and capacity

40  Read and interpret bar, line and circle graphs as well as maps and charts and use these skills to answer verbal problems and read maps to scales

41  Find patterns and sequences of numbers such as odds, evens and multiples of a given number and recognize patterns and sequences of shapes

42  Read Celsius and Fahrenheit thermometers

43  Convert from one English unit of measure to another in length, weight and capacity

44  Find perimeter and area of triangles, squares, rectangles, and circles

(circumference)

45  Find perimeter of hexagons and parallelograms

46  Find volumes of prisms and cylinders

47  Find a percent when a part and the whole are known (division)

48  Find a part of the whole when the percent and the whole are known (multiplication)

49  Find the whole when you know the percent and the part of the whole

50  Extend the topics of ratio and proportion

51  Extend the topic of operations with fractions

52  Extend the topic of operation with decimals

53  Extend the topic of solution of equations

54  Define exponents

## 7th grade math skills

1 Read, write and express numerals up to the millions using expanded notations including exponents

2 Distinguish between natural, counting, and whole numbers

3 Round off whole numbers

4 Apply order of operations

5 Calculate time differences

6 Recognize patterns and sequences

7 Read and round decimals up to the thousandths place

8 Solve exercises and verbal problems involving length, weight, and capacity using the metric system

9 Add and subtract whole numbers; applying skills to verbal problems

10 Multiply and divide whole numbers

11 Solve word problems using commutative, associative, identify prop. of 1, multiplication prop. of zero, non-divisibility by zero, and remainders expressed as fractions

12 Determine the greater or smaller of 2 whole numbers, using the symbols for greater than, less than(> <) and locates their positions on a number line

13 Add, subtract, multiply and divide decimals to the hundred thousandths place, including verbal problems and money

14 Factor sets of numbers into their primes

15 Change proper and improper fractions to their equivalents

16 Solve exercises and word problems involving ratio and proportion

17 Add and subtract common fractions and mixed numerals with like and unlike denominators including word problems

18 Multiply and divide common fractions and mixed numerals including word problems

19 Convert common fractions, decimals and percents one to the other

20 Find the percentage when the percent and the number are known, including word problems

21 Find the number when the percent and percentage of it are known including word problems

22 Find the percent when the percentage and number are known including word problems

23 Name angles using three letters

24 Measure to the nearest degree and classify according to their measure, acute, right, obtuse, and straight angles

25 Identify parallelograms, rectangles, squares, and triangles and their component parts including altitude

26 Find perimeters and areas of rectangles, squares, and triangles

27 Identify congruent triangles

28 Find circumferences and areas of circles

29 Find volumes of cubes, rectangular solids and cylinders

30 Identify cones, pyramids and spheres

31 Find the mean (average) of sets of numerals

32 Read and interpret bar, line, circle, and pictographs; maps and charts

33 Add, subtract, and multiply and divide positive and negative numbers and show their position on a number line

34 Graph points on a Cartesian plane

35 Use and read a thermometer

36 Solve exercises and verbal problems involving length, weight capacity using the English system and the concept of a dozen

37 Find least common multiples and greatest common factor

**8th grade math skills**

1 Apply the four fundamental operations to whole numbers; round, estimate and apply to word problems

2 Work with patterns and sequences (odd, even, square, square root and prime factors)

3 Apply the four fundamental operations to decimals; round estimates, and apply to word problems

4 Express numbers in expanded form using exponents and rename as integers

5 Measure and change to equivalent units in the metric system and English system and apply to practical examples

6 Find the greatest common factor and the lowest common denominator (GCF and LCD) and apply where appropriate

7 Apply the four fundamental operations to fractions and mixed numbers, simplify results and apply to word problems

8 Give absolute values of positive and negative numbers as well as zero and locate their positions on a number line

9 Apply the four fundamental operations to positive and negative numbers

10 Solve linear equations and orders unequal variables (ie X<Y<Z is the same as Z>Y>X)

11 Measure angles with a protractor, read using 3 letters

12 Classify angles and triangles, quadrilaterals, and polygons

13 Find perimeters and areas of triangles, rectangles, parallelograms, and circles (circumference)

14 Define the radius, diameter relationship in a circle

15 Evaluate algebraic expressions and formulas

16 Solve problems involving ratio and proportion and apply them to related problems and scales

17 Convert common fractions, decimals, and percents, one to the other

18 Find the percentage of a number when the number and percent are given, including word problems

19  Find the percent when the percentage and number are known, including word problems

20  Find the number when the percent and percentage of it are known, including word problems

21  Find squares of positive numbers

22  Find square roots of numbers using the estimation or algorithm method

23  Apply both to the Pythagorean theorem

24  Find surface areas and volumes of rectangular prisms and cylinders

25  Find ordered pairs that satisfy a linear equation in two variables and graph on a Cartesian plane

26  Read and interpret bar, line, circle, and pictographs; maps and charts

27  Find the mean, median, and mode of a group of numbers and apply to practical situations

28  Determine simple probability

29  Read temperature from Fahrenheit and Celsius thermometers

30  Determine the passage of time and hour related to same

31  Apply measurement concepts of dozen and gross and perform operations with all denominate numbers

32  Simplify algebraic expressions without or with parentheses

33  Multiply and divide numbers in exponential form

34  Find volumes of cones, pyramids, and spheres in both English and Metric systems

35  Identify complimentary, supplementary, and vertical angles

36  Determine the union and intersection of sets, draw and interpret a related Venn diagram

37  Define the commutative and associative properties; identify elements for addition and multiplication; and order of operations

38  Identify those angles associated with two parallel lines cut by a transversal

# *LANGUAGE ARTS-PREK TO GRADE 8*

## Pre-Kindergarten communication skills

1  Identify pictured objects by pointing

2  Identify pictured objects by naming

3  Follow simple directions

4  Express basic needs in simple phrases

5  Say and perform action to a finger-play

6  State his/her first and last name

7  Classify and name objects by use

8  Name colors (red, yellow, blue)

9  Sing a simple song

10  Respond in phrases to what/when/where/why/questions

11  Identify prepositions; on/off, in/out, up/down, behind/in front, beside/next to

12  Discriminate common sounds

13  Name colors

14  Express ideas in sentences

15  Discriminate between words that sound the same or different

16  Supply a rhymed response to a verbal cue

17  Discriminate similarities and differences of pictures and designs

18  Identify opposites: hot/cold, soft/hard, wet/dry, etc.

19  Use plural "S" form appropriately

20  Recall facts after hearing a story

21  Recite alphabet

22  Classify by categories rough/smooth, wet/dry, etc.

23  Recognize his/her own name in print

24  Smile

25  Show a facial response to the ringing of a bell or other sudden noise

26  Smile when spoken to

27  Laugh aloud

28  Raise arms when mother or caregiver says, "Come here" or "Up" while reaching toward child

29  Shake head "no" at the appropriate time to indicate comprehension

30  Wave "bye-bye" at the appropriate time to indicate comprehension

31  Give affection by kissing, hugging or patting

32  Nod head for "yes" indicating the recognition of a simple question

33  Squeal

34  Vocalize to a toy or pet

35  Make "singing" tones

36  Babble using several consonants

37  Say "mama" or "dada" without specific meaning

38  Imitate sounds or words of others

39  Say "mama" or "dada" or other family names with purpose and meaning

40  Use jabbering as if talking, although the sounds are unintelligible to adults

41  Give his/her first name

42  Give his/her full name

43  Tell his/her age

44  Tell if he/she is a boy or girl

45  Name his/her siblings

46  Deliver a simple message

47  Show an interest in the conversation of others

48  Make verbal greeting (e.g., "hi")

49  Acknowledge compliments or thanks

50  Say "excuse me" when disturbing or interrupting

51  Point to the body parts: mouth, eyes, nose, feet, hair, tongue, teeth, etc.

52  Use a time line to distinguish today, last night, tonight, yesterday, tomorrow, tomorrow night, day before yesterday, day after tomorrow, etc.

53  Distinguish between little/big, short/long, tall/short, few/many, empty/full, less/more, thin/fat, thick/thin, narrow/wide, light/heavy, shallow/deep

54  Distinguish between direction/position concepts: up/down, out/in, bottom/top, over/under, far/near, go/stop, low/high, inside/outside, off/on, beginning/end, closed/open, above/below

55  Distinguish between direction/position concepts: forward/backward, away from/toward, center/corner, straight/crooked, through/around, going/coming, front/back,

right/left, to/from, here/there

56  Sort designs by color (blue, yellow, red)

57  Sort designs by shape (circle, square, triangle)

58  Sort designs by size (large, medium, small)

59  Identify types of weather: rainy, sunny, hot, cold, windy, cloudy

60  Classify items concretely: toys, numbers, people, things to read, animals, clothes, colors, things to ride, tools, food, dishes, furniture, designs, fruit, musical instruments, vegetables

61  Classify items by function: toys, numbers, people, things to read, animals, clothes, colors, things to ride, tools, food, dishes, furniture, designs, fruit, musical instruments, vegetables

62  Classify items abstractly: toys, numbers, people, things to read, animals, clothes, colors, things to ride in, tools, food, dishes, furniture, designs, fruit, music instruments, vegetables

63  Give reasonable response to cause and effect questions

64  Identify community helpers by pointing to: doctors, nurses, fire fighters, police officers, mail carriers, dentists, teachers, mechanics, carpenters, painters, and storekeepers

65  Identify places in the community we can go when we: are sick, buy milk, buy clothes, buy medicine, borrow a book, buy stamps, need a haircut, want our car fixed

## Kindergarten communication skills

1  Identify pictured actions by naming

2  Identify pictured emotions by naming

3  State his/her full name

4  Follow 1 and 2 step directions

5  Classify by kind and use

6  Name colors of objects

7  Identify and match shapes, colors, letters, words, and pairs of pictures

8  State his/her address

9  Identify capital and lower case letters A-F

10  Print or trace capital and lower case letters A-F

11  State his/her telephone number

12  Print or trace his/her first name

13  Supply rhyming response to riddles

14  Identify a picture that matches an oral statement

15  Relate a story or event

16  Exhibit his/her right and left hand

17  Compare concrete objects (bigger/smaller/heavier/lighter)

18  Respond in complete sentences to picture cue

19  Match capital and lower case letters G-L

20  Identify capital and lower case letters G-L

21  Print or trace capital/lower case letters G-L

22  Recall details about a selection

23  Recognize rhyming words and patterns of rhyme

24  Recognize and repeat a sequence (objects, pictures, patterns)

25  Arrange pictures to show a sequence

26  Use prepositions in describing location of objects (on/off, close/near/far, behind/in/out, front/back, inside/outside, over/under)

27  Use pronouns appropriately according to sex or number

28  Use plural forms of nouns

29  Use time relationships (before/after, morning/afternoon/night)

30  Identify opposites (boy/girl, light/dark, up/down, etc.)

31  Match capital and lower case letters M-S

32  Identify capital and lower case letters M-S

33  Print or trace capital and lower case letters M-S

34  Identify spatial relationships top/bottom, first/middle/last

35  Respond in sentences to who/what/when/where/why questions

36  Predict outcome of a story

37  Use time concepts appropriately (yesterday/today/tomorrow)

38  Discriminate between words that sound the same or different

39  Interpret school vocabulary (pencil, chalk, bulletin board)

40  Use vocabulary appropriate to his/her age and grade

41  Listen for specific information

42  Match capital and lower case letters T-Z

43  Identify capital and lower case letters T-Z

44  Print or trace capital and lower case letters T-Z

45  Identify capital and lower case letters A-Z in random order

46  Print first and last name

47  Recall and retell story in correct sequence (first/next/last)

## 1st grade language arts skills

1 Capitalize first word in sentence

2 Capitalize "I"

3 Capitalize proper names

4 Use period at end of telling sentence

5 Use question mark at end of asking sentence

6 Develop oral language based on use of complete thoughts

7 Tell stories that have a beginning/middle/end

8 Form letters correctly using appropriate size and shape

9 Use exclamation point when strong feelings are expressed

10 Use inflectional endings correctly (ed, ing, s)

11 Place letters on line correctly

12 Recognize and use comparative forms of adjectives correctly

13 Recognize and use personal, possessive pronouns correctly

14 Identify pronoun antecedent

15 Recognize and use correct verb tense in sentence

16 Write a simple sentence

17 Develop writing process

18 Space between letters correctly

19 Use s and es to from noun plurals

20 Use singular form of noun correctly

21 Space between words correctly

22 Correctly print words using upper and lower case

23 Write numerals correctly

## 2nd grade language arts skills

1 Develop writing process

2 Write for different audiences

3 Use written forms

4 Write simple sentences

5 Capitalize correctly

6 Recognize and use period correctly

7 Recognize and use question mark correctly

8 Recognize correct noun forms in sentence

9 Recognize possessive pronouns in sentence

10 Recognize correctly and incorrectly spelled words

11 Maintain uniform spacing between letters and words

12 Recognize and use comma correctly

13 Recognize abbreviations (days, months)

14 Recognize and use correct inflectional endings (ing, ed, y to i)

15 Recognize contractions

16 Use possessive form of noun correctly

17 Recognize noun/verb agreement in number

18 Recognize noun/verb agreement in tense

19 Recognize correct comparative adjective in sentence

20 Recognize correct use of exclamation point

21 Recognize correct sentence capitalization and punctuation

22 Recognize correct comparative adjective in sentence

23 Space between words correctly

24 Correctly write first and last name in cursive writing

25 Correctly write numerals

26 Recognize correct verb tense in sentence

27 Demonstrate the difference between manuscript and cursive writing in terms of stroke, slant, and form

28 Form cursive letters correctly

29 Place cursive letters on line correctly

30 Space between cursive letters correctly

## 3rd grade language arts skills

1  Develop writing process

2  Write for different audiences

3  Use written forms

4  Write simple stories

5  Capitalize correctly

6  Use commas

7  Recognize and use period

8  Recognize and use question mark

9  Recognize and use exclamation point

10  Identify verb in a sentence

11  Identify subject of a sentence

12  Identify correctly and incorrectly spelled words

13  Develop oral language based on use of complete thoughts

14  Complete transition to cursive writing

15  Write paragraphs

16  Recognize and use adjectives correctly

17  Recognize and use pronouns correctly

18  Recognize and use correct verb

19  Recognize and use adverbs correctly

20  Form cursive letters of uniform height

21  Form cursive letters of uniform slant

22  Recognize correctly punctuated sentences

23  Maintain uniform spacing between letters and words

24  Align letters carefully on the base line

25  Identify correctly capitalized sentences

26  Correctly proofread one's own cursive writing mistakes

## 4th grade language arts skills

1  Develop the writing process

2  Write for different audiences

3  Use written forms

4  Write simple and compound sentences

5  Identify correct use of period

6  Identify correct use of question mark

7  Identify correct use of exclamation point

8  Identify and use possessive forms of nouns (singular/plural)

9  Identify and use pronouns correctly

10  Identify and use correct subject/verb agreement

11  Identify and use correct verb tenses

12  Identify correctly and incorrectly spelled words

13  Speak in complete thoughts

14  Review and reinforce cursive handwriting

15  Apply cursive handwriting to all written work

16  Write paragraphs

17  Identify correct use of comma

18  Identify and use correct comparative adjectives

19  Identify and use correct modifying adjectives

20  Identify and use adverbs correctly

21  Identify correctly the subject of a sentence

22  Identify correctly the verb of a sentence

23  Identify correctly the appropriate transitional words

24  Identify correct sequence of sentences in a paragraph

25  Identify topic sentence/sequence of other sentences in a paragraph

26  Capitalize correctly

27  Identify correct use of quotation marks

28  Identify correctly punctuated sentences

29  Identify sentence as complete, incomplete, run-on

30  Capitalize correctly

31  Identify correct use of comma

32  Identify and use correct comparative adjectives

33  Identify and use correct modifying adjectives

34  Identify and use adverbs correctly

35  Identify correctly the subject of a sentence

36  Identify correctly the verb of a sentence

37  Identify correctly the appropriate transitional words

38  Identify correct sequence of sentences in a paragraph

39  Correctly proofread his/her own writing mistakes

## 5th grade language arts skills

1  Develop the writing process

2  Write for different audiences

3  Use written forms

4  Write simple sentences correctly

5  Write compound sentences

6  Capitalize correctly

7  Identify correct use of period

8  Identify correct use of question mark

9  Identify correct use of exclamation point

10  Identify and use possessive nouns correctly

11  Identify and use pronouns correctly

12  Identify and use verbs correctly

13  Identify correctly and incorrectly spelled words

14  Speak in complete thoughts

15  Improve fluency of handwriting

16  Identify correct use of quotation mark

17  Identify correctly punctuated sentences

18  Identify and use comparative forms of adjectives correctly

19  Identify and use adjectives correctly to modify

20  Identify and use adverbs correctly

21  Identify the subject of the sentence

22  Identify the verb of the sentence

23  Recognize subject/verb agreement

24  Recognize and use transitional words (however, therefore, etc.)

25  Develop a neat legible handwriting style

26  Write paragraphs

27  Recognize correctly capitalized words and sentences

28  Identify correct use of comma

29  Identify sentences as complete, incomplete, or run-on

30  Identify correct sequence of sentences

31  Develop aspects of handwriting style with proper margins and indentation

## 6th grade language arts skills

1  Develop the writing process

2  Write for different audiences

3  Use written forms

4  Write paragraphs

5  Identify correct use of end marks

6  Identify correct use of quotation marks

7  Identify correct use of irregular plural nouns

8  Identify correct use of pronouns

9  Identify correct use of verbs

10  Identify correct use of adjectives (comparative/modifying)

11  Identify correct use of adverbs

12  Identify subject of a sentence

13  Identify verb of a sentence

14  Identify correctly/incorrectly spelled words

15  Speak clearly in complete thoughts

16  Review and reinforce correct letter formation in handwriting

17  Write a report of several paragraphs with a title

18  Capitalize correctly

19  Recognize correctly capitalized sentences

20  Identify and use comma correctly

21  Identify correct use of transitional words

22  Identify sentences as complete, incomplete, or run-on

23  Identify correct sequence of sentences in a paragraph

24  Identify relevant details to support a topic sentence

25  Organize information for speaking

26  Identify correctly punctuated sentences

27  Identify correct use of transitional words

28  Write a story of several paragraphs with a title

29  Write sentences

30  Use correct oral language to present an oral report

31  Maintain the quality of handwriting

## 7th grade language arts skills

1  Develop the writing process

2  Write for different audiences

3  Use written forms

4  Write simple sentences

5  Write compound sentences

6  Write complex sentences

7  Write declarative, interrogative and imperative sentences

8  Write paragraphs

9  Capitalize correctly

10  Punctuate sentences correctly

11  Use quotation marks correctly in sentences

12  Identify correct use of nouns (common/proper)

13  Identify correct use of pronouns (objective/nominative)

14  Identify correctly and incorrectly spelled words

15  Use spoken language clearly

16  Organize information for speaking

17  Use spoken language clearly and correctly in short oral reports

18  Apply the rules of good handwriting to all written work

19  Identify character's feelings, motives, actions

20  Identify plot of the story

21  Identify setting of the story

22  Identify mood of the story

23  Write a report of several paragraphs with a title

24  Write a story of several paragraphs with a title (book/content area)

25  Recognize correctly capitalized sentences

26  Identify correctly punctuated sentences

27  Recognize verbosity in sentences

28  Recognize excessive repetition in sentences

29  Recognize misplaced and correctly placed modifiers in sentences

30  Recognize nonparallel and parallel construction in sentences

31 Identify correct sequence of sentences in a paragraph

32 Identify correct supporting detail for a topic sentence

33 Identify correct concluding sentence of a paragraph

34 Identify correct use of commas

35 Identify and use irregular verb forms correctly in sentences

36 Identify and use adverbs correctly in sentences

37 Identify sentences as complete, incomplete, or run-on

38 Demonstrate appropriate neatness and arrangement for outlines, reports, letters and essays

## 8th grade language arts skills

1 Develop the writing process

2 Write for different audiences

3 Use written forms

4 Capitalize correctly

5 Recognize correctly capitalized sentences

6 Identify the correct use of punctuation

7 Identify correct use of quotation marks

8 Identify and use possessive nouns correctly

9 Identify correct pronoun antecedent

10 Identify and use personal, demonstrative and relative pronouns correctly

11 Identify sentences as complete, incomplete, or run-on

12 Identify correctly and incorrectly spelled words

13 Use spoken language clearly

14 Organize information for speaking

15 Use spoken language clearly and correctly in short oral reports

16 Self-evaluate written work in all subject areas for neatness, proper letter formation, spacing, and alignment

17 Apply the rules of good handwriting to all written work

18 Identify character's feelings, motives, actions

19 Identify plot of the story

20 Identify setting of the story

21 Identify mood of the story

22 Identify correct use of commas

23 Identify correctly punctuated sentences

24 Identify and use linking verbs correctly

25 Discriminate between contractions and possessives

26 Identify and use correct verb tenses

27 Identify and use irregular verb forms correctly

28 Identify correct use of possessive nouns and pronouns in sentences

29 Identify correct adjective in a sentence

30  Identify correct use of adverbs

31  Identify subject of sentence

32  Identify verb of sentence

33  Identify subject/verb agreement

34  Recognize and use appropriate transitional words

35  Recognize verbosity in a sentence

36  Recognize excessive repetition in a sentence

37  Recognize misplaced and correctly placed modifiers

38  Identify correctly and incorrectly spelled words

39  Recognize nonparallel construction

40  Recognize and correct double negatives

41  Identify correct sequence of sentences in a paragraph

42  Identify correct supporting details for the topic

43  Identify correct concluding sentence of a paragraph

# SCIENCE- *K-8*

## Kindergarten science skills

1 Identify weather conditions as cloudy, rainy, snowy and sunny and keep account of the weather on a day to day basis

2 Identify the order in which the seasons occur and match weather conditions with the seasons

3 Relate clothing to weather conditions, seasons,

4 Relate weather to good health care

5 Distinguish between work and play and recognize that work is moving something

6 Identify pushing and pulling as forces, and recognize that forces do work

7 Recognize that machines make work easier

8 Recognize machines used for work and play

9 Identify common animals as suitable or unsuitable as pets

10 Recognize pet characteristics

11 Classify pets as large or small

12 Relate pets with specific pet homes

13 Recognize the need for pet care

14 Recognize that there are stages of growth in plants

15 Identify the growth sequence in living things

16 Recognize that plants provide things for use by animals and humans

17 State that the earth is round, that it is going around all the time and that we live on the earth

18 Identify land and water on a globe

19 Identify the sun as a star and explain why it looks different from other stars

20 Relate two facts about the sun and one fact about the moon

21 State that astronauts have visited the moon

## 1st grade science skills

1 Demonstrate an awareness of the environment and the means through which it is perceived

2 Describe the functions of the sense organs and demonstrate related safety habits

3 Observe and classify activities according to which sense is being used

4 Describe and compare the uses and values of the information received by the various sense organs

5 Describe characteristics unique to living things

6 Describe body coverings, body parts, shape and colors of different animals

7 Compare the relative sizes of common animals

8 Describe the many ways in which animals move

9 State that all animals need a certain diet, water and sleep and that some animals need play

10 Identify the stages that animals go through during metamorphosis

11 Describe the care given to baby animals by their parents

12 Describe and plan a proper home for a pet

13 Describe and compare similarities and differences of prehistoric and present day animals

14 Describe some of the ways fossils are formed

15 Classify kinds of motion used in doing work

16 Describe and compare machines that people use to help them do work

17 Describe and compare types of simple machines and tools

18 Classify machines as simple or complex

19 Describe the kinds of energy used to operate machines

20 Identify parts of plants (stems, roots, leaves, flowers and seeds)

21 Identify the factors necessary for plant growth

22 State that most plants come from seeds

23 Classify seeds by the ways in which they are scattered

24 Name some plants people eat

## 2nd grade science skills

1  Observe and describe where water is found on the earth

2  Compare fresh and salt water and the life that is supported by each

3  Predict what may happen to plants and animals if they are taken out of their natural environment

4  Explain changes in states of matter

5  Demonstrate and observe an experiment to show a change in the state of water

6  Compare reactions of substances placed in water

7  Describe solutions, solutes and evaporation

8  Describe how water is polluted

9  Describe and compare animals

10  Describe the physical characteristics of various habitats and compare animals according to their habitat

11  Observe, describe, and classify the coverings of common animals

12  Compare functions of body coverings

13  Compare and classify animals by their body structures

14  Compare and classify food-getting structures of animals and describe feeding habits

15  Describe links of a food web and predict what might happen if one part of the web were destroyed

16  Classify animals as plant-eaters, animal eaters, or animals that eat both plants and animals

17  Observe and compare methods of animal locomotion

18  Describe tracks left by animals as they move

19  Compare skeletal systems of a number of familiar vertebrates

20  Compare air with other (visible) examples of matter and conclude that air has weight and takes up space

21  Describe the characteristics of air pressure

22  Observe and explain air pressure

23  Compare and contrast animal structures designed to take in air

24  Compare polluted air with clean air and explain reasons for differences

25  Classify heat and light as forms of energy

26  Recall that when sunlight is absorbed by matter, it is changed into heat

27  Describe the use and functions of thermometers as instruments to measure temperature changes

28  Compare and describe heat transfer by convection, conduction and radiation

29  Describe how heat is transferred through solids, gases, and liquids

30  Compare safe and unsafe ways of handling fire

31  Observe and describe a number of common sources of both heat and light

32  Classify objects as to kinds of energy they emit

33  Compare light sources as to their intensity

34  Explain light reflection

35  Classify objects as being opaque, translucent, or transparent

36  Describe safety practices that should be followed in handling heat and light sources

**Goal: 3rd grade science skills**

1  Locate science terms in the glossary and index

2  Identify, in pictures, terms used in the lesson

3  Describe the elements of a picture

4  Describe how a thermometer is used

5  Describe several of the conditions necessary for life on a planet

6  Compare planet characteristics and demonstrate the orbits of the planets

7  Describe meteors and meteorites

8  Demonstrate, through experimentation, a kilometer and the distance it covers

9  Describe rotation and revolution

10  Explain why we have night and day

11  Give examples of how earth is changing and name the forces that cause changes

12  Identify the layers of the earth's crust

13  Describe the action of a volcano

14  Explain how sedimentary rock layers are formed

15  Describe varying forces that cause erosion

16  Describe how soil is formed and the features of rocks

17  Compare the different kinds of soil and rank their water holding ability

18  Classify human activities as "work" or "non-work" according to the scientific definition

19  Identify the six types of simple machines

20  Describe and compare the kinds of work done by simple machines

21  Describe how a force may be applied to an object

22  Measure the distance an object is moved

23  Observe and describe how machines use energy

24  Observe and describe the heat energy that results from friction

25  Observe and record characteristics of plants

26  Describe conditions necessary for plant growth in different environments

27  Name some differences and similarities in kinds of leaves

28  Identify factors necessary for the growth of plants

29  Identify parts of plants used as food

30  Explain uses of non-green plants

31  Explain the growth of fungi

32  Describe differences in the growth of molds

## 4th grade science skills

1  Name the three major gases that compose our atmosphere

2  Tell why rust will form on certain metals

3  Identify substances other than gases contained in the atmosphere

4  Demonstrate that a flame cannot burn without oxygen

5  Explain how compressed air can be used to do work

6  Determine the scientific principle of an airfoil

7  Describe the operation of propeller and jet engines

8  Classify metals as magnetic and nonmagnetic

9  Describe how electrical energy is changed to mechanical energy

10  Observe static electricity and draw conclusions about it

11  Identify static and current electricity

12  Describe a simple circuit and explain its operation

13  Identify materials which are conductors

14  Identify materials which are insulators

15  State safety rules for using electrical appliances

16  List the resources which man must have to stay alive

17  Describe sources of energy

18  List the ways in which man has changed his environment

19  Define the terms "extinct" and "endangered"

20  Name examples of animals that have become extinct and endangered

21  List activities which will preserve the environment

22  Explain the origin of warm and cold air masses

23  Explain why soil absorbs more sunlight than water

24  Describe what happens when cold air meets warm air

25  Define "humidity"

26  Describe how changes in weather and climate affect various kinds of plants and animals

27  Identify animals as warmblooded or cold-blooded

## 5th grade science skills

1  Describe the structure of the earth's crust
2  Classify some common minerals by their hardness
3  Distinguish between rocks and minerals
4  Name some of the important minerals and how they are obtained from the earth
5  Compare some of the properties of fresh and ocean water
6  Outline a food chain from plant life to carnivores
7  Describe the effects of pollution on ecosystems
8  Describe the process of salt water desalination
9  Describe some of the problems that arise in obtaining salt and other minerals from salt water
10  Describe and compare two ways of using the oceans to produce electrical energy
11  Deduce the contents of a closed package
12  Tell how atoms combine to form molecules
13  Describe how temperature affects particle motion
14  Identify some of the major elements and their symbols
15  Explain that a molecule is a combination of two or more atoms
16  Read and write simple chemical formulae
17  Separate components of a mixture by filtering
18  Compare water samples with respect to hardness
19  Discuss the relationship of the moon to the earth
20  List the phases of the moon
21  Describe the motions of the earth and the moon that cause solar and lunar eclipses
22  Identify the planets in the order of their distance from the sun
23  Identify the planets in the order of their size
24  Describe the characteristics of a planet, an asteroid, a comet and a meteorite
25  Make inferences about travel beyond the solar system
26  Describe the process of photosynthesis
27  List the important elements necessary for photosynthesis
28  Identify molds, algae, fungi, mosses, ferns, and a variety of flowering plants
29  Identify the major plant parts: stem, root, leaf, and flower
30  Explain the reproductive system of flowers
31  Explain how plants reproduce by spores

## 6th grade science skills

1  Define several kinds of radiant energy

2  Identify and describe amplitude, frequency and wave length in waves

3  Compare and contrast the three methods of heat transfer

4  Describe the relationships between friction and static electricity, and magnetism and current electricity

5  Compare and contrast static and current electricity

6  Describe how electrical energy can be produced from chemical, mechanical and radiant energy

7  Describe and relate the measurement properties of current electricity

8  Identify electric safety equipment and explain how it protects us

9  Explain the difference between weight and mass

10  Compare and contrast physical and chemical changes

11  Identify the parts of an atom and classify them according to their electrical charges

12  Identify the elements in a compound

13  Compare and contrast kinetic and potential energy

14  Describe the processes of fission and fusion

15  Compare and contrast the characteristics of the atmosphere

16  Name the major factors that affect weather

17  Explain the formation and movement of air masses

18  Explain the nature and causes of weather phenomena

19  Identify and describe weather instruments

20  Read and interpret weather maps and charts

21  Analyze ways in which living and nonliving things are alike and different

22  Explain how plants are affected by various external stimuli

23  Describe the process of plant growth

24  Relate the effect of light in the growth of plants

25  Develop hypotheses to explain the adaptations of plants to their environment

26  Identify the important characteristics of survival based on instinct

27  Distinguish between learned and instinctive behaviors

28  Explain how body structures affect animal behavior

29  Compare the survival needs of animals

30  Identify, describe and draw conclusions about the procedures and results of an animal training experience

31  Identify types of fossil fuels and discuss the reasons for their shortage

32  Compare and contrast alternative energy sources

33  Describe the importance of living, nonliving and once-living things in meeting human needs

34  Identify forms of matter and energy that are wasted

35  Make inferences about the need to protect the oceans due to their increasing importance as a source of food and energy

## 7th grade science skills

1 Describe the relationship between energy and living things

2 Explain the scientific classification system

3 Explain scientific method

4 Explain the metric measurements of length, mass, volume and temperature

5 Define and explain spontaneous generation

6 List the essential conditions for life to exist

7 Describe the parts and functions of a microscope

8 Describe and compare the functions of cell structures

9 Describe the movement of materials in and between cells

10 Explain cell division

11 Define the term "tissue"

12 Explain the scientific classification system

13 Draw conclusions about animals based on scientific classifications

14 Compare the characteristics and functions of animal structures

15 Compare the two types of animal reproduction

16 Compare and contrast the reproductive process in frogs and mammals

17 Describe the stages of reproduction in animals

18 Describe and compare inborn and acquired behavior

19 Explain the functions of the sensory organs

20 Draw conclusions about the importance of living clocks

21 Define ecology terms including biosphere, community habitat, succession and biome

22 Compare food chains and food webs  Draw conclusions about levels in a food chain

23 Describe levels in a food chain

24 Describe and compare the six biomes

25 Define conservation terms such as weathering, endangered, extinct, pollution and photochemical

26 Compare conservation methods for soil, forest, wildlife and water

27 Compare sources and ways to control air and water pollution

28 Describe ways to increase food and energy supplies

29 Describe the effects of population growth on food, energy and land supplies

30 Draw conclusions about plants based on their scientific classifications

31 Compare the characteristics and functions of plant structures (roots, stems, leaves)

32 Explain the process of photosynthesis

33 Compare and contrast seed production in conifers and flowering plants

34 Explain seed dispersal and germination

35 Explain plant propagation

36 Describe the effect of fertilization on soils

## 8th grade science skills

1 Explain the uses of measurement standards and list the units used to measure length, volume, mass and temperature

2 Conduct activities to develop skill in measurement practices

3 Distinguish between theory and law in science

4 Explain how work is related to force and distance

5 List the six simple machines and give examples of each

6 Solve numerical problems related to work, mechanical advantage, power, and efficiency

7 Differentiate between weight and mass

8 Define gravity as a property of all matter

9 Compare and contrast speed, velocity, and average speed

10 State Newton's three laws and give examples of each

11 Explain the effect of gravity on falling objects

12 Define centripetal force and describe situations in which this force acts on an object

13 Compare physical and chemical properties

14 Compare physical and chemical changes

15 Define the four states of matter

16 Determine the density of an object

17 Define an element and give symbols for the common elements

18 List and explain the basic parts of an atom

19 Relate atomic number to number of protons in the nucleus

20 Define compounds and recognize formulas for compounds

21 Explain how atoms combine and contrast the transfer and sharing process of bonding

22 Use oxidation numbers to write formulas for compounds

23 Define the characteristics of a wave length, amplitude, frequency, and speed

24 Using the relationship among wavelength, frequency, and speed, find one when the two are given

25 Define the electromagnetic spectrum and list examples from various points in the spectrum

26  Describe the action of a prism in producing the visible light spectrum

27  Distinguish between primary light colors and primary pigment colors

28  List the spectrum colors by order of wavelength

29  Distinguish between the properties of convex and concave lenses

30  Detail the differences and similarities between a microscope and a telescope

31  Describe how lenses correct vision defects

32  Explain the relationships of sound, volume, and amplitude; pitch and frequency

33  List examples of noise pollution and indicate some methods for controlling this kind of pollution

34  Define the Doppler effect

35  Distinguish between potential and kinetic energy

36  Describe the relationship between temperature and heat

37  Define specific heat

38  Differentiate among conduction, convection, and radiation as methods of heat movement

39  Explain how insulation controls heat transfer

40  Describe various cooling systems and explain the role of evaporation

41  Contrast wet and dry cells

42  Compare conduction (static) and current as sources of electric charge

43  Use Ohm's law to solve simple problems in current-resistance relationships

44  Describe the behavior of magnets

45  Explain how an electric current and a magnet set up similar magnetic fields

46  Describe various electronic devices

# SOCIAL STUDIES- GRADES 9-12

## World History:  1000 A.D. to the Present

1  Summarize the development of feudalism in Europe and the rise of towns and commerce

2  Identify the major kingdoms of western Europe in feudal times

3  Distinguish the location and cultures of the Byzantine and Muslim empires

4  Outline the role of the Roman Catholic Church in Europe

5  Identify the causes of the conflict between the Christian and Muslim cultures

6  Outline the emergence of European nation-states and their political development

7  Outline the conflicts related to the Crusades, Mongol conquests, and expansion of the Ottoman Turks

8  Relate the spread and impact of the Black Death

9  Explain the preservation of the Greek and Roman philosophy, medicine, science, and law

10  Describe the economic foundations of the Renaissance

11  Outline the rise of Italian city-states

12  Contrast the artistic, literary, and intellectual creativity of the Medieval and the Renaissance periods

13  Describe the impact of Machiavelli's theory of government

14  Describe the roots and impact of the Protestant reformation

15  Describe the impact of religious differences on European governments

16  Describe the period of European expansion into the Americas, Africa,  and Asia in the 16th-19th centuries

17  Describe the development and spread of slavery in the 16th-19th centuries

18  Describe the causes of revolution in England and France

19  Describe the impact of religious differences on the founders of the United States

20  Outline the impact of new scientific discoveries by Galileo, Newton, Kepler, Harvey, etc.

21  Describe the impact on 19th century Europe of Congress of Vienna,  British reform laws, and the unifications of Italy and Germany

22  Describe the origins of the Industrial Revolution and its effect on  imperialism and colonialism

23  Describe the emergence of capitalism and free enterprise as dominant economic patterns

24  Describe the relation of capitalism to the rise of Marxism, socialism,       and utopianism

25 Describe the effect of the Industrial Revolution on the status of women and children

26  Describe the causes and rise of the workers' union

27  Describe the causes and results of World Wars I and II

28  Describe the causes and result of the Russian Revolution

29  Describe the economic and military power shifts since 1945 in Europe, Japan, China, and the third world

30  Describe the rise and fall of the USSR

### World Geography

1   Identify the different map projections and their distortions

2   Explain map scale and orientation

3   Define and illustrate latitude and longitude

4   Relate the major regional climatic zones

5   Relate the climatic zones to events in the modern world

6   Describe how various environments have affected man's political and economic status

7   Describe man's effect on the world environment

8   Describe the effect of geographical factors on cultures, religions, social and economic systems

9   Describe the major human migrations

10  Describe the impact of the locations of important natural resources on regional economics

11  Outline the development and location of city and town location

12  Identify specific problems related to human mobility, social structure, and the environment

13  Describe the patterns and networks of economic interdependence of multinational groups

## US History I

1  Identify European nations' motivation for early exploration

2  Describe the development of the colonies

3  Identify the causes and results of the French and Indian War

4  Chart the events from 1763-76 which led to the Declaration of Independence

5  Explain the events of the American Revolution and their consequences

6  List the results of the American Revolution

7  Identify the weaknesses and strengths of the government under the Articles of Confederation

8  Analyze the problems in framing the Constitution

9  List the parts of the United States Constitution

10  Explain the functions of the three branches of government

11  Identify the problems faced by President Washington

12  Identify the causes and results of the War of 1812

13  List the democratic advances made during the Jackson Era

14  Explain "Manifest Destiny"

15  Describe the major issues and events that led to sectional differences in the 19th century

16  Identify the short term causes of the Civil War

17  Analyze the successes and failures of the Union and Confederacy during the Civil War

18  List the factors which altered American Society during the Reconstruction Period

19  Explain the influences and impact of Post-Civil War Westward movement on American History

20  Identify the causes, effects and impact of industrialization on American life

21  State the reasons for the growth and effectiveness of labor unions

22  Analyze the political events of the Gilded Age

### US History II

1  Identify problems of immigrants trying to assimilate into US society of early 1900's

2  State reasons for the Spanish-American War and the emergence of the USA as a world power

3  Identify the concepts of Progressivism and its impact on American life

4  Identify and describe causes and results of US involvement in World War I

5  Analyze the political, economic and social life of the 1920's

6  Analyze the causes of the Great Depression and the impact of the New Deal

7  Reconstruct worldwide conditions of the 1920's and 30's which led to World War II

8  Analyze the causes and effects of the period known as the Holocaust

9  Trace US involvement in World War II on the home front and world battlefields

10  Summarize the results of World War II

11  Compare and contrast the ideological differences between the US and the Soviet Union that led to the Cold War and the Korean Conflict

12  Interpret political, social and economic events of the 1950's

13  List the reasons for the turmoil and protests of the 1960's

14  Define the purpose of Congress

15  Outline the steps that Congress takes to turn a bill into law

16  Identify the major powers of the President

17  List the primary and secondary function of our American legal system

18  Identify the problems that each Constitutional Amendment resolves

40  Chart the powers which are shared by State and Federal governments, and powers reserved only for the State Government

19  Identify needed research skills

20  Analyze the civic rights and responsibilities of 18 year olds

21  Identify some major causes for crime, the rights of the accused, the steps in the criminal justice process and the strengths and weaknesses of our judicial system

22  Prepare a research paper

23 Analyze the causes of juvenile delinquency, the problem of treatment and offer possible solutions

23 Compare and contrast varied attitudes toward punishment

24 Analyze problems found in a correctional institution

25 Identify the principles of American democracy

26 Trace the development of the powers of government

## Economics

1  Identify characteristics of: American Capitalism, Socialism, Communism

2  Explain the basic ideas of inflation and recession

3  Explain stocks and bonds, as well as their trading on the stock exchange

4  Evaluate economic information

5  Explain how wants lead to demand and then to production

6  Explain pricing in a free market economy, as a result of supply and demand curves

7  List and explain the role of: land, labor, capital, entrepreneurship

8  Explain the nature of proprietorship, partnership and the corporation

9  Explain the advantages and disadvantages of competition and monopoly and/or the need for government regulation

10  Explain how various taxes pay for various governmental services

## Sociology

1  Describe your social environment in relation to a working definition of Sociology

2  Define the meaning of culture and cultural diversity

3  List the major causes for cultural change

4  Differentiate among values, norms and sanctions by purpose

5  Explain the concept of social self and how it differs from personality

6  Describe how adolescents form relationships

7  Identify the well-defined stages of adulthood

8  State the major factors necessary for a group to exist

9  Identify the social classes in American society

10  Differentiate between statistical minorities and other kinds of minorities

11  Describe the effects of changing sex roles on both men and women

12  Identify the five social institutions

13  Distinguish between various family types, patterns, and kinship

14  Explain the primary and secondary functions of education and religion

15  List the functions of the institutions on economy and government

16  Distinguish between the various approaches to change

17  Define a social problem

18  Discuss the relationships between mass media, collective behavior and    social movement

19  Explain the relationship between population growth and ecological problems

## Psychology

1  Identify and explain how psychology compares to other sciences and  six fields on which psychologists work

2  List at least six methods which psychologists use to obtain their data

3  Identify the six main areas of development and the main contributions of heredity and environment to the developmental process

4  Distinguish among: norms, values, deviance, and sanctions

5  Identify four theories of personality

6  Identify the person responsible for the theory along with the main aspects of personality development which each theory stresses

7  Define learning by means of classical conditioning, operant conditioning, and cognitive learning

8  Identify and explain three important theories of emotions and at least three measures of emotional states

9  Identify motivation and three ways in which psychologists explain motivation

10  Identify at least three major types of conflict situations and at least five emotional disorders in our society

11  Explain how social groups form and how they operate

12  Identify specific methods used by psychologists to measure personality

# ENGLISH GRADES 9-12

## English 9

1 Explain the relationships between and among: characters, plot, tone, point of view, and theme

2 Identify the following figures of speech in literary selections: simile, metaphor, personification, and onomatopoeia

3 Identify the characteristics which distinguish literary forms

4 Use literary terms in describing and analyzing selections

5 Demonstrate mastery of grammar and usage skills

6 Demonstrate satisfactory growth in vocabulary

7 Explain the difference between an author's style and literary effect

8 Describe the use of images and sounds to elicit readers' emotions

9 Identify an hypothesis

10 Evaluate clarity and accuracy of information in a selection

11 Identify the two basic parts of drama

12 Describe how stage directions help the reader understand a play's setting, mood, plot, and theme

13 Write clear, varied sentences

14 Arrange paragraphs in logical sequence

15 Revise writing for clarity, use of language, spelling, punctuation, and capitalization

16 Define plagiarism

17 Describe the consequences of plagiarism

## English 10

1 Explain the uses of symbolism in literature, particularly through the study of the novels 'The Old Man and the Sea' and 'A Separate Peace'

2 Explain prepositional, verbal, and appositive phrases, independent and subordinate clauses, correct agreement, and correct use of modifiers

3 Identify universal themes prevalent in literature of many cultures

4 From printed consumer materials identify essential information related to operation, cautions, contents, and warranties

5 Skim manuals or consumer texts to locate information

6 Compare and contrast product information in advertisements with manuals and warranties

7 Compare the use of rhyme, rhythm, and sound in poetry to convey a message

8 Paraphrase the meaning of selected poems

9 Explain the use of asides in drama

10 Explain the role of a director in stage work

11 Compare character development in a play as compared to other literary forms

12 Elaborate ideas through word choice and vividness

13 Write clear, varied sentences

14 Edit final copy for correct grammar, spelling, punctuation, and capitalization

15 Describe how writing achieves its intended purposes

16 Analyze the writing of others

17 Explain concepts contained in literature

18 Translate concepts from a selection into simpler and more easily understood terms

## English 11

1  Organize evidence to support a position in an oral presentation

2  Critique the accuracy, relevance, and organization of evidence

3  Critique the clarity and effectiveness of an oral presentation

4  Describe contributions of different cultures to American literature

5  Describe the development of American literature from the 17th to the 20th century

6  Identify and contrast periods in American literature

7  Describe the major themes of American literature

8 Read and follow directions to complete an application (employment, college admission, etc.)

9  Explain the use of a Thesaurus to extend vocabulary for writing

10  Analyze the poetic elements of classic poems

11  Identify the elements and techniques which make poetry most enjoyable

12  Compare specific poems of American writers

13  Describe the relation between farce and characterization

14  Explain the use of monologue and soliloquy

15  Explain the use of verbal and dramatic irony

16  Organize written ideas in a logical manner

17  Elaborate an idea in writing clearly and accurately

18  Adapt content and vocabulary to audience, purpose, and situation

19  Edit final copy for grammar, spelling, punctuation, and capitalization

20  Develop a plan for research

21  Collect information to support a thesis

22  Evaluate quality and accuracy of information

23  Arrange information in a logical sequence

24  Revise copy for clarity and content

## English 12

1 Orally defend a position

2 Orally explain information

3 Use detail and analogy to support an oral position

4 Critique oral presentations

5 Recognize major literary forms and techniques in British and other world literature

6 Relate works and authors of British and other literature to major themes and issues of the time

7 Identify information needed for a lab experiment

8 Identify information needed to evaluate a produce or service

9 Evaluate the quality of informational texts and manuals

10 Explain how the choice of words in a poem fits the character

11 Explain how the rhyme, rhythm, meter, alliteration, parallelism and assonance support the subject and mood of a poem

12 Explain how imagery and figures of speech appeal to a reader's senses and experience

13 Compare the works of poets from traditional and contemporary cultures

14 Present written ideas in a logical order

15 Elaborate a written idea clearly and accurately

16 Revise writing for depth and technique of presentation

17 Edit final copy for correct grammar, spelling, punctuation, and capitalization

18 Collect information to support a thesis

19 Evaluate quality and accuracy of information

20 Arrange information in a logical sequence

# MATHEMATICS: GRADES 9-12

## Basic Math

1 Add up to 5 digits and 6 numbers including regrouping

2 Subtract up to 5 digits including regrouping

3 Multiply up to 4 digits times 3 digits

4 Divide up to a 2 digit divisor, 5 digit dividend with remainders

5 Perform the four major operations with decimals:

6 Add mixtures of decimal/decimal and decimal/whole numbers up to 4 place decimals

7 Subtract decimal/decimal, decimal/whole numbers up to 4 decimal places

8 Multiply up to 3 digit multiplier and a 4 decimal place product

9 Divide the three basic types of problems up to a 2 digit divisor and 4 digit dividend

10 Add up to 3 addends including unlike denominators

11 Subtract with like and unlike denominators including regrouping

12 Multiply 2 fractions or mixed numbers

13 Divide 2 fractions or mixed numbers

14 Add/subtract 3 fractions in same problem

15 Compare fractions

16 Calculate fractional equivalents (including whole numbers and decimals)

17 Identify a set of prime numbers

18 Convert decimals, fractions, and percents

19 Find the percentage of a number

20 Find a percent given two numbers

21 Use percent to find discounts, sales tax, commission, and interest

22 Recognize and use the inequality symbols

23 Solve one step and two step word problems

24 Estimate answers to problems

25 Round whole and decimal numbers

26 Recognize exponents, square number

27 Find perimeters and areas of squares, rectangles, triangles, and circles

28 Find volume of a rectangle, prism, cylinder, cone, pyramid, and sphere

29 Compare English and Metric linear, liquid, mass, and temperature measurements

30 Measure, construct, and classify angles using a protractor

31 Find complements and supplements of angles

32 Read a bar, line, and circle graph

33 Construct a bar and line graph

34 Write and use ratios and proportions

35 Calculate correct change from a purchase

36 Write out a sales slip and figure tax

37 Find average of several numbers

38 Find missing number, given the average and all but one of the numbers

39 Find the missing angle of a triangle, given two angles

40 Add, subtract, multiply, and divide signed numbers

41 Explain parallel and perpendicular

42 Explain finite and infinite

43 Solve simple equations with one variable

44 Plot points on a coordinate graph

45 Evaluate simple formulas

46 Solve simple set problems using a Venn Diagram

47 Solve a simple problem involving probability

## Consumer Math

1 Perform the basic operations with whole numbers, fractions, and decimals

2 Solve percent computations

3 Write a deposit and withdrawal slip

4 Write a check and check stub

5 Read a bank statement

6 Reconcile an account

7 Compute simple interest

8 Read and interpret a pay slip

9 Compute gross and net pay

10 Compute commission

11 Fill out and read a time card

12 Take a sample employment test

13 Fill out an income tax form (standard deduction)

14 Read and use tax tables

15 Prepare a budget

16 Keep simple records

17 Make and use a shopping list

18 Compute discount

19 Use unit pricing for comparative shopping

20 Explain discount coupons for shopping

21 Fill out an order blank

22 Calculate change

23 Find the best buy

24 Explain the cost of using a credit card

25 Determine the actual cost of an item bought using financing

26 Compute sales tax

27 Read and interpret a bill or an invoice

28 Compute the balance due on a charge account statement

29 Compute a real estate commission

30 Use a table to find mortgage payments

31 Use table to find insurance premiums

32 Differentiate among various types of investments

33 Differentiate among various types of insurance

34 Read and interpret graphs

## Business Math

1  Keep a personal cash record including a checking account

2  Reconcile a checking account

3  Fill out a sales slip

4  Compute prices of fractional parts of quantities

5  Compute unit price

6  Determine wages based on hourly rate, regular time, and overtime

7  Calculate FICA tax

8  Read and interpret a time card record

9  Determine wages based on a piece-rate basis

10  Compute salesman's commission

11  Calculate interest on a loan - yearly, monthly, daily basis

12  Differentiate among using credit union, finance borrowing, and installment buying

13  Distinguish among various types of taxes: property, sales, excise,  income

14  Calculate home expenses: taxes, insurance, utilities, groceries

15  Calculate transportation and travel expenses

16  List normal office costs

17  Keep records of a small business: balance sheet, income statement, and  payroll

18  Determine purchase cost of a retailer

19  Compute the pricing of goods

20  Calculate sales and profits

21  Explain the operations of the retailer, wholesaler, and manufacturer

22  Identify the retailer's problems in buying and selling merchandise

23  Identify the major types of investments: stocks and bonds

24  Demonstrate how to determine changes in value from the financial page

25  Explain how to buy and sell stocks and bonds

## Algebra I

1  Perform the four basic operations with positive and negative numbers

2  Evaluate expressions

3  Identify coefficients, constants, and variables

4  Simplify expressions using the distributive property and combining like terms

5  Solve linear equations including those with the variable on both sides

6  Translate English phrases into mathematical terms

7  Solve word problems, involving number relationships, coins, uniform motion, perimeter, consecutive integers, work, age, mixture, digits, direct and indirect variations, area

8  Solve equations with fractions and decimals

9  Solve equations with absolute values

10  Solve literal equations

11  Solve quadratic equations by factoring, completing the square and quadratic formula

12  Solve linear inequalities

13  Define finite, infinite, and equal sets

14  Find subsets, unions, and intersections of sets

15  Graph unions and intersections of sets

16  Simplify and evaluate expressions containing exponents

17  Classify and simplify polynomials

18  Add, subtract, multiply, and divide polynomials

19  Factor binomials and trinomials completely

20  Add, subtract, multiply, and divide algebraic fractions

21  Simplify complex fractions

22  Solve fractional equations

23  Use formulas to solve problems

24  Plot points and graph linear equations on a coordinate plane

25  Recognize and use the slope/intercept form of an equation

26  Calculate the slope of a line

27  Write the equation of a line given two points on the line

28  Identify and use ratios and proportions to solve problems

29  Solve systems of equations by graphing and algebraically

30  Find square roots of numbers using a table

31  Perform these operations with radical expressions: simplify, combine like radicals, multiply radicals, and rationalize denominators

32  Solve equations containing radicals

33  Use the computer and appropriate software where applicable to the course

## Intermediate Algebra

1  Solve first degree equations and inequalities, equations with absolute values, and fractional equations

2  Use the Pythagorean Theorem and solve problems using it

3  Solve problems dealing with direct and inverse variation

4  Calculate with exponents

5  Identify and classify polynomials

6  Perform the four basic operations with polynomials

7  Square and cube a binomial

8  Factor polynomials

9  Simplify and do the four major operations with rational expressions

10  Simplify complex rational expressions

11  Solve literal equations

12  Evaluate expressions and formulas

13  Convert repeating decimals and fractions

14  Define complex numbers

15  Simplify and do the four basic operations with irrational numbers

16  Solve quadratic equations by factoring, completing the square, and the quadratic formula

17  Identify and use the discriminant

18  Identify and use roots (sum and product)

19  Solve radical equations

20 Graph a linear equation using slope intercept and a table or values

21  Use the distance formula, slope formula, midpoint formula, and solve related problems

22  Write the equation of a line given two points and given a point and a slope

23 Identify parallel and perpendicular lines through the use of slope

24  Identify and graph functions and relations

25  Identify the domain and range of a given function

26 Use functional notation

27 Identify the conic sections and their equations

28  Graph and do problems related to the conic sections

29  Solve linear and quadratic systems and inequalities graphically and algebraically

30  Use a table of logarithms to multiply, divide, raise to power, extract roots to do combined operations

31  Evaluate formulas using logarithms

32  Solve exponential equations

33  Use the computer when appropriate in the development of course skills

## Geometry

1  Explain the role of undefined terms, definitions, postulates and theorems in a mathematical system

2  Use Algebra skills to solve numerical type geometric problems

3  Identify and name sets of points, lines, segments, angles, and planes

4  Define, classify, and measure angles

5  Define and apply concept of angle and segment bisectors

6  Define and apply the properties of parallel lines and related angles

7  Define and classify triangles

8  Define and apply properties of congruent triangles

9  Define and utilize concepts of altitudes and medians of a triangle

10  Define and apply properties of similar triangles

11  Apply the Pythagorean Theorem

12  Identify and utilize properties of polygons and regular polygons

13  Define and apply the properties of the various quadrilaterals

14  Apply formulas for surface area and volume of solid figures

15  Identify and apply concepts associated with circles, congruent circles, arcs, chords, secants, and tangents

16  Perform constructions for segments, angles, and triangles

17  Devise a formal geometric proof in the various areas studied

18  Prove and apply the major theorems studied throughout the course

19  Use the computer when appropriate in the development of course skills

293

## Computer Literacy

1  Turn the computer on and off

2  Use the printer and disk

3  Use immediate mode to do arithmetic problems

4  Type in and run programs which demonstrate the necessary statements and commands in BASIC

5. Identify areas where the computer is being used today

6  List names of various computer languages

7  Identify major events and important persons in historical development of computers

8  Use a variety of software for various purposes

9  Identify things a computer can and cannot do

10  Load and run programs from disk

12  Identify the component parts of a computer system

13  Write and debug a simple program

14  Use a desktop publishing program

15  Demonstrate use of word processing, use wrapping, insert, delete, and print options

16  Predict the outcome of a simple BASIC program

17  Identify career opportunities in the computer field

18  Recognize major historical events in the development of computers

19  Identify some future uses for computers

20  Use software for CAI, drill and  CTC simulations, enrichment and discovery

21  Evaluate a piece of software

22  Develop a vocabulary of computer related terms

23  Explain what a data base is

24  Explain the applications of a data base

25  Create a data base

26  Access and print material from a data base

27  Explain what an electronic spreadsheet is

28  Enter and change data for an electronic spreadsheet

29  Print output from an electronic spreadsheet

30  Delete, insert, replace, transpose characters, words, and paragraphs using a word processor

31  Save his/her work on a disk

32  Format and print his/her word processing documents

33  Retrieve a file

34  Create a graphic design on CRT

35  Explain the uses of computers in music

36  Explain the impact of the computer in society

37  List uses of computer technology in business, education, and science

295

# HEALTH: GRADES 9-12

## Health 9

1 Demonstrate his/her knowledge of anatomy and physiology of the respiratory and skeletal system

2 Identify diseases of the lung

3 Explain the relationship of the respiratory system and physical exercise

4 Explain the cause and prevention factors of heart disease, cancer, and venereal disease

5 Explain the scientific medical advancements made on the treatment of heart disease and cancer

6 Demonstrate his/her knowledge of basic concepts of communicable and noncommunicable diseases as measured by teacher devised tests

7 Describe the anatomy and physiology of the male and female reproductive system, fetal development

8 Development a positive attitude concerning human sexuality

9 Describe basic medical procedures of abortion

10 Describe the physical and psychological factors in abortion

11 Explain why HIV is not transmitted through casual contact in the school, home, or work environment

12 Explain why HIV is not transmitted by objects in one's environment

13 Explain why HIV is not transmitted through food or food handlers

14 Discuss the ways in which HIV transmission can be blocked

15 Explain why abstinence is the only sure way of preventing sexual transmission of HIV

16 Explain how condoms can help prevent infection with HIV

## Health 10

1 Identify the needs, values and general directions for first aid

2 Describe the nature of a variety of wounds, their causes, types, symptoms, and appropriate first aid

3 Describe specific first aid treatment for injury to the eyes, head, chest, abdomen, back, genitals, legs, feet, and hands

4 Describe the cause, symptoms, and treatment of shock

5 Identify the symptoms and treatment for choking (Heimlich)

6 Demonstrate cardiopulmonary resuscitation and artificial respiration

7 Distinguish between safe and unsafe boating and swimming procedures

8 Describe symptoms, prevention, and first aid for poisoning

9 Classify and identify dangerous substances

10 Describe the classification, cause and first aid for burns

11 Identify cold and hot water emergencies

12 Identify and be able to respond to sudden illness such as heart attack, stroke, fainting, convulsion, and epilepsy

13 Demonstrate dressing and bandaging specific wounds

14 Demonstrate methods of control of bleeding

15 Name and identify bone and joint disorders

16 List emergency rescue and transfer procedures

17 Define the mental mechanisms of rationalization, projection, repression, compensation, sublimation, displacement, conversion, and regression

18 List methods of coping with stress within and outside the family

19 List ways to make sound decisions regarding peer pressure, career choices and environmental decisions

20 Explain why HIV is not transmitted by objects in one's environment

21 Identify safety steps used by medical staff to prevent HIV infection

## Health 11

1  Pass the Motor Vehicle Department written and road test

2  List basic administrative and traffic laws

3  List the rules of the road and right of way procedures

4  List basic service and maintenance need of an automobile

5  Identify traffic control signs, signals, and roadway markings

6  Identify safety factors on the public highways and the influences that lead to accidents

7  Describe various types of automobile insurance

8  Describe proper procedure at the scene of an accident

9  List component parts of an automobile

10  Demonstrate the basic maneuver skills for behind-the-wheel performance

11  Identify proper driving under adverse conditions and coping with emergencies

12  Demonstrate an ability to see, identify, and predict in traffic

13  Perform required driving skills

14  Demonstrate refusal skills to reinforce responsible decision making

## Health 12

1  Describe the use of contraceptives

2  List the symptoms of pregnancy and tests for pregnancy

3  Describe fetal development and birth

4  Explain types of birth, multiple births, sex determination, Rh factor and inherited characteristics

5  Identify basic medical procedures of abortion

6  Identify specific male and female medical tests and operations

7  Examine the emotional aspects of dating as preparation for the long term relationship of marriage

8  Identify the legal, emotional, social, and financial concerns in preparing for marriage

9  Identify sound money management for a family

10  Explain artificial insemination, surrogate mother, and adoption

11  List the responsibilities of parenthood

12  Identify the types of child abuse, causes and legal responsibilities

13  Explain the emotional and financial effects of the death of someone close

14  List the pros and cons of single life

15  Explain the physiology of the AIDS virus

16  Explain safe and unsafe sex practices as they relate to AIDS

# SCIENCE: GRADES 9-12

## Earth Science

1  Differentiate between hypothesis and theory

2  List physical properties, motions, and gravity fields of earth and moon

3  Describe the structure of matter and the forms of matter

4  Identify minerals as elements and compounds

5  Describe the forces that control the formation and properties of igneous and metamorphic rocks

6  Describe the formation and composition and structure of the atmosphere

7  Describe the composition and structure of the atmosphere

8  Identify major factors that influence climate and weather

9  Diagram the water cycle

10  Describe effects of currents, tides, and waves

11  Identify agents of erosion

12  Define river systems and ground water systems

13  Describe formation of glaciers and their effects

14  Describe cause and effects of earthquakes

15  Describe major land forms and topography maps

16  Explain how scientists study the age of the earth

17  Define renewable and nonrenewable resources

18  Describe supply and uses of earth's resources

19  Define stars and galaxies

20  Describe our solar system

21  Identify major steps in space exploration

## General Science

1 Define physical science

2 List methods used by scientists in developing and testing scientific knowledge

3 Conduct activities to demonstrate measurement abilities

4 List at least six simple machines and give examples of each

5 Solve numerical problems related to work, mechanical advantage, power and force

6 Differentiate between weight and mass

7 Compare and contrast speed, velocity, and average speed

8 State Newton's three laws

9 Demonstrate how the velocity of a projectile changes in flight

10 Define matter

11 Define the four states of matter

12 Determine physical properties of matter

13 Compare physical and chemical properties

14 Define an element and give symbols for the common elements

15 List and explain the basic parts of an atom

16 Relate atomic number to the number of protons in a nuclei

17 Describe the relationship between atomic mass and isotope

18 Define compounds and formulas for compounds

19 Use oxidation numbers to write formulas for compounds

20 Explain how atoms combine to form compounds

21 List properties of metals

22 Describe the properties of families and transitional elements

23 Distinguish between metals and metalloids

24 List properties of nonmetals

25 Compare and contrast the properties of the various families of nonmetals

26 Explain why there are so many compounds derived from carbon

27 Define isomers and diagram compounds

28 List and describe various classes of compounds of carbon

29 Distinguish among three types of solutions

30 Contrast organic and inorganic solvents

31  Use the solubility rules to determine whether certain compounds are soluble in water

32  Describe the effect of a solute on the boiling and freezing points of a solvent

33  Write and balance equations

34  Distinguish between exothermic and endothermic reactions

35  List and distinguish properties of the common acids and bases

36  Describe the relationship among ion concentration, pH, and acid-base strength

37  Define the characteristics of a wave: length, amplitude, frequency, and speed

38  Differentiate between reflection and refraction of waves

39  Define electromagnetic radiation and spectrum

40  Explain the importance of light to living things

41  Describe the action of a prism in producing the visible light spectrum

42  Describe how a person sees color

43  Define interference

44  Distinguish between the properties of convex and concave lenses

45  Describe how lenses correct vision defects

46  Diagram the workings of a telescope

47  Define laser and describe how it functions

48  Define compression waves and compare them to transverse waves

49  Solve simple numerical problems relating to the speed of sound

50  List and explain properties of musical sound

51  Define the Doppler effect

52  List examples of noise pollution and methods of alleviating the problem

53  Describe the relationship between temperature and heat

54  Define specific heat

55  Describe the process of melting and vaporization

56  Explain Boyle's and Charles' Laws

57  Differentiate among conduction, conversion, and radiation as methods of heat movement

58  Explain how insulation affects heat transfer

59  Describe how internal combustion engines work

60  Explain the problems of waste heat and the resulting thermal pollution

61 Describe various methods for obtaining and identifying static charges

62 Contrast wet and dry cells

63 Define volt

64 Use Ohm's Law to solve simple problems in current-resistance relationships

65 Compare and contrast voltmeter and ammeter

66 Explain how a magnet and coil produce alternating current

67 Explain the operation of amplifiers

68 List some radioactive elements

69 Compare three types of nuclear radiation

70 Define half-life of a radioactive nuclide

71 Compare fusion and fission

72 List the major fossil fuels

73 Explain the use of the sun for energy

74 Describe the hydroelectric, geothermal, and nuclear powers

75 List the advantages and disadvantages of nuclear power

76 List ten ways that people can conserve energy

## Chemistry

1 Demonstrate the proper use of the Bunsen burner,

2 Identify the scent of an unknown using proper techniques

3 Cut and fire-polish glass tubing

4 Measure liquids in various glass containers

5 Relate mass to energy

6 Explain how matter is classified and the various changes undergone by matter

7 Identify basic measurements of length, time and mass in the metric system and perform related calculations

8 Identify an element by its chemical symbol

9 Balance and interpret chemical equations

10 Convert a given word equation into a balanced formula equation

11 Define a mole or Avogadro's number

12 Express a given mass of an element in moles and vice versa

13 Demonstrate formula writing and naming of compounds

14 Explain chemical terminology involving simple compounds, e.g. molecular and formula weights

15 Determine the percentage composition if given the formula of a compound

16 Determine the molecular and empirical formula of a compound when given its percentage composition and its molecular weight

17 Explain how the present atomic model was derived

18 Draw the shell model of the atom

19 Interpret the information given by the four quantum numbers that define the location of an electron

20 Indicate the distribution of electrons in an appropriate notation when given the atomic number of an element

21 Describe some physical characteristics of an element by its location in the periodic table

22 Name certain series and groups of the periodic chart in terms of accepted chemical families

23 Predict the sizes and ionization characteristics of one element relative to another

within a group or series on the basis of nuclear field strength and electronic distribution

24 Define valence electrons and predict the properties of an element based on the number of valence electrons

25 Characterize the nature of bonding between two elements from their location on the periodic chart

26 Draw certain basic molecular structures based on chemical bonding

27 Describe the concept of pressure

28 Read a barometer

29 Give examples of Boyle's and Charles' laws

30 Define a solid and liquid both macroscopically and microscopically

31 Compare the properties of metals, ionic solids, covalent solids and network solids

32 Describe van der Waals forces and hydrogen bonds,

33 Compare the strength of various chemical bonds

34 Define solute, solvent and solution

35 Contrast a physical mixture and a solution

36 Use the mole concept to solve stoichiometric equations and mole conversions

## Biology

1  Explain the characteristics and organization of living things and the cells of which they are made

2  Explain the elements of the scientific method and its uses in conducting a controlled experiment

3  Explain the proper use of the compound light microscope and other tools and techniques used in the study of biology

4  Explain the nature of matter and the energy and chemical changes important

5  to living things

6  Explain the inorganic and organic compounds involved in the chemistry of life

7  Explain the discovery and basic parts of cells and the differences in cells

8  Explain the movement of materials in and out of the cell by means of diffusion, active transport and other means of transport

9  Describe the energy for living cells and the capture and release of energy in such processes as photosynthesis, glycolysis, fermentation, and aerobic respiration

10  Define cell division, mitosis, and meiosis and their part in asexual and sexual reproduction

11  Apply the principles of Mendelian genetics by probability

12  Explain the chromosome theory, sex determination by chromosomes, sex-linked traits, and the behavior of genes

13  Describe the replication of DNA, protein synthesis and the effects and frequencies of mutations

14  Explain the inheritance of human traits and the detection of genetic disorders

15  Describe the techniques of controlled breeding, cloning, polyploidy and recombinant DNA

16  List the theories about the origin of the universe, earth and life and the fossil record as an evidence of evolution

17  Contrast Lamarck vs Darwin's theory of evolution and the Hardy-Weinberg Principle as a mechanism of studying evolution

18  Describe the concepts of early and modern evolution

19  Explain the Linnaeus System of Classification and the ongoing science of modern

taxonomy

20  Describe the size, structure, shape, and reproductive cycles of viruses and the relationship of viruses to disease

21  Describe the characteristics and classification of the kingdom of Monera and the size, shape, structure, and life processes of bacteria

22  Describe the habitats, ways of life and classification of protozoa

23  List the characteristics, habitats and classification of algae

24  List the characteristics, habitats and ecological and economical roles of fungi

25  Describe the origins and adaptations of vascular and non-vascular plants

26  Explain the reproduction and adaptations in seedless vascular plants gymnosperms and angiosperms

27  Describe the kinds of plant tissue and the structure and function of roots, stems, and leaves

28  Explain reproduction in flowering plants, the formation of fruit and seed germination and dispersal

29  List the factors affecting plant growth, tropisms, and nastic movements

30  Describe the use of plants for food, forestry, fibers, medicine, and seasonings

31  Describe the symmetry and body plans of sponges and coelenterates

32  Describe the structural characteristics of flatworms, roundworms, and segmented worms

33  Describe the structural characteristics of mollusks and echinoderms

34  Describe the characteristics and classification of the phylum of Arthropoda and distinctions among arachnids, crustaceans, and myriapods

35  Describe external and internal structure of insects and complete and incomplete metamorphosis

36  List the characteristics of chordates and vertebrates and differences in structure among jawless cartilaginous and bony fishes

37  Describe the characteristics of amphibians and all systems of the frog

38  Outline the history of reptiles and the characteristics of modern reptiles

39  Describe the origin and characteristics and all systems of birds

40  Identify the characteristics of mammals and the functioning of their respiratory, circulatory, nervous, and reproductive systems

41 Describe the physical and behavioral characteristics of humans and the organization of the tissues, organs, and systems of the body

42 Describe the human skeletal, muscular, and integumentary system

43 Specify the role of food and nutrition in human life and the structure and functioning of the human digestive system

44 List the composition and types of blood, circulation through the body and defenses against disease

45 Explain the structure and function of the respiratory and circulatory systems

46 Explain the structure and function of the human central nervous and peripheral nervous systems

47 Describe how receptors, sense organs, and the entire human nervous system works together

48 List the major endocrine glands, the hormones they produce, and endocrine system regulation

49 Contrast human male and female reproductive systems

50 Describe the menstrual cycle, fetal development, and birth

51 Differentiate among infectious, sexually transmitted, degenerative, and hereditary diseases

52 Describe the characteristics of drugs, alcohol, and tobacco, and their effects on the body

## Physics

1 Distinguish between science and technology

2 Distinguish the meaning of Law and Hypothesis, and appreciate the scientific method

3 Define matter, mass, inertia, density, energy

4 Explain the relation of energy and physics

5 List the subdivisions of physics

6 Distinguish the meaning of accuracy and precision

7 Identify the units of measurement in physics

8 Explain scientific notation

9 Demonstrate the usefulness of the vector in physical notation

10 Relate the concepts of speed and velocity

11 Explain acceleration

12 Define velocity and acceleration using graphs

13 State Newton's Laws of Motion

14 State Newton's Law of Universal Gravitation

15 Define the scientific meaning of force

16 Solve problems using vectors to represent forces

17 Find the resultant force of concurrent forces

18 Explain the importance of friction in physics

19 Define parallel forces, torque and couple, and the conditions of equilibrium

20 State the meaning of curvilinear motion

21 State the definition of centripetal acceleration and centripetal force

22 Explain the concept of "frame of reference"

23 Differentiate between frequency and periodicity

24 Identify Simple Harmonic Motion in specific physical occurrences

25 Explain the mathematical relationship of the parameters governing the motion of the pendulum

26 Explain the meaning of work

27 Define the scientific meaning of power

28 Explain elastic and gravitational potential energy

29  Explain the relationship between momentum and impulse

30  Explain the concepts of Conservation of Energy and Conservation of Momentum

31  Define ductility, malleability, elasticity, Hooke's Law, cohesion, adhesion, surface tension, meniscus, capillarity, melting, and freezing of liquids

32  Describe vaporization, equilibrium, and condensation of gases

33  Explain the distinction between heat and thermal energy

34  Compare three temperature scales - Fahrenheit, Celsius, and Kelvin  Absolute zero

35  State Boyle's Law and Charles' Law

36  Explain relationship between heat and work

37  State the First and Second Laws of Thermodynamics

38  State properties of waves - reflection, refraction, diffraction, interference

39  Describe how sound is produced

40  Describe how sound is transmitted

41  Compare the speed of sound and light

42  Relate frequency and pitch

43  Explain the Doppler Effect

44  Explain the relationship of physics and various musical instruments

45  Compare the properties and fundamentals of waves with light

46  Contrast the corpuscular and wave theories of light

47  Distinguish between photometry-intensity and illumination

48  Apply the Laws of Reflection in the laboratory

49  Demonstrate image formation by plane mirrors, concave and convex mirrors

50  Form object-image relationships using curved mirrors

51  Use ray diagrams to explain situation of images

52  Define the phenomenon of optical refraction

53  State the relationship between refraction and speed of light in media

54  Diagram image-object relationships formed by converging and diverging lenses

55  Use ray diagrams to locate images

56  Explain image formation in telescopes and microscopes

57  List the properties of color

58  Explain interference patterns of light

59  Show the mathematical relationship between slits and interference fringes, and the wavelength of light

60  Explain polarization of transverse waves by means of reflection, refraction, and scattering

61  Explain the attractive and repulsive forces which operate in electrostatics

62  Test the nature and magnitude of charges using the electroscope

63  Explain Coulomb's Law of Electrostatics

64  Explain the nature of electric fields, electric lines of force, and field intensity

65  Explain the importance of the concept of electric potential energy

66  List the various sources of continuous current

67  Explain the design of the dry cell as a source of current

68  Draw circuit diagrams to study and explain relationships between electromotive force of cells and internal resistance in series and parallel circuits

69  Solve problems of potential difference, current, resistance, and power in various circuits using Ohm's Law and circuit diagrams

70  Measure resistance using the Wheatstone Bridge and voltmeter-ammeter method

712  Explain the relationship between production of heat and dissipation of power in electrical circuits

72  Calculate the cost of purchasing home electrical energy when the rate for the kilowatt hour is known

73  Explain the domain theory of magnetism

74  Explain magnetic lines of force using lines of flux

75  Explain terrestrial magnetism

76  Relate electric current to magnetism using Ampere's rule for a solenoid

77  Relate the principles of operation of the galvanometer

78  Explain the principles of operation of the simple d-c generator and the simple d-c motor

79  State the principles of inductance

80  Explain the importance of the transformer to regulate voltage in  alternating current

81  Explain the sinusoidal representation of alternating current

82  Explain the development of the vacuum tube and be aware of its applications

83  Relate the development of the transistor and its characteristics

84  Explain how magnetic fields can control charged particles, as in cathode-ray tubes and television

85  Outline the significant steps in the development of atomic physics

86  Explain the concept of radioactive isotopes, their technology, and applications

87  Use nuclear symbols and equations in order to further study nuclear reactions

88  Explain radioactive decay and half-life and some applications

314

# APPENDIX

315

316

# Special Conditions

1   With/without visual cues
2   With/without supervision
3   With/without prompting
4   With/without directions
5   With/without verbal cues
6   With/without a visual model
7   With/without tactile cues
8   With/without  assistance
9   With/without adaptive equipment
10   Repeatedly
11   Only upon request
12   Independently

# Criteria

1   Every time
2   Consistently
3   On grade level
4   Whenever necessary
5   At the___th percentile
6   With a score of ___%
7   In __ out of __ trials
8   Increase by ___
9   Decrease by ___
10 With ___% accuracy
11 ___ times out of ___
12 ___% of the time
13 Every period
14 Every day
15 Each marking period
16 For ___ seconds
17 For ___ minutes
18 For an entire (day/week/month)

# Normed (Standardized) Tests and Measures

1  Abbreviated Symptom Questionnaire
2. ADD-H Comprehensive Teacher Rating Scale
3. Attention Deficit Disorders Evaluation Scale
4  Batelle
5  Basic Achievement Skills Individual Screener
6  Bender-Gestalt Visual Motor Test
7  Brigance
8  Bruininks-Oseretsky Test of Motor Proficiency
9  California Achievement Test
10  California Test of Basic Skills
11  Child Behavior Checklist
12  Cognitive Ability Test
13  Connors Rating Scale
14  Cumberland Vocational Evaluation for Trainable Students
15  Developmental Test of Visual Motor Integration (Berry)
16  Developmental Test of Visual Perception (Frostig)
17  Differential Aptitude Test
18  DISTAR Program
19  Denver Developmental Screening Test
20  Detroit Test of Learning Aptitude
21  Early Learning Accomplishment Profile
22  Emotional and Behavior Problem Scale
23  Erhardt Hand Function
24  Fiorenpino's Reflex Test
25  Glass Analysis
26  Gordon Diagnostic System
27  Hand Sensory Test
28  Hawaii Early Learning Profile
29  Heath Reading Inventory
30  Iowa Test of Basic Skills
31  Key Math Test
32  Larsen/Hammill Test of Written Spelling
33  Marshalltown Behavioral Developmental Profile
34  Matching Familiar Figures
35  McCarthy Scale of Children's Abilities

36  Metropolitan Achievement Test
37  Metropolitan Reading Test
38  Montgomery Richter
39  Movement Assessment of Infants
40  O/T Evaluation Scale
41  Peabody Individual Achievement Test
42  Peabody Fine Motor Assessment
43  Peabody Picture Vocabulary Test
44  Piat
45  Piers-Harris Children's Self-Concept Scale
46  Postrotary Nystagmus
47  Project Active Motor Ability Tests
48  Regular Learning Accomplishment Profile
49  Rossetti Infant-Toddler Language Scale
50  Slingerland Screening Test for Identifying Children with Specific Language Disability
51  Slosson Intelligence test
52  SRA Corrective Reading Program
53  Test of Achievement and Proficiency
54  Thematic Apperception Test
55  Trombly Scott
56  Vane Kindergarten Test
57  VASCO Vocational Assessment System
58  Wide Range Achievement Test (WRAT)
59  Woodcock-Johnson Psychoeducational Battery
60  Woodcock Reading Mastery Test
61  Wechsler Intelligence Scale for Children (WISC-R)
62  Wechsler Intelligence Scale for Preschool (WISP)
63  Wepman Auditory Discrimination Test
64  Wepman Auditory Sequential memory Test
65  Yale Children's Inventory

# Generic Tests and Measures

1  Anecdotal record
2  Appropriate topic test
3  Attitude inventory
4  Attendance record
5  Behavioral profile
6  Behavior rating forms
7  Communication and speech assessment
8  Criterion referenced test
9  Developmental checklist
10  Disciplinary record
11  District testing program
12  End-of-year exam
13  Extracurricular acivities participation record
14  Human figure drawing
15  Independent living assessment
16  Laboratory situation
17  Parent checklist
18  Personality profile
19  Physical tolerance evaluation
20  Pre and post behavioral scale
21  Semester exam
22  Sentence completion test
23  Skills inventory
24  Social skills and leisure assessment
25  State minimum competency test
26  Structured observation
27  Student checklist
28  Student self-report or evaluation
29  Teacher checklist
30  Teacher-made test

# Accommodations

1  Seat (him/her) near to the teacher
2  Provide specially adapted seat
3  Move (his/her) seat away from visual and auditory distractions
4  Provide individualized training in study skills
5  Provide individualized training in test taking strategies
6  Provide individualized training in note taking
7  Provide individualized training in time management skills
8  Provide individualized training in organizing materials
9  Provide individualized training in classroom conduct
10  Provide lesson outlines
11  Provide weekly lesson outlines
12  Provide sheet of homework assignment(s)
13  Provide organizers for materials and notes
14  Adapt requirements for homework
15  Adapt requirements for classwork
16  Adapt requirements for mastering objectives
17  Adapt requirements for seat retention
18  Adapt requirements for spelling
19  Adapt requirements for handwriting
20  Adapt requirements for talking
21  Adapt requirements for test answers
22  Adapt requirements for grading
23  Adapt requirements for task completion
24  Adapt requirements for acceptable behavior
25  Adapt requirements for deadlines
26  Provide tests in Braille version
26  Allow extra time in testing
27  Allow use of calculator in testing
28  Provide outline of topics for each test
29  Provide individualized test administration
30  Provide take-home tests
31  Provide more frequent, less extensive tests
32  Allow recording of test answers on tape recorder

## Accommodations (Continued)

33  Allow essay answers to be given orally
34  Provide aide to record student's oral answers
35  Administer tests orally
36  Exempt from standardized tests
37  Provide test questions on audio cassette
38  Allow (him/her) to answer on audio cassette
39  Provide recorder of oral answers
40  Provide interpreter of test directions
41  Multiple test sessions
42  Testing in separate room
43  Frequent breaks from work
44  Visual masking of portions of the test booklet
45  Repetition and review of test directions
46  Transparencies and desk overlays
47  Test proctoring by a familiar teacher
48  Provide a large pencil or other special grip device
49  Assign an in-class tutor
50  Highlight the textbook
51  Color code student's notes
52  Provide extra set of textbooks for home
53  Provide instructional support notes to parent(s), advocate(s)
54  Accept typewritten/word processed homework
55  Allow extra time for assignments
56  Provide alternative assignments
57  Provide materials with lower reading level
58  Provide computerized instructional materials
59  Provide study materials appropriate to (his/her) primary learning modality
60  Reduce the need for verbalization
61  Reduce the need for written communication
62  Reduce the need for auditory communication
63  Reduce the need for visual attention to learning task

64  Provide large print material
65  Provide Braille text materials
66  Provide Braille printer
67  Provide a talking computer system
68  Extend (his/her) school year
69  Abbreviate (his/her) school year
60  Label objects in the room
61  Adjust the school day
62  Provide large print materials
63  Independent study carrel

# Teaching Methods

1 Organic method
2 Sight word approach
3 Glasser technique
4 Phonetic approach
5 Multisensory presentations
6 VAKT method
7 Close method
8 Provide manipulative representations
9 Consistent daily routine
10 Language experience method
11 Daily chart of behavior
12 Encourage creative drama
13 Provide immediate feedback
14 Ignore inappropriate behavior
15 Set clear limits and consequences
16 Use proximity techniques to improve behavior
17 Provide immediate rewards
18 Behavior modification
19 Establish eye contact before giving directions
20 Color code materials
21 Color code words
22 Devise mnemonics for procedures
23 Picture clues
24 Emphasize the auditory modality
25 Emphasize the kinesthetic modality
26 Emphasize the tactile modality
27 Emphasize the visual modality
28 Involve him/her in group discussions
29 Involve him/her in group projects
30 Assign responsibility to the student for leadership role
31 Have a peer tutor (him/her)
32 Have (him/her) tutor a peer
33 Encourage role-playing
34 Have (him/her) read to a younger class
35 Correlate with content area subjects
36 Award points for work completed
37 Apply skills to everyday experiences
38 Short, highly structured assignments
39 Allow additional time for completion
40 Have (him/her) repeat directions every time
41 Correlate with regular classroom skills and materials
42 Stress relation of skills to vocational goals
43 Discrimination, visual and auditory
44 Given tactile auditory and visual stimulation, practice target phoneme in isolation
45 Practice target phoneme in syllables
46 Practice target phoneme in initial, medial, and final positions in words
47 Exercises to improve swallowing pattern-charts and patient supervision at home
48 Auditory self-monitoring techniques
49 Recitation of familiar lists
50 Play therapy
51 Relaxation exercises
52 Parental counseling
53 Practice with feared words
54 Practice with feared situations
55 Practice air flow sigh technique before speech
56 Practice using rate reference
57 Appropriate language games
58 Enacting a particular language situation
59 Auditory memory games
60 Discrimination between sounds presented audibly
61 Singing exercises
62 Listen to self on tape recorder and identify vocal qualities
63 Match pitch to pitch pipe and model voice
64 Practice varied loudness levels and monitor on tape recorder
65 Practice increased/decreased rate of speech and monitor with stop watch and/or tape recorder
66 Practice use of controlled breathing in phonation, word lists, sentences, paragraphs

## Teaching Methods (continued)

67   Yawn-sigh approach to reduce hyperfunction
68   Chewing exercises to reduce hyperfunction
69   Abdominal diaphragmatic breathing techniques
70   Home program to identify vocal abuse/misuse
71   Altering tongue position
72   Chant talk
73   Open mouth posture
74   Pushing approach

## Placement Options

1 Regular Classroom
2 Part day regular, part day special classroom
3 Regular classroom, out of district
4 Self-contained special education classroom in another school of the district
5 Self-contained special education classroom in out of district school
6 Residential school
7 Residential hospital

# Special Services

1  Psychological counseling
2  Guidance counseling
3  Transition counseling
4  Occupational counseling
5  Individual classroom aide
6  Wheelchair aide
7  Neurological testing
8  Speech therapy
9  Occupational therapy
10  Physical therapy
11  Auditory testing
12  Vision testing
13  Special aide
14  Transportation aide to and from school
15  Special transportation to and from school
16  Special transportation within school
17  Community counseling/training for
parent(s), advocate(s)

# Index

328